Henry Ossawa
TANNER

NEGRO AMERICAN

BIOGRAPHIES AND

AUTOBIOGRAPHIES

John Hope Franklin / Series Editor

Henry Ossawa TANNER

AMERICAN ARTIST

Marcia M. Mathews

The University of Chicago Press

CHICAGO AND LONDON

Library of Congress Catalog Card Number: 69-19279

The University of Chicago Press, Chicago 60637

The University of Chicago Press, Ltd., London W. C. 1

Published 1969

Printed in the United States of America

CONTENTS

Contents

PLATES

Plates

EDITOR'S FOREWORD

Henry Ossawa Tanner, one of the nation's leading artists at the turn of the century, has enjoyed in recent years a marked revival of interest in his works. This revival is in part because of the great current interest in the accomplishments of Negro Americans. Tanner and the subjects of many of his paintings are most attractive to those who seek to know more of the aesthetic and cultural history of Negro Americans. It is also, in part, because Tanner numbered among his favorite subjects the lands and peoples of today's troubled Middle East and North Africa. Some of his most memorable achievements are his religious paintings of the Holy Land, heads of men and women in Palestine, and landscapes and other scenes of Morocco. And it is in part due to the abiding faith of a small group of devotees who have insisted on keeping alive the memory of the man and his works. For more than half a century Tanner's friends and supporters at the Grand Central Art Galleries in New York and at several Negro colleges and universities have continued to exhibit his works. To many admirers no revival was ever necessary, for they had never fogotten him.

A member of a distinguished family, Tanner had a burning desire to fulfill his ambitions as a painter. He became an expatriate, not merely because of the limited opportunities in his native America for persons of African descent, but also because Europe, and especially France, beckoned to any American whose talents and training in the New World indicated that he might more fully develop his potential in the Old World. But even in the midst of the many honors that came to him in Europe, Tanner never completely forsook his native land and its problems. He remained closely associated with W. E. B. DuBois, was a faithful member of the National Association for the Advancement of Colored People, and encouraged numerous young Negro artists, such as Edwin Harleston and Laura Wheeling.

Marcia Mathews has brought to her task of portraying the life of Henry Ossawa Tanner many years of study of the history of American and European art and of the problems that beset young artists, black and white. She has explored every facet of Tanner's long and complex life; and in this she has had the full cooperation of the Tanner family, especially of Henry's son, Jesse Ossawa Tanner. She has provided us with the first full-length portrait of the artist who still ranks not only as the first truly distinguished Negro American artist but as one of America's first outstanding successes in the salons of Europe. In this work she has significantly added to our knowledge of the history of American art.

JOHN HOPE FRANKLIN

INTRODUCTION

It is with the greatest pleasure that I am writing an introduction to Mrs. Mathews's most interesting book on my father, Henry Ossawa Tanner. He was a great artist, and Mrs. Mathews has with considerable skill and perseverance brought together facts that were in danger of being forgotten. He was also a wonderful man whom I admired very much and I was and am very proud to have been his son.

My father was the son of Benjamin Tucker Tanner, a bishop in the African Methodist Episcopal Church and a fourth-generation American of Negro extraction. But he always felt himself to be an American first and a Negro second. This was quite natural, as our family was of mixed blood with Red Indian, Negro, and white ancestors.

If my father lived so much abroad it was owing to the fact that he felt the white people in America were not ready to face acceptance of the colored races, especially the Negro race. He believed this acceptance would eventually be worked out through education and equal opportunity, though it might take many years.

In Europe my father was taken for what he was, a talented artist whose "colour" did not add to or detract from his talent. Not only did he not feel any racial prejudice, but in Europe other Americans acted as though racial prejudice did not exist in their own country.

My father's studio in Paris was always crowded with interesting people and at Etaples in the Pas de Calais, he practically created the Etaples Art Colony. I have seen up to a hundred people, many of them Americans, invited to tea at his summer home at Trépied, near Etaples. In view of his position and popularity it is not surprising that my father married, as he thought, quite the prettiest girl in Paris, a member of the large American colony.

My mother was very happy all of her life. She was happy in her marriage and she saw her son become a graduate of Cambridge University, in England, and of the Royal School of Mines, London, as well as win his "colours" in the 100 yards and the quarter mile at Cambridge, and row in the eight on the Thames for the Royal School of Mines.

What a destiny indeed was that of my father! What an adventure that of my mother! How justified is the saying of my father that a race traces its own destiny. "Judge a tree by its fruits," he would say.

My father always worked very hard on his pictures and they were painted very slowly. If you study them you keep discovering new things about them—a new form is revealed, a new star seems to shine, a new shadow stretches out—in a word, his pictures are very much alive. A Tanner can do more than give you enjoyment, it can come to your rescue, it can reaffirm your confidence in man and his destiny, it can help you to surmount your difficulties or console you in your distress. A picture by Tanner is really a part of the artist himself, a mystic whose visions are deeply personal yet universal in significance.

My father was a father indeed! All the family knew that they could count on him. His patience was loving and the example he gave so impressive that when at the age of eight years I told my father a childish lie to avoid some punishment, I wet my handkerchief with tears that night, so great was my distress at not having told him the truth. I was not above a childish lie at that age, but I knew that to him it was a sacrilege.

There is no doubt that he felt the tragedy of the First World War very deeply. He was horrified at the terrible loss of life and at the suffering of the wounded. At first he could not paint, but after America entered the war he volunteered for work in the American Red Cross. Some of his work was done as an artist attached to the Red Cross.

He was very distressed at the extremes to which man's passions can lead him and believed that only the "few" who listened to the word of God might be saved. However, my father was not concerned with religious dogma; he felt there was a unity in human aspirations and revealed faith. He had many Jewish and Catholic friends. A French priest once gave him a very beautiful old Bible, which he treasured.

Though my father felt that the presence of God stretches out through the cosmos and his love extends to other worlds than our own, he also felt that man has an active role to play and should not submit passively to his fate. Christ watches over his flock ("The Good Shepherd" was a favorite subject of his), but evil is a tangible thing and *God needs us* to help fight with him against evil and *we need God* to guide us. (We all have a little of God in us.)

My father did not believe in praying for individual needs. Prayer was, to him, a powerful factor in man's destiny, but we should pray for a clearer perception of what our actions should be rather than for better health or greater wealth.

"Let God guide us" was his principal reason for prayer. This guidance was achieved, he believed, through a receptive state of mind that allows us to know God's will. It is this sort of mystical fourth dimension that my father attempted to give his religious paintings, and which is sensed by so many of his admirers.

JESSE OSSAWA TANNER

Le Douhet, France

ACKNOWLEDGMENTS

IT IS MY PLEASURE TO ACKNOWLEDGE HERE THE ENCOURAGEment and assistance that I received during my research and writing of the biography of Henry Ossawa Tanner.

The initial research for the biography was sponsored by the American Philosophical Society. To them I owe a debt of gratitude.

I am equally indebted to Mr. Jesse Ossawa Tanner, the artist's son, who kindly placed at my disposal his father's papers, which he had carefully preserved over the years. He also gave me the benefit of his personal recollections.

Dr. Thomas English, professor emeritus at Emory University, and Dr. Benjamin E. Mays, president emeritus of Morehouse College, read portions of the first draft of the book and offered helpful criticism.

Professor James A. Porter, director of the College of Fine

Arts at Howard University, gave a careful reading to the final manuscript and made valuable suggestions. I am particularly grateful to him for the information about the portrait of Richard Allen at Howard University.

Mr. Erwin S. Barrie, director of the Grand Central Art Galleries in New York, which handled Henry Tanner's paintings in the United States for many years, gave helpful information on Tanner as a man and as an artist.

Mrs. Margaret Clifford Bryant gave permission to quote from letters in the Atlanta University Library.

Dr. James P. Brawley, president emeritus of Clark College, went through old college records with me to ascertain facts pertaining to Tanner's connection with Clark University (now Clark College).

Mr. Romare Bearden, artist, kindly wrote the appraisal of Henry Tanner that is included in the last chapter of the book.

Mr. John D. Hatch, art historian, maintained an interest throughout the writing of the book.

The personnel of several libraries, both in the United States and in Europe, assisted me in my research. To Miss Ruth Walling, associate librarian of Emory University, however, I am most indebted.

The following museums gave their permission to use reproductions of paintings in their possession: Hampton Institute College Museum, *The Banjo Lesson;* Los Angeles County Museum (William Preston Harrison Collection), *Daniel in the Lions' Den;* Philadelphia Museum of Art (W. P. Wilstach Collection), *Annunciation;* Pennsylvania Academy of the Fine Arts, *Nicodemus;* Milwaukee Art Center (Gift of Mr. and Mrs. Whipple Dunbar), *Moonlight, Hebron* and *Sunlight, Tangiers;* High Museum of Art (J. J. Haverty Collection), *Etaples Fisher Folk;* Frederick Douglass Institute of Negro Arts and History (Collection of Mr. and Mrs. Norman B. Robbins), *Abraham's Oak;* Atlanta University Museum (Waddell Collection), *Disciples Healing the Sick;* Howard University Museum, *Return from the Crucifixion;* Art Institute of Chicago, *Two Disciples at the Tomb.*

Mr. Haig Tashjian, owner of the painting *Sodom and Gomorrah*, kindly contributed the color engraving of this painting as an illustration for the book.

Permission was granted by their publishers and authors to quote from the following books:

Edwin Austin Abbey by E. V. Lucas (Methuen and Company, Ltd.), *Bohemian Literary and Social Life in Paris* by Sisley Huddleston (J. B. Lippincott Company), *Modern Negro Art* by James A. Porter (Dryden Press), *John Elliott* by Maud Howe Elliott (Houghton Mifflin Company), *Recollections of a Picture Dealer* by Ambroise Vollard (Little, Brown and Company), *An American Artist's Story* by George Biddle (Little, Brown and Company), *The Art Spirit* by Robert Henri (Lippincott Company), *The American Artist and His Times* by Homer St. Gaudens (Dodd, Mead and Company), *Thomas Eakins: His Life and Work* by Lloyd Goodrich (Whitney Museum of American Art).

Last, but in no sense least, my thanks go to Dr. John Hope Franklin, Editor of the series of Negro American Biographies and Autobiographies, of which *Henry Ossawa Tanner: American Artist* is one, and to Joseph J. Mathews, my husband, whose wisdom and patience guided my efforts throughout the writing of this book.

Henry Ossawa
TANNER

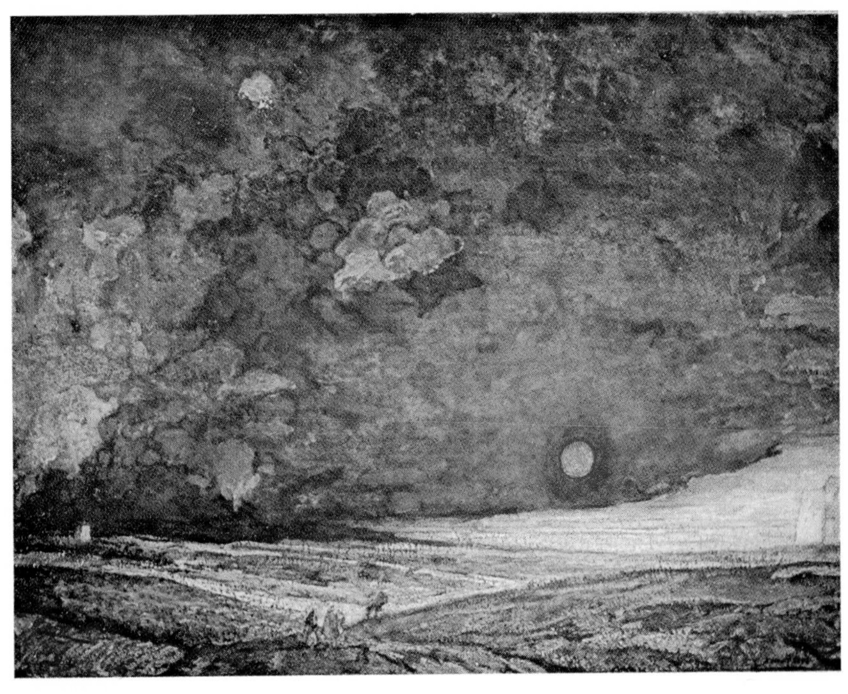

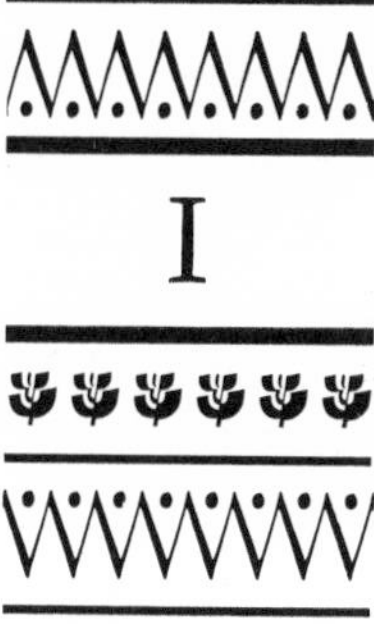

Early Years

In Pittsburgh, Pennsylvania, on June 21, 1860, Benjamin Tucker Tanner, twenty-five years old and a minister in the African Methodist Church, wrote in his "Day Book":[1]

> This is the first birthday my dear little son Henry Ossawa Tanner ever saw. The Lord has blessed him and us wonderfully, he has never been sick a day.

Then the proud father went on to enumerate other babies, born about the same time as Henry, who had already been called to Heaven, and added:

> Whether the preservation of Henry's life and health will prove a blessing the Lord only knows. For how can I, a mortal man, look into the future and see his life, see whether he will love God and man, or whether he will be an enemy of

1. "Day Book" of Benjamin Tucker Tanner, Manuscript Division, Library of Congress.

both. The Lord give us, O give us wisdom to bring him up, if at all in the understanding and admonishment of God.

The Reverend Mr. Tanner was a man of deep religious convictions, as his diary indicates. The month before Henry's first birthday he had received his pastoral certificate from the African Methodist bishop, Daniel Payne, by which he was ordered to the distant station of Sacramento, California—in those days about as remote as the valleys of the moon. Whether he had planned to take his wife, Sarah Elizabeth Miller Tanner, and young Henry he does not say, but the question is academic since attempts in Cincinnati, Philadelphia, New York, and Baltimore to raise the necessary funds for the long sea voyage proved fruitless.

Instead he went to Washington, D. C.—sent "on loan" by Bishop Payne to serve as pastor of the 15th Street Presbyterian Church, the leading Negro Presbyterian church in the city. This church, established in 1841, divided honors with the Israel Church as the most influential church in the Negro community. Among its organizers were two African Methodists, members of Union Bethel Church, so in taking over his new duties the Reverend Mr. Tanner was not alienating himself completely from his own church. It was an exceptionally fine start for a young minister.

Times were exciting in the nation's capital, with the Presidential election coming up and war clouds heavy on the horizon. Benjamin Tanner noted in his "Day Book" on November 7, 1860:

> Abraham Lincoln is elected President of the U.S. As far as I am judge it is for good great excitement. So much so that I was advised not to have church.

And, again, on November 23:

> The political and financial condition of the country is terrible. Rumors of secession, war, trouble, etc., are rife.

But the young husband's concern was less for national happenings than separation from his wife and child. On November 19, after receiving his quarterly allotment, he wrote:

> I went to the Metropolis and got a check and sent $16.00 to Pittsburgh to bring my wife on here. May God give her a safe and comfortable journey.

On November 21:

> . . . wrote the last letter, I hope, at least for sometime, to my beloved wife. I told her that I would go to Balt. and meet her there.

On November 28 he joyfully went to Baltimore to meet his little family. Sarah was tired from the long journey, but after breakfast at "Bro. Read's" and a brief rest they went on to Washington by the 4:30 train. Of the journey Tanner cryptically remarks: "In the cars American prejudice."

The "Day Book" gives a few glimpses of their first year in Washington:

> Mrs. Tanner and myself took tea up at Mrs. Phists' last evening on Capitol Hill. It is quite a walk from 14th Street.
>
> Returned home about 11 O'clock and accompanied Mrs. T. down to Friend Brown's where we spent a pleasant afternoon. While there I read Redpath's Guide to Hayti. That promises to be a great country.

We learn from the diary that Benjamin Tanner worked regularly in his study at least six hours a day, going home when necessary to relieve Sarah in the care of young Henry. The following entries indicate the young father's devotion to his family:

> I was visiting about 8 o'clock when I returned home to guard little Henry while S. washed.
>
> Prepared an address. Then repaired home about one to nurse the baby, little Henry, while Sadie worked.
>
> I was confined to my study till nearly two o'clock when I returned home to watch over Henry while Sadie ironed.

National events, nevertheless, impinged themselves on his thoughts. On December 24 he wrote:

> The country seems to be bordering on a civil war all on account of slavery. I pray God to rule and overrule all to his own glory and the good of man.

But the impending crisis cast no gloom on his personal fortunes. On December 31 he made the following entry:

> Last day of this year which hath been the most eventful of all my life. God Jesus give me some proper conception of thy goodness toward me.

In view of the status of most free Negroes in the U. S., only about one-half of whom were literate, Benjamin Tanner had reason to thank the Lord. He had two prized possessions—a heritage of freedom and a good education. His paternal grandfather is named in the 1800 census of the state of Pennsylvania, the first that included Negroes. His parents, Hugh S. and Isabel Tanner, had given him an education superior to that of most white youth, sending him first to Avery College, in Allegheny, Pennsylvania, from which he graduated, and subsequently to Western Theological Seminary, in the same town.

On his mother's side Henry Tanner was the grandson of Charles Jefferson Miller, born in 1808, the mulatto son of a white planter in Winchester, Virginia. Charles Miller left Virginia in 1846 for the free state of Pennsylvania, taking his family with him in an oxcart. It was in Pittsburgh that his daughter Sarah met Benjamin Tanner, whom she married in 1858. The fact that Benjamin Tanner was a short man, about five feet two inches tall, and Sarah a woman of five feet eight, did not bother either of them. During their more than fifty years of married life Tanner's feeling of protectiveness toward his wife never slackened.

As the young minister became more involved in church affairs the references in his "Day Book" to Sarah, Henry, and aspects of his personal life grew fewer. His entries were soon transformed into theological discussions, possibly the bases of sermons, and add nothing to the picture of his personal life, though they tell a good deal of his religious bent.

During Henry's early years his father's activities were many and varied and his changes of residence frequent. In 1861 he founded a school for freedmen in the U. S. Navy Yards, Washington, D. C. Three years later he was in Frederick, Maryland, where he temporarily abandoned preaching to take charge of another school for freedmen. On May 8, 1866, he wrote in the "Day Book":

> Have been appointed to the charge of Bethel Church [Philadelphia]. May God give me peace and strength to perform the onerous duties devolving upon me.

By then he had two additional children, Hallie, born in 1863, and Mary Louise, born in 1865. His references to them in his diary lack the tenderness with which he wrote of Henry. That of January 30, 1866, states:

> Another little girl has been given me. And for what O Lord? I already have two, and really I am so poor that I sometimes wonder how I shall meet my responsibilities but I know that God is good and He will continue to provide for me and mine.

Less than thirteen months later there is another entry:

> My wife this morning at 5 o'clock gave birth to her fifth child, Isabella Turner. May God help her.

His concern for money arose less from an inability to care for his family, however, than from his deep feeling of responsibility for them. Whenever he went on a trip he was troubled for fear he would meet accidental death and leave Sarah and the children without a provider. Shortly after Isabella's birth he had to go to Washington to see about the publication of his book, *An Apology for African Methodism.* Before leaving he wrote in the "Day Book":

> I am terribly pushed for money to pay the printer. I renewed my life insurance for $2000 and sent it back to my bank. It is my wish that if I die for her [Sarah] to return to Pittsburgh and buy a small home for about $1200 put $500 in the Bank of Pittsburgh settle down on the other $300. Keep all my books for the children.

On an earlier occasion he had thought it best for Sarah to settle near Wilberforce in the event of his death.

During these years only once, in July of 1866, did he refer directly to Henry.

> My little boy was disappointed in the number of chickens hatched. Ah, said I, my son, you are only certain of two things, that virtues will be rewarded and sins punished.

Whether seven-year-old Henry was properly impressed by his father's disquisition can only be surmised. He had reached an age when it must have been apparent to him that the Lord did not always distribute his blessings evenly—that Negroes, no matter how upright in their behavior, were given short shrift compared to white people. He had no doubt seen his own father, a man looked up to by Negroes, treated with condescension by people of less merit whose complexions were white.

The Reverend Mr. Tanner may have found it difficult to provide Henry with an explanation, based on God's goodness, of the inequities that prevailed about him, for in the "Day Book" his allusions to racial prejudice are marked with a note of bitterness.

> If the colored people would only do right is the cry from the parlor to the kitchen, from the Senate Hall to the country squire shanty. "Colored people won't do right."
>
> Right, what do they mean by right, is it to see white yet their eyes have been put out, to love labor while yet they are taught none but the meanest work—to love their country, while yet it brands them the most infamous on earth. To love their race while yet from infancy they are taught to believe their natural inferiority. If colored people would do right. Oh yes, to do that "right" we would not be men.

> but rather we would have to be a race not a little lower but if anything a little above the Seraphim.

On another occasion he wrote of the intolerable position of cultivated Negroes in American society, when emigration from abroad was pouring thousands of Germans and Irish into the country, taking employment that formerly the Negroes had enjoyed.

> What business has a man of polished mind in a dining room as a servant?

He believed that well-educated Negro children, girls in particular, suffered the most from this intolerable situation.

> What? must they go into some knave's kitchen to cook for some numbskulls. It is not proper for the superior to act servant to the inferior, not even the equal.

However hard their father may have tried to reconcile his religious views with reality, Henry and his sisters could not have been insulated from the hard facts of life. They had only to open their eyes to see the injustice that prevailed about them. And what they did not see with their eyes they heard about. Henry Tanner's hatred of racial prejudice remained with him through life. He felt no animosity toward the white race—his dearest and closest friends were white people—but toward those individuals who blindly or cruelly inflicted pain and humiliation on others because of race or color. Long after Tanner had left the United States and discrimination no longer affected him personally, he would jot down instances of racial prejudice that he remembered or that came to his notice. Whether he thought to incorporate them someday in an essay, whether they were to relieve his own tensions, or to use as illustrations in letters to friends is not clear. In any event, they give an insight into his thinking.

One of these "jottings" concerns his mother when he was a baby. His parents were living in Alexandria, Virginia, at the time. Mrs. Tanner had gone into Washington to shop and had taken her year-old child with her. A single track of street cars ran between the two cities but Negroes were not allowed to ride the cars. Tanner does not say how the trip was usually negotiated, possibly by horse and buggy, but on the day in question a severe snow storm came up and Mrs. Tanner was stranded in the city, with the street car her only hope for getting home. She decided to take her chance and, pulling her veil down over her face and uncovering the baby's head, for Henry's skin was light and his hair had an auburn tinge, she mounted the street car. About half way to Alexandria Mrs. Tanner noticed two men looking at her and talking to one another. Finally one of them came over, pulled up her veil and said, "Who, what have we here a nigger, stop the car" and, amid guffaws, Henry and his mother were hustled out into the night. At the end of this "jotting" Tanner wrote: "May God forgive them for even at this distant day it is hard for me to do so."

Below the narrative he added a longer note:

> I never knew this story till I was a grown man and we were in our Diamond Street house in Phila near East Park. I left the house immediately and it took several hours walking in among the trees and under the night skies to cool the heat and hatred that surged in my bosom. I have no recollection of ever going back there [Washington] till on a trip from Paris I found my mother living there with my sister and I went there for a few days. One day we took a St. car and a distinguished looking middle age man of the same race that had formerly ejected that same mother and son arose and gave my mother a seat. My mother said it was not a very rare thing, but I always thanked God I had seen it.[2]

Of Henry's earliest years there are few mementoes. A photograph taken when he was four years old shows a handsome,

2. The letters, notes, and "jottings" in this book that are not footnoted are all taken from Henry Tanner's personal papers which were collected by his son and are now located in the Archives of American Art in Detroit, Michigan.

Tanner had the habit of making rough drafts of his letters and of saving them for reference. Some of the letters quoted, therefore, may not be in the exact form of the letters he finally wrote. Nevertheless, it may be assumed that the ideas expressed in them are fundamentally the same.

well-dressed little boy in satin trousers, white frilled shirt, and checked jacket. There is a slightly troubled expression on his face, induced perhaps by the ordeal of having his picture taken, but suggestive of the sensitivity that was to be characteristic of him.

When Henry Tanner's own son was six years old he wrote a little story for him, in which he describes what must have been his first home in Philadelphia.

> When I was a small boy I lived in Phila near 3rd and Pine. It was one of those alternate old black and red brick houses so common at that time. It was a very old house, in fact it was said that it had been an old bakery. I imagine that it was here that Franklin bought that famous loaf of bread that he carried under his arm.
>
> In the sidewalk was a manhole down which was put the coal and through it came the only light into the cellar. It was more or less my duty to bring the coal upstairs from the underground dungeon. The day in question which I am going to tell you about my mother was engaged in making pies and cakes for Thanksgiving. Now if there was anything I loved to do it was to be in the kitchen and watch my mother make pies and aid to cut out cakes with the forms. It was unalloyed pleasure and if there was anything I did not like it was to go down in the cellar—dark but for a little ray of light that came down from the street. So that these words, "Now, Henry go down and get me a bucket of coal" were anything but welcome. Had I rushed off I could have done it in 3 minutes but it seemed to me that it was a terrible affair and I started up slowly, very slowly. . . .[3]

Henry was just six when the Civil War ended, and his memories of it are vague, but one incident remained with him. The Tanners were living in Frederick, Maryland, at the time.

> From our attic window the rebel camp and soldiers could be seen. Once my father for some cause was at the little station and by his clothes was recognized as a minister. "Hello!

3. This story exists only in an unfinished rough draft and is among the personal papers located in the Archives of American Art.

Sambo, what are you doing with those duds on, take this," and he was kicked out of the station. I believe my father said he was drunk.

Rebel soldiers passed their house all day long, but the Reverend Mr. Tanner took the precaution of nailing up the windows to make it look vacant. Only once did a rebel soldier stop and bang on the door—but an officer sent him on.

Henry first learned his letters from a Mr. Jones, "a patient individual" who, according to Tanner, had "a task such as the Egyptians required of the Israelites." His real education began in Philadelphia, where he attended the Randolph Street School, whose principal was Jacob C. White, a graduate of the Institute for Colored Youth and a man in whom Benjamin Tanner had great faith. The school was part of the public school system, but was attended exclusively by Negro children, since not until 1881 was an act passed allowing them to attend public schools with white children. In a letter written from Paris in 1909 to an old schoolmate, Charles Forten, Henry Tanner refers to this school.

> The thing that places it in my mind are the drawings we made on our slates. The outstanding fact—one boy whose name I have forgotten could according to our ideas draw anything—whole lines of soldiers charging—run away horses, houses on fire, people escaping by the roof and doors, a day at a Circus. There seemed nothing he could not draw in such speed—in our eyes a Michelangelo. I have many times wondered what became of him—did he live, if so his talent . . . . [illegible] I am sure he was so far ahead of the rest of our efforts that we all felt ourselves outclassed. But I have learned it is very hard to pick a winner. When I look back on my Julien days in Paris not more than one out of five of the "idols" of the school were ever heard of and I can recall both French and Americans whose easels were always besieged by onlookers who have simply faded out of sight leaving no traces upon the sands of time.

It was not until 1872, when Henry was thirteen, that the Tanners were established in what was to be their permanent home. In that year Benjamin Tanner purchased an eight-room house at 2708 Diamond Street in North Philadelphia from James H. Coburn. The price he paid for it—$3,500—was substantial for those days. But the Reverend Mr. Tanner had risen in the church and was now a man of distinction in the Negro world. In addition to his pastoral duties he was editor of the *Christian Recorder* and two years before had been honored by his old school, Avery College, with an honorary M. A. degree.

The Philadelphia that Henry Tanner knew as a boy was a sober place still bearing the marks of its Quaker origin. On the streets ladies were seen in Quaker bonnets and gray gowns and men in shad-bellied coats and broad-brimmed hats. Unlike New York there were few millionaires in Philadelphia, and aside from the Negroes the inhabitants were mostly Anglo-Saxon. It was a large city, with a population of some three quarters of a million people, but many parts still had a quietly rural appearance. Fairmont Park, covering more than 3,000 acres on both banks of the Schuylkill River and Wissahickon Creek, was still new when the Tanners settled in the Diamond Street home.

One day Henry was walking in this park with his father when he observed an artist painting a landscape. According to his account it was the first time he had seen a professional artist at work, and he was intrigued by the fact that the man stationed himself so far from the tree he was painting.

"Why does he not have a spy-glass so that he can see that big tree more distinctly? Why does he get so far away?" he asked, in the inquisitive manner of children.[4]

He does not give his father's explanation, but evidently it did not dampen his interest in art because he writes that

> a long conversation that night produced fifteen cents and this, early the next morning, secured from a common paint shop some dry colors and a couple of scraggy brushes. Then I was out immediately for a sketch. I went straight to the spot where I had seen the artist the day before.... Coming

4. Henry Ossawa Tanner, "The Story of an Artist's Life," *World's Work*, 18 (June and July, 1909): 11662.

> home that night, I examined the sketch from all points of view, upside down and down side up decidedly admiring and well content with my first effort.[5]

Thereafter Henry delighted in walking down Chestnut Street to see the pictures in Earle's Galleries or in the window of Bailey's jewelry shop.

> How well I remember "A Foggy Morning" by Cowell . . . or "A Morning at Long Beach," by Senat; how much better the numerous "Storm at Sea" by Hamilton and the still more numerous "Breezy Day off Dieppe," by Brescoe; how, after drinking my full of these art wonders, I would hurry home and paint what I had seen and what fun it was.[6]

Initially Henry decided he would be a marine painter. Something occurred to change his plan, however, and this, he writes

> was my meeting with an animal painter, Mr. J. M. Hess, now dead. From him I learned that animal painters were even less numerous in America than marine painters. I renounced the inviting field of marine painting to become the great American Landseer. By this time I must have been fourteen.[7]

James Hess, the "animal painter," was exactly Henry's own age and a cripple, with one leg shorter than the other, having suffered when very young from what was presumed to be typhoid fever. His father, a house painter, had died when he was a baby and as a small boy James Hess had sold newspapers on the streets for a living. Although later, through the help of a benefactor, he attended the Pennsylvania Academy of the Fine Arts and sold some of his paintings, he died in 1890 without ever making a name for himself. In 1925, his son, George Hess, learning from a friend that Henry Tanner, the famous artist, had expressed an interest in knowing the details of his father's

5. Ibid., p. 11662.
6. Ibid., p. 11663.
7. Ibid., p. 11663.

life, wrote Tanner what he knew, and added: "Probably you remember coming to see him laid away—about the time that you first sailed for France."

It may have been young James Hess who inspired Henry Tanner to study art one summer vacation. Finding a teacher was not a happy experience. For the first time he learned what it was to explore wider horizons than those delineated by his color.

> No man or boy to whom this country is a land of "equal chances" can realize what heartache this question caused me, and with what trepidation I made the rounds of the studios. The question was not, would the desired teacher have a boy who knew nothing and had little money, but would he have me, or would he keep me after he found out who I was.[8]

After unsuccessful visits to one or two studios, a local white artist, Mr. Isaac L. Williams, agreed to take him for two dollars a lesson. The lessons proved a great disappointment, for they consisted almost entirely of mechanical drawing, a subject that held no interest for Henry. After a day or so, although he liked the atmosphere of Mr. Williams's studio, he gave up his lessons and plodded along by himself.

During another high school vacation he got a job at a hotel in Atlantic City, and, momentarily, forgot his decision to give up marine painting. He did a sketch of a wrecked schooner driven ashore by a storm which so impressed an amateur artist by the name of Henry Price that Price invited him to his studio and encouraged him to work there between his duties at the hotel. When Mr. Price returned to Philadelphia in the fall he took Henry with him and for nearly a year he slept in Mr. Price's studio, going home only from Saturday until Monday.

But Mr. Price was either whimsical or selfish. He opposed Henry's suggestion that he study at the Pennsylvania Academy of the Fine Arts, and their relationship came to an abrupt end. Tanner says he never knew the reason for the break—whether

8. Ibid., p. 11663.

he inadvertently offended Mr. Price or whether his benefactor merely tired of him. Henry returned to his parents' home and "in the regular course of events" left school.

He was now seventeen, of an age to decide on a career. His father, who had looked favorably on art as a pastime, was not at all in sympathy with the idea of his son taking it up as a life work. He knew how scarce opportunities were for the gifted Negro, and since Henry was not minded to enter the church, the "safest" career, he placed him with a friend in the flour business. Henry found the work uninteresting and physically taxing. In spite of that first year of life during which he had "never been sick a day" Henry was not a robust boy. He may have made the most of the flour business as a drain on his energies, for when he became ill following a stint of work, he won his father's consent to make art his profession.

At this rather critical stage of Henry Tanner's youth a great event took place in Philadelphia—the Centennial Exposition of 1876. It was the first World's Fair ever held in America and, from the point of view of size, was the greatest that had ever been held anywhere. Two hundred and thirty-six acres of land in Fairmont Park were set aside on the west bank of the Schuylkill River for the big show, and seven colossal exhibition halls, annexes, pavilions, and offices were erected to take care of the displays and the governmental representatives that accompanied them.

One of the exhibition halls—Memorial Hall—was an art gallery with 75,000 square feet of wall space for pictures. Never before had such a comprehensive display of art been assembled in the United States. Edwin Austin Abbey later wrote to his friend, Will Low, that the Centennial Exposition was his great "eye-opener" and that he believed the birth of modern American art could be dated from the Philadephia Centennial Exhibition. Henry Tanner's memory of the exhibition was probably much the same as Abbey's.

Seen in retrospect the art displayed was not representative of the best of any country with the exception of England and the United States. A critic writing for the *Nation* declared:

> It is painful to pass the French rooms. Not a single example of Ingres, Gleyre, Millet, Rousseau, Gérôme, Baudry, Flandrin, Delaroche, Hébert, Meissonier, Corot, Daubigny père, Couture, Regnault, Bonnat.[9]

Yet the French exhibition was not without merit, adds the critic, since none of the "wild experimentalists" were there either—meaning Manet, Degas, Monet, and the other impressionists.

Italy sent as her pièce de résistance a plaster figure of George Washington perched on an eagle too small for his six feet of form. "Having no occasion for legs in the attitude chosen, Washington thriftily dispenses with them," caustically noted William Dean Howells.[10]

The English exhibition was excellent. The Gainsboroughs alone were worth the fifty-cent admission price to the fairgrounds.

The most surprising aspect of the art exhibition, however, was the fine showing made by the United States. The American paintings may have lacked the literary appeal of the British and in this "wanted charm," according to Mr. Howells, but American art was technically fine, and, in the case of older artists like John S. Copley, Gilbert Stuart, C. W. Peale, and S. F. B. Morse, had an added historical interest. Of the living artists represented—John LaFarge, Eastman Johnson, Winslow Homer, Thomas Eakins, John Bridgman, among others—only Eastman Johnson received a "first" award.

It was in connection with the awards that the following

9. "International Exhibition—XVI," *Nation*, September 28, 1876, p. 193.

10. "A Sennight of the Centennial," *Atlantic Monthly*, 38 (July, 1876): 93.

incident took place in Memorial Hall and may well have reached the ears of the Tanner family.[11]

The day after the awards were announced a Negro man, well dressed and of dignified bearing, hurried into the hall with a newspaper in his hand.

"What is that colored person in here for?" was the general attitude of the spectators when they saw him pushing forward to study the pictures.

The official in charge went over and asked his business, with the admonition to "speak lively."

"I want to inquire concerning No. 54," the man replied.

"What's that to you?" was the retort. When the Negro disclosed that he was the artist of a landscape entitled "Under the Oaks" that had won a medal, the attitude of the attendant as well as the spectators underwent a change. It was possibly the first time that a Negro artist spontaneously won the respect and admiration of disinterested white people on the basis of creative talent. They were soon bowing politely and making way for him to pass. The artist was Edward Mitchell Bannister, from Providence, Rhode Island.

There are few names of Negro artists in the history of American art before the twentieth century. Most are as anonymous as the artist for whom business was sought in the *Boston News-Letter* of January 7, 1773:

> A Negro man whose extraordinary genius has been attested by the best masters in London; he takes faces at the lowest rates.

The first known Negro artist is Joshua Johnston, who worked in Baltimore and whose *Portrait of a Cleric* in the Bowdoin College Museum of Art, while imitative of colonial portraiture in general, is an excellent character portrayal. But

11. The incident was related to me by Mr. William Alden Brown of Providence, Rhode Island. Mr. Brown, noted collector of American art, was a friend and one-time pupil of Edward Bannister.

little can be gleaned of him except his name. According to Homer St. Gaudens, whose attention was directed to the artist by Dr. J. Hall Pleasants:

> A misty allegation exists that Joshua Johnston belonged to one of several Maryland families. For all we know he served too in the household of an artist from whom he picked up the rudiments of his craft. Certainly his painting has a touch of the Peale group. It may have been Charles W. Peale, or Rembrandt, or even Charles Peale Polk. They all worked at odd times in Maryland during Johnston's years between 1796 and 1826.[12]

Robert Douglass, Jr., born in 1809, though less gifted than Johnston, also attained considerable reputation as an artist. He studied under Sully and, except for visits to Europe and Haiti, seems to have worked exclusively in Philadelphia. Henry Tanner was acquainted with his art, though he may not have known him personally. Douglass died in 1887.

Robert Duncanson, from Cincinnati, was better known than either Johnston or Douglass. He was sent to Europe by the Anti-Slavery League to study, exhibited his rather fanciful landscapes in England and Scotland, and was invited by Lord Tennyson to bring his painting of *The Lotus Eaters* to his home on the Isle of Wight. Before Duncanson died in 1871 he returned to America and did a series of murals for Nicholas Longworth at his home in Cincinnati.

Edward Bannister, the centennial medal winner, was a Canadian from St. Andrews, New Brunswick, who had gone to Boston as a young man where, for a time, he shared a studio with the artist Edwin Lord Weeks. After marrying Christiana Carteaux, an American Indian from Providence, he settled in that city and became not only a well-known artist but a man of high standing in the community. It was at the instigation of

12. *The American Artist and His Times* (New York: Dodd, Mead and Co., 1941), p. 50.

some "society ladies" in Providence that his picture *Under the Oaks* had been sent to the centennial. It was not known to the judges to be the painting of a Negro artist.

Art in America was not at that time thought of as a means of pointing up social injustices. An artist used his talent to transmute a sense of beauty into pictorial form, without regard to its sociological significance.

One young Negro artist, however, had already revealed within the limits prescribed by accepted classical canons her feeling about slavery. She was Edmonia Lewis, born near Albany, New York, in 1845. Her bust of Colonel Shaw exhibited at a fair held in Boston during the Civil War for the Soldiers' Relief Fund had attracted a considerable amount of attention, and subsequently she had gone to Rome where she studied sculpture and became acquainted with Harriet Hosmer and other neo-classicists. Her version of the Negro's attitude toward emancipation in a sculpture entitled *Forever Free*, executed in 1866, struck a muted note of racial protest.

There can be little doubt that Henry Tanner knew of Edmonia Lewis and of the other Negro artists who had attained distinction. Edmonia Lewis's statue of a dying *Cleopatra* at the Centennial Exhibition was one of the show's attractions. The Reverend Mr. Tanner was well informed in matters of Negro culture and would have seen to it that his children were similarly informed. In his eyes no goal was too high for a Negro to aim at and although he would have preferred for his son Henry to follow in his footsteps and become a minister of the church, he was quite prepared to assist him in his ambition to become an artist.

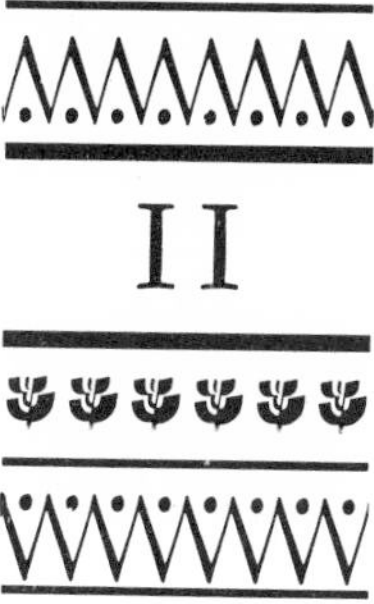

Studies under Thomas Eakins

During Henry Tanner's boyhood the most common method of studying art was the one he had followed briefly with Isaac L. Williams, that of working in the studio of an established artist and learning from him the principles of drawing and painting. Often a student did nothing more than copy his teacher's own pictures. There were art schools, but these were limited to a few large cities like New York, Philadelphia, and Cincinnati, and even here the teaching was more or less desultory.

The oldest professional art school in the United States was Philadelphia's Pennsylvania Academy of the Fine Arts, founded by Charles Willson Peale in the early years of the century. This domed-roof, Doric-style building far out on Chestnut Street "standing in a kind of solitude" where "paying guests were few and far between,"[1] was not an art school in the modern sense of the word. Students were permitted to draw from its collection of casts, to copy the paintings that hung on its walls, and to attend the lectures given there on "artistic anatomy." What instruction there was was based largely on a study of the antique, a method that induced in Thomas Eakins, a one-time student at the old academy, a lifelong hatred of cast drawing.

Edwin Austin Abbey wrote to his future wife apropos of his classes at the academy:

> What a fusty, fudgy place that Pennsylvania Academy was in my day! The trail of Rembrandt Peale and of Charles Leslie, of Benjamin West, and all the dismal persons who thought themselves "Old Masters" was over the place, and the worthy young men who caught colds in the dank basement with me, and who slumbered peacefully by my side during long anatomical lectures, all thought the only thing worth doing was the grand business, the "High Art" that Haydon was raving about. . . .[2]

In 1868, however, fresh breezes were blowing about the city and a new direction was taken to improve the training of young artists. The board of directors of the Pennsylvania Academy of the Fine Arts concurred with an idea suggested by John Sartain, the artist, to establish proper art schools. These were put in operation in 1870, but it soon became apparent that space in the old academy was too cramped for efficient teaching. A lot was bought on Broad Street, at the corner of Cherry, and the cornerstone of a new academy was laid on December 7, 1872. The new building—"the most complete, best lighted, heated and divided building of its kind on the Continent"[3]—was to house the most progressive art school in the United States. It opened its doors with a large art exhibi-

1. John Sartain, *Reminiscences of a Very Old Man* (New York: S. Appleton and Co., 1899), p. 144.

2. Edward Verrall Lucas, *Edwin Austin Abbey*, 2 vol. (London: Methuen and Co., 1921), 1: 13.

3. *Art Journal*, 29 (1876): 202.

tion in April, 1876, one month prior to the opening of the Centennial Exposition.

Henry Tanner did not enroll immediately at the new school. Mr. Price, his former benefactor, had discouraged him from attending the old academy, and it may be that the discouragement lingered on. Or, he may have felt that his race would be held against him in the school's competitive atmosphere. This is unlikely, however, since Henry Tanner was not the first Negro to attend the Pennsylvania Academy—Robert Douglass had that distinction.

During his late teens Henry Tanner sketched the animals at the Philadelphia Zoo and made clay models of animals and people, apparently disinterested in further professional training. He wrote many years later that at this time his health was not good and that when he was eighteen he was advised to go to the Adirondacks for "relaxation and a change of climate."[4] His parents, solicitous of their son's health, sent him to Rainbow Lake in upstate New York, where he made "many good friends,"[5] and did a number of paintings. The results are seen in *Burnt Pines in the Adirondacks* and *Adirondack Reminiscence*—rather sketchy and impressionistic landscapes that showed promise rather than distinction. They were later exhibited at the Pennsylvania Academy of the Fine Arts.

Tanner was pleased with his trip to the Adirondacks and, after returning to Philadelphia, decided to follow it with one to Florida. This was his first venture into the South, but what he saw or did there is not recorded. In a short time he returned to Philadelphia to continue his independent career. He was conscious of the obstacles in the path of an artist and bitterly conscious of the additional trials that beset a Negro artist, for unlike his father he did not find in his identification with the Negro race the support he needed to sustain him against pre-

4. Henry Ossawa Tanner, "The Story of An Artist's Life," *World's Work*, 18 (June and July, 1909): 11664.

5. Ibid., p. 11664.

vailing prejudice. For this apparent weakness he has been harshly criticized by some Negroes, who lose sight of his sensibilities as an artist and of the fact that his talent needed the kind of stimulus that only acceptance could give him.

His bitterness, however, was tempered with gratitude for the favors that fortune seemed to hold for him. Henry Tanner was blessed with a personality that inspired affection and confidence and throughout his life he never lacked friends at a time when he needed them. One of these times came shortly after he returned from Florida. He made the acquaintance of C. H. Shearer, a landscape painter from Reading, Pennsylvania, who had studied abroad and whose stories of life in Düsseldorf and Munich fired Tanner's imagination and stirred him with a longing to go abroad.

He did more for Tanner than fire his imagination:

> A visit to him always renewed my courage, not that courage which was necessary to my work but the courage that was necessary to overcome some of the unkind things I had to struggle with. He would remove, at least for a time, that repressing load which I carried, a load that was as trying to me as that carried by poor Pilgrim. I was extremely timid, and to be made to feel that I was not wanted, although in a place where I had every right to be, even months afterward caused me sometimes weeks of pain. Every time any one of these disagreeable incidents came into my mind, my heart sank, and I was anew tortured by the thought of what I had endured, almost as much as by the incident itself.[6]

It may have been Shearer, or possibly his old friend James Hess, who persuaded him to study at the Pennsylvania Academy of the Fine Arts. In any case, in 1880, when Henry Tanner was twenty-one years old, he was enrolled as a student in the new academy.

He could not have studied at a better school or, fortunately for him, at a better time. Thomas Eakins, one of the finest art

6. Ibid., p. 11664.

teachers in the United States and considered by many critics one of America's most promising artists—he was then thirty-six years old—was in charge of instruction at the academy with the title of "Professor of drawing and painting." He had succeeded to this position the year before when old, half-paralysed Professor Christian Schussele, his former teacher, had died, thereby breaking a final bond with the "fusty, fudgy" Pennsylvania Academy of former years.

The appointment of Eakins to Schussele's position was not looked on favorably by the board of directors of the academy. These men were not artists, but the elite of Philadelphia society, a society that had little interest in the new American intellectual life arising from immigrant sources. Conservatism was its keynote. The directors of the academy, representing this narrow outlook, were understandably suspicious of a young "radical" who showed such little propriety as to paint *The Gross Clinic*, a realistic portrayal of an operation directed by the prominent surgeon, Dr. Samuel D. Gross, at the Jefferson Medical College, and a picture the centennial judges had refused to hang in the art gallery on the grounds of "bad taste." Nor did they approve of his methods of teaching, in which he subordinated the study of the antique to that of the living model. Further, he emphasized the importance of studying the nude and was as forthright in discussing the structure of the human body in the women's life class as in the men's. Under Eakins's progressive leadership students no longer organized their own life classes with the curator standing over them to see that a decorous silence was maintained between the class and the female model, who wore a mask to protect her modesty. Eakins also had his more advanced students dissect cadavers, as he had done at Jefferson Medical College and in Paris, in order to give them a better understanding of human anatomy.

But the dissenting board members had little choice in the matter of Eakins's appointment. He had proved his ability and popularity as a teacher during Schussele's long illness, and Fairman Rogers, the wealthy and influential chairman of the committee of instruction, was a close friend and advocate of his. Nevertheless, the conservative members remained antagonistic to Eakins's liberal ideas and in February, 1886—a little over two years after Fairman Rogers had retired—they forced Eakins's resignation. It was a blow to his students, who backed him almost unanimously, as well as to his reputation and prestige as an artist.

There can be no doubt that Eakins was a teacher rarely surpassed in excellence. Robert Henri wrote:

> . . . it was an excitement to hear his pupils talk of him. They believed in him as a great master, and there were stories of his power, his will in the pursuit of study, his unswerving adherence to his ideals, his great willingness to give, to help, and the pleasure he had in seeing the original and worthy crop out in the students' work.[7]

Cecilia Beaux, who "watched him from behind staircases and corners, a curious instinct of self-preservation" keeping her outside the magic circle, commented:

> No one who studied under him ever forgot his precepts, or could be interested in any principles of Art that did not include his. They were rock-bottom, fundamental, but somehow reached regions, by research, that others could not gain by flight.[8]

He was the kind of teacher to appeal to a young Negro of sensitive nature, and it is not surprising that Henry Tanner quickly fell under the spell of his magic. Tanner became so eager to please his teacher that after receiving a word of praise about a picture, he says he would sometimes not touch it for a week. But Eakins could not put up with indecisiveness.

7. *The Art Spirit* (Philadelphia and London: J. B. Lippincott Co., 1923), p. 87.

8. *Background With Figures* (New York: Houghton Mifflin Co., 1930), p. 96.

"What have you been doing?" he once said. "Get it—get it better or get it worse. No middle ground of compromise."[9] This was a lesson that Tanner learned with difficulty, for at this stage of his life he needed praise to sustain his self-confidence in a way that would have been incomprehensible to the single-minded Eakins.

What Tanner did learn from Eakins was a feeling for the structure and weight of the human body and a knowledge of how to express this in two dimensions. Eakins believed this possibly the most important aspect of art that a painter could master. W. C. Brownell, the critic, who visited Eakins's class, wrote that "When Mr. Eakins finds any of his pupils painting flat, losing sight of the solidity, weight and roundness of the figure, he sends him across the hall to the modelling room for a few weeks."[10]

Tanner also learned the importance of light in the construction of his pictures—not the impressionist's light that blurs and disintegrates form, but light that reveals the character and nature of things, whether it is a group of French fishermen, the gnarled trunk of an old tree, or the head of a Biblical prophet.

At the time Henry Tanner was his pupil, Eakins's pictures were showing a change in subject matter and style from those painted a few years earlier. He was less interested in such vigorous subjects as rowing, sailing, and hunting, and more interested in pastoral scenes. The scientific draftsmanship and low-key color of *Max Schmitt in a Single Scull* (1871) had given way to the softer, more subtle atmospheric effects of *Mending the Net* (1881).

The change was also apparent in Eakins's growing interest in indoor scenes like *The Chess Players* (1876), *Courtship* (1879), *Retrospection* (1880) and *The Pathetic Song* (1881)—pictures that are as close to genre as Eakins ever got.

9. Tanner, "Story of an Artist's Life," p. 11665.

10. Cited in Lloyd Goodrich, *Thomas Eakins* (New York: Whitney Muesum of American Art, 1933), p. 77.

The new approach marked a stage in Eakins's transition from an artist preoccupied with physical activity and the human body to one in whom character was a dominant interest. It was a stage that found a responsive chord in Henry Tanner who, unlike his teacher, was neither a scientist nor an independent thinker. Raised in the bosom of African Methodism and acutely conscious from early childhood of the Negro's inferior position in American society, Tanner sought in his painting an emotional escape from the unhappy realities of life. His teacher's temporary allegiance to a more romantic approach to art proved fortunate for him since it provided him with the discipline he needed in a style that was peculiarly congenial.

The Crucifixion, painted in 1881 and the only picture on a religious theme that Eakins ever painted, was an exception to this style. But it did not inspire Tanner to find in the Bible the kind of subject for which he was later to become famous. By religion Eakins was an agnostic, and his *Crucifixion*, far from being religious in tone, was the highly realistic study of a figure hanging on a cross. One of his students posed for the picture, strapped to a cross and hoisted up out of doors, and from this simulation of a crucifixion, Eakins studied the effect of the sagging weight on the nailed hands and exhausted muscles of the body. It is powerful and dramatic in its naturalism, yet would have appealed less to Tanner than those pictures of Eakins's, painted about the same time, that evoke a quiet sentiment.

One aspect of Eakins's scientific bent, however, had important consequences for Henry Tanner. This was his interest in photography. Initiated by Daguerre in 1839, photography had reached a stage of development that made it a practical asset to artists. No one, for instance, really knew what a horse's four legs did while in a gallop. The keenest eye could not decide whether the traditional gallop, with all legs extended simultaneously, was correct. It was believed that instantaneous photography could solve the controversy as well as other problems of rapid locomotion, and various devices were invented for taking photographs of moving objects. The man most outstanding in the field was Eadweard Muybridge, who photographed a galloping horse by using a series of cameras placed side by side on a track that took successive pictures as the horse went by. Eakins corresponded with Muybridge about this experiment and as a result of the correspondence invited him to give a series of lectures on photography at the Pennsylvania Academy of the Fine Arts.[11]

Tanner had left the academy by then (1883), but he was aware of Eakins's own experiments with the camera and was himself attracted to photography about this time. As one might expect, it was not the scientific side of photography that intrigued Tanner but its pictorial possibilities.

Henry Tanner spent only two years at the Pennsylvania Academy of the Fine Arts, and why he left after so short a time is not clear. It has sometimes been attributed to the fact that he won no awards and hence felt discriminated against. This could hardly have been the case. At the time he was enrolled at the school there were no awards given. The Charles Tappan prize was put up in 1881 when Tanner had been at the academy only one year, and the Temple Competition in Historical Painting, with a first prize of $3,000, was not given until 1883. Eakins himself did not believe in awards. He thought that a student who needed a prize to stimulate his interest in art was not genuinely interested—an understandable attitude in a man who himself had been a professional artist for ten years and, aside from his teaching, had received only $2,000 from his art. He had sold just eight of his paintings.

In "The Story of an Artist's Life" and in his various "jottings" Tanner says little about his days as a student at the academy, so it is difficult to reconstruct his life there except

11. W. J. Homer and J. Talbot, "Eakins, Muybridge and the Motion Picture Process," *Art Quarterly*, 26 (Summer, 1963): 203.

as one of two hundred-odd students. He was the only Negro in the school, and this in itself would have set him apart. But Tanner was a tall, cultivated, fine-looking man with a pleasing, gracious manner that won people, and in the enlightened atmosphere of Thomas Eakin's classes it is unreasonable to believe that he made no friends or was not generally accepted.

Eakins himself, though temperamentally poles apart from Tanner, had great respect for his student's ability as an artist and great liking for him as a person. This is verified by the fact that he accorded him an honor bestowed on only a few of his students—he painted his portrait.[12] It was not painted during the years Tanner was his pupil, but more than a decade later on one of Tanner's infrequent trips home from Europe, after he had made a reputation for himself in Paris. It is only incidentally the portrait of a Negro. The face that Eakins recorded is that of a distinguished gentleman, thoughtful and assured. A great deal had happened to change the timid, sensitive, Negro youth into the man who was one of the most talked-about artists in Paris.

12. The portrait of Henry O. Tanner by Thomas Eakins is in the Hyde collection, Glens Falls, New York. It is an oil on canvas, 24⅛ by 20¼ in.

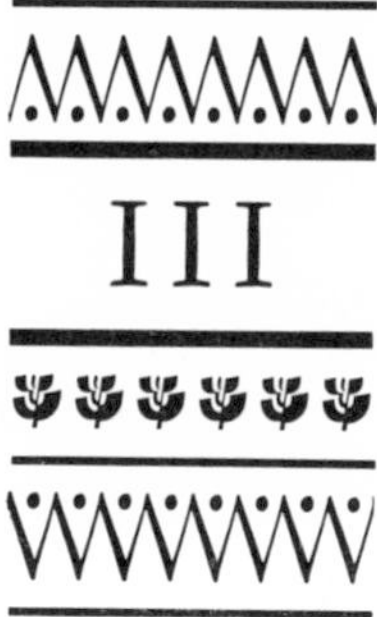

Life in the South

For seven years after leaving the Pennsylvania Academy of the Fine Arts Henry Tanner remained in Philadelphia, trying to establish himself as a professional artist. He turned to illustration, as did many young artists hoping to make a living by their art, and dispatched his black and white drawings with fair regularity to New York publishers. They came back with discouraging promptness but, "as fast as they would be returned with thanks by one they were off to another."[1] The first illustration that "stayed," and for which he received a check for $40, made him wonder how publishers could pay such big prices.

One illustration drew $50 and appeared as a full page illustration in the January 10, 1888, issue of *Harper's Young People.*

1. Henry Ossawa Tanner, "The Story of an Artist's Life," *World's Work*, 18 (June and July, 1909): 11665.

In this pen-and-ink drawing Tanner showed his ability to give poetic charm to what, at the hands of a lesser artist, would have been a pedestrian sketch. In the picture two little girls are standing beside a railed enclosure at the zoo watching some friendly and inquisitive deer come toward them. The older child holds the younger one protectively by the arm as she prepares to make an offering to the nearest animal. It is not the children or the elderly lady with the muff in the background that give appeal to the picture, but the bare trees etched with snow, the twilight sky, and the gentle animals. In the drawing of the deer Tanner showed his sensitive feeling for animal life, a feeling shared by Thomas Eakins, who also spent much time at the Philadelphia Zoo. However different in temperament Eakins and Tanner were, in their response to animals they had a great deal in common.

Besides his illustrations Tanner sold an occasional landscape or animal painting, not only to Bishop Payne and other of his father's friends but to the anonymous public who knew nothing about him. One of his best sales was a painting of *A Lion at Home*, which was sold by the Academy of Design for $80.

But the reputation he hoped for did not materialize; nor were his sales very encouraging. By 1888, when the Reverend Benjamin Tanner was elected a bishop in the African Methodist Church, it began to look as though his artist-son was getting nowhere in spite of the fact that his pictures were shown at the annual exhibits of the Pennsylvania Academy of the Fine Arts and the National Academy of Design in New York.

It had been Tanner's hope to follow in the footsteps of Thomas Eakins and other American artists and go abroad for additional study. He knew that European study not only improved an artist's skill but gave him the kind of prestige that was invaluable in establishing a reputation at home. He also knew that in the great art centers of Europe a man's race was no obstacle to his success as an artist. His father went to

London in 1881 to attend the Ecumenical Council meeting and no doubt corroborated much that Henry had heard about the freedom and equality a Negro enjoyed abroad.

As the years passed, however, there seemed little likelihood that Henry Tanner could get to Europe without imposing a great financial burden on his father who, though well off, had a large family to provide for, including another son, Carlton, born in 1870. He saw only one solution and that was to combine business with art. He had a reasonable degree of skill in photography, and as a commercial photographer he thought he might not only free himself from financial obligation to his father but save something toward a trip abroad. Photography had an advantage over other businesses in that it could give him the leisure to do some painting and modelling on the side.

He evidently thought Philadelphia too large and competitive a city for his business enterprise and wished to settle in a smaller community, though one with a large Negro population since white people were not apt to patronize a Negro photographer. He selected Atlanta, Georgia, as the site for his photographic venture.

There were other reasons for his selection of Atlanta. It was a city noted for its progressiveness, having grown remarkably in size and wealth since the end of the war. A number of Negroes, born in slavery, had accumulated property and were conducting successful businesses there. And it was an important seat of Negro education. Through his father and Bishop Payne he was acquainted with Morris Brown College, founded by the African Methodist Church in 1880, and with the other Negro schools located in Atlanta: Spelman College for Girls, Gammon Theological Seminary, the Baptist Seminary that had moved to Atlanta from Augusta in 1879, and Clark and Atlanta Universities. This last, which had originated as a small school in a railroad boxcar, had graduated its first college class in 1876 and drew to its faculty graduates of Harvard, Yale, Wellesley, and other well-known eastern institutions. Atlanta seemed, on the face of things, to offer the kind of contacts that would be helpful to Tanner in a business venture.

The idea of living in the South could hardly have appealed otherwise to a man like Henry Tanner. He had been to Florida and experienced the patronizing condescension, more cutting than outright hostility, that prevailed in the southern states. He knew that no amount of talent could break down the rigid barriers of racial prejudice that existed there. But discrimination was of less importance to him than making the money that would take him to Europe. Henry Tanner went to Georgia sometime in 1888, probably in the late summer or fall.

Atlanta, by 1888, had a population close to 65,000. It was no longer a wooden, muddy, gas-lit town but a thriving, modern city with many brick buildings and some streets that were paved and lighted by electricity. It had as yet no hospital or art gallery or public library—which would have been closed to Tanner in any case—but it had a Chatauqua, located at Lithia Springs, and the beginning of a Georgia School of Technology. The *Atlanta Constitution*, on July 29, 1889, boasted that Atlanta was unrivalled, "the gate-city of the South."

Atlanta had begun as "Terminus," a railroad settlement, in 1837. As a railroad and distributing center it had prospered. Atlantans, basking in the illusion that they were part of an old southern culture, had developed as time went on a typical Old South nostalgia for their romantic prewar past. But it is highly doubtful whether that past was characterized by anything but a hard-bitten spirit of enterprise which even the Union forces could not destroy.

This spirit had its effect on Negroes as well as whites. Perhaps in no other southern city were they as active in business or as thrifty and astute in handling their money as in Atlanta. In 1890 R. D. Badger, a Negro dentist, paid taxes on $9,600 worth of property—not to be compared with the millions some white men had made since the war, but a considerable sum for a man who had been a slave less than three decades before. Badger was not the only Negro who had established a degree of financial security.

The progressive outlook of Atlanta Negroes was nowhere more apparent than in their attitude toward education. The first schools for Negro children were sponsored in the sixties by the benevolent American Missionary Association and the Freedmen's Aid Society, but Negroes in Atlanta were soon contributing significant sums to educate their children, as well as to build churches and homes. Nor was it many years before they were teaching their own people. Teaching was one of the few professions open to educated Negroes, for white southerners, who equated a desire for professional standing with a demand for racial and social equality, were determined to limit their opportunities. Only the more venturesome went into business.

By most white people, credit for a Negro's success was given to the institution of slavery, not personal enterprise. In a series of interviews with Negroes who had done well in business the *Atlanta Constitution* of August 31, 1890, commented that as slaves Negroes had learned "culture and refinement," as well as to be "respectable and unobtrusive upon the planes of life which were not their own."

Henry Tanner, when he set up his photographic gallery in Atlanta, had no desire to obtrude himself on any plane of life not his own. Not, however, because he felt in any way inferior—the reverse would surely have been true—but because he invariably shrank from exposing himself to slights and indignities. Yet slights and indignities were, in the South, the Negro's lot, however he might seek to avoid them.

The location of Tanner's "very modest photographic gallery" in Atlanta cannot be determined. No letter describes it, nor is it listed in any city directory. For that matter, the name "Tanner" does not even appear. We do know, however—we have Tanner's word for it—that the photographic venture was a failure. He got the leisure he had hoped for in such abundance that he grew depressed and for a time could do no work at all.

> What had perhaps helped to make the situation more tantalizing was the fact that a picture of mine had been sold in Philadelphia at an auction sale for two hundred and fifty dollars. True, I had received but fifteen, but the incident had given me hope and made me more than ever dissatisfied with the four or five dollars a week I was making in that miserable gallery. . . .[2]

It was at this very distressing period of Tanner's life that he had the good fortune to meet Bishop and Mrs. Hartzell, who for the next few years became his patrons. Bishop Joseph Crane Hartzell—"the man who put the Methodist Episcopal Church on the map of Africa and invested twenty years of his life in the interests of the black race over there"[3]—was at that time a trustee of Methodist Clark University. He was forty-seven years old, a strong and vigorously liberal Christian to whom all men were brothers. His interest in the Negro race, which led him in 1896 to found the Hartzell Training School at Old Umtali in Rhodesia, was deep-seated and ardent. He and his wife often came to Atlanta to attend trustee meetings at Clark. Mrs. Hartzell heard of young Henry Tanner, and seeing his art, recognized in him an unusual talent. Her husband needed no persuasion to see that Tanner was offered a position as teacher of art at Clark University. Tanner gladly accepted, sold his "miserable gallery," and breathed freely again. It was apparent to him that by nature he was not designed for business.

Months stretched ahead of him, however, before his classes would begin. He had heard of the beauty and bracing air of

2. Ibid., p. 11666.
3. Quoted from a folder on Bishop Joseph Hartzell, Tanner Collection, Archives of American Art, Detroit.

the North Carolina mountains, and decided to go to Highlands, hoping to make his expenses there with his camera. He rented a small cabin—"fragrant from the new pine logs used in its construction"[4]—and for a time enjoyed the natives' bill of fare, corn bread and applesauce. But there was an oasis in this bare existence—some white friends by the name of Clifford. Wesley Clifford was a teacher at Clark University, and he and his family were vacationing at Highlands. They not only invited Henry to dinner but through their friendly overtures secured an order for him to photograph a small cottage. Other orders followed.

> I made photos of the whole immediate region—a most lovely country and as no photographer had ever visited it before, they were a success, and my hard times—very hard times—vanished as the mountain mists do before the sun.[5]

The lovely scenery of the Blue Ridge Mountains was alone enough to inspire him with a desire to take up painting again. But he had an added inspiration. In the small mountain cabins of the poor Negroes Henry Tanner found new and appealing subjects. It is from his experiences at Highlands that one of his finest paintings is derived—*The Banjo Lesson*—now hanging at Hampton Institute in Virginia. Though the style of the painting indicates a somewhat later date than 1889, it was apparently done from one of the many sketches he made at Highlands.

In *The Banjo Lesson* Tanner, for the first time, came close to rivaling his teacher, Thomas Eakins, in a sincere expression of life. It has been called "sentimental genre" by some critics, but like Eakins's *The Pathetic Song* it has a quality the ordinary storytelling picture lacks. In the figure of the old Negro man teaching the little boy to play the banjo the dignity and pathos of old age are expressed in a manner that has none of the banality of ordinary genre. It has been lamented by critics that

4. "Story of an Artist's Life," p. 11666.
5. Ibid., p. 11666.

Tanner turned his back on this type of painting, which elevates the poor Negro to a higher role than that of the simpleminded darky. But at the time this picture was painted Henry Tanner's career was still ahead of him.

When Tanner returned to Atlanta from the Blue Ridge he had pleasant associates to look forward to and a studio in which to work. Clark University, begun as a primary school in 1869, was a liberal arts college located on 400 acres of land a few miles south of the city. It was staffed in the main with well-trained white teachers, but the most notable teacher at the school was a Negro, William H. Crogman, who had been one of the first six students to graduate from Atlanta University. The first commission that Henry Tanner was given in the fall of 1889 was for a portrait of Professor Crogman.

In the minutes of the tenth Annual Trustees Meeting held on May 29, 1889, at Clark University no special mention is made of Henry Tanner, and he is not listed among the fourteen teachers for whose combined salaries $7,670 was set aside by the Freedmen's Aid Society.[6] It is believed that his classes were composed almost entirely of teachers who paid the special fee that was usually required for "extras" like art or music.

It is an interesting commentary on the times that Atlanta, conscious of its shortcomings in having no art society that was felt needed "to give still larger expression and further embodiment to the rapidly widening culture of Atlantans,"[7] completely ignored the one man who might have added distinction to the city as an artist of rare talent. In the *Atlanta Constitution* of November 30, 1890, there was a long write-up of the purveyors of art in Atlanta, and Tanner's name, that was to become famous in the greatest art center in the world, is notable by its absence. Those mentioned, instead, are the now forgotten names of Miss Minnie McAfee, whose "work shows

6. Minutes, 10th Annual Trustees' Meeting, May 29, 1889, Clark University, Atlanta,Ga.

7. Quoted from a letter by J. G. Armstrong, in the *Atlanta Constitution*, August 3, 1888.

delicacy of touch and a fine finish rarely seen outside the Academies," Mrs. Charles Loring, who "has had instructions in the finest schools in the country," Mrs. J. R. Gregory, whose portraits of Stephens and Johnson were hanging in the State House, and Miss Mamie Griggs, "a graceful, pleasant little lady, whose winning manners render her a popular favorite." Also, Mrs. Chisolm, "our flower artist," and Miss Hattie Ellis, "who teaches art at the Capitol Female College."

There were gentlemen devotees of the arts as well, notably Mr. Hal Morrison, whose "charming rooms on Peachtree are a favorite resort for many of our young people who admire pretty things," and Mr. Orion Frazee, who had created the death mask of Jefferson and the bust of Henry Grady. But the best known of all was Mr. William Lycett, "an indispensible [*sic*] factor of Atlanta society." His was the first art school in Atlanta, started in 1863.

It would be interesting to know whether Henry Tanner and William Lycett ever met. Lycett was not a southerner, not even American born. He had come with his father and brothers from Staffordshire as a boy and had graduated from Cooper Union School in New York. But as one of the leading citizens in Atlanta, a prominent Mason, and a member of the old Governor's Horse Guard, whose patrons were among the elite of the state, it seems unlikely that he would have taken more than a passing interest in a young Negro artist, even one who had been privileged to study under Thomas Eakins. Mr. Eakins was, after all, under something of a cloud at that time and seemed unlikely to emerge. But Tanner knew that in coming south he would not be accepted, so anonymity was expected. Ignored by the citizens of Atlanta, he was nevertheless happy in his associates at Clark University, two of whom remained his lifelong friends, Wesley Clifford and Bishop Hartzell.

Years later, in the late 1920's, an Atlanta businessman by the name of Joseph Haverty took an interest in Tanner's art and bought several of his paintings for the High Museum in Atlanta. In a letter dated December 12, 1931, he sent Tanner a check for $451, the balance due on three pictures he had received the previous month. In this letter he makes the comment:

> We had a very nice reception of the three new pictures at our Museum and considerable publicity was given them. In discussing the painter with some of our friends at the Museum on last Sunday week, I was told that at one time you were teaching art in the Clarke [*sic*] University in Atlanta. Is this true?

It is an unspoken commentary that Tanner had not mentioned his life in Atlanta to Mr. Haverty.

During the year that Henry Tanner spent at Clark University he not only taught art but painted portraits and made some interesting plaster models of Negroes. Among these was a bust of Bishop Payne, now located at Central State College in Ohio.

His friends at Clark were encouraging, and there were two who were determined for him to have the opportunity to develop his talent beyond the level it had already reached. These were Bishop Hartzell and his wife. Mrs. Hartzell was a woman of discrimination who believed firmly that Henry Tanner should realize the dreams he imparted to her of studying in Italy. She suggested having an exhibition of his art in Cincinnati, the headquarters of the board of education of the Methodist Church. It was arranged for the fall of 1890 and for three weeks the people of Cincinnati, especially the Methodists, were invited to enjoy the pictures of the talented young artist, Henry Ossawa Tanner. But, like the photographic gallery on which Tanner had pinned his hopes, the exhibition was a failure —not one picture was sold. It seemed as though Tanner was doomed never to reach his promised land.

Bishop and Mrs. Hartzell, however, had other ideas. They were convinced that he was no ordinary artist and were willing to invest in his talent. They bought the entire lot of his pictures for about $300, and this, with a commission of $75 from a "Mr. E—— of Phila" was sufficient to start him on his travels and support him briefly in Europe. Bishop Tanner agreed to assist his son with additional funds, enough to sustain him modestly while he carried on his studies abroad. So, at the age of thirty-one, Henry Tanner was finally on the road he wanted most to travel. He sailed out of New York on the *City of Chester* January 4, 1891, headed for Rome via Liverpool, London, and Paris, taking with him memories of a life that by racial standards then existing had been fortunate but which to him was far from satisfactory.

IV

The Artist in America 1891

WHEN HENRY OSSAWA TANNER SAILED FOR EUROPE IN 1891 he was following a fashion set by the colonial painter, Benjamin West, in 1759. Since then each generation of aspiring artists had seen some of their numbers cross the ocean to find in the Old World the training and artistic stimulus they felt were missing in America. In colonial days they had gone to England, then had left the new republic for Italy, Germany, and France. Some of these artists, having independent means or realizing professional success in Europe, remained abroad permanently, preferring exile in a land where art was recognized and honored to life in a country without artistic standards. Others came home and taught what they had learned or set up studios only to find that wealthy Americans usually preferred to invest their money in the works of European artists rather than in those of their own compatriots. The atmosphere was not a happy one for artists. Matthew Arnold wrote in 1885:

> I asked a German portrait painter, whom I found painting and prospering in America, how he liked the country. "How *can* an artist like it?" was his answer. "The American artists live chiefly in Europe; all Americans of cultivation and wealth visit Europe more and more constantly. The mere nomenclature of the country acts upon a cultivated person like the incessant pricking of pins."[1]

By 1891 it was no longer London or Rome or Düsseldorf that attracted American artists but Munich and especially Paris, where the rooms of the Beaux Arts school and numerous academies were thronged with American art students, sons of the wealthy and prominent as well as the less privileged. During the holidays and summer vacations they set up their easels in Normandy, Brittany, Fontainebleau, and along the banks of the Seine and painted French landscapes and French peasants and fishermen, in the intimate style of the Barbizon painters or the plein-air manner of Monet.

There were art schools at home, of course—the National Academy, the Art Students' League, the Pennsylvania Academy of the Fine Arts, the private schools run by Chase and Henri—where life classes were conducted and the technical aspects of painting taught; but the atmosphere was not the same as in Paris. An artist's career was not considered important in America.

The "studio piece" of an American artist—the historical or allegorical painting so favored by the Beaux Arts and admired in the Salons—found few buyers among the American middle class. These imposing pictures made a fine showing on exhibition walls but they were too large for most living rooms, and their subject matter did not appeal to the average American. If an American had a taste for lofty sentiments, and could

1. *Civilization in the United States* (Boston: De Wolfe, Fiske and Co., 1888), p. 175.

afford it, the chances are he preferred to buy the genuine European product by an artist with an established reputation.

Those artists who wished to express great thoughts or kindle noble feelings—the Idealists—had to find additional means of adding to their livelihood. Some, the more fortunate, received commissions to paint mural decorations for public buildings, but most turned to illustration as the surest way to earn a living. Will H. Low, describing the situation, quoted an artist friend:

> Yes, we return from Europe, undecided whether we'll go back to Paris for the rest of our life, or stay here and build a studio big enough for our work; and then, after a little, we're blamed glad to make drawings for some magazine at thirty dollars a drawing.[2]

It was perhaps no great loss to American art that many of these artists were diverted from their flights of fancy. The subject-matter of their pictures is, for the most part, vapid and contrived. Even the paintings of Edwin Austin Abbey and John LaFarge, who rose above the prevailing level of mediocrity in their skillful drawing and fine decorative sense, fail to reveal the depth of expression necessary to great imaginative painting. Nevertheless, they drew high praise from the critics. Abbott Thayer's *Madonna Enthroned* and Kenyon Cox's *Painting and Poetry* were lavished with praise at the 1893 Chicago Exposition and Thayer's *Caritas* won the $3,000 prize in 1896 at the Pennsylvania Academy of the Fine Arts. In these "ideal" pictures the decorous, vacuous, well-draped young female figure is a favorite; no hint of sensuous appeal mars the "purity" of her form. It was an age of sterile morality and the artist helped to preserve the illusion.

The nude figure was, of course, unacceptable. America, it was said repeatedly, was not France. Those robust, unashamed, naked women by Courbet and Manet might be tolerated in

2. *A Chronicle of Friendships* (New York: Charles Scribner's Sons, 1908), p. 231.

Paris, but they were considered degenerate and immoral in New York. As late as 1912 a review of an art exhibition in the *Nation* states, "of paintings with the nude there are no less than seven; it quite takes the breath away—one in every eighty."[3]

It was safer, for reputation as well as for pocket, for an artist to turn to genre painting. Anecdotal pictures were always popular. Popular too were the engraving and lithographic reproductions of them that could be sold by the thousands. Yet no artist then living could present ordinary scenes with quite the spirit of William Sidney Mount or Caleb Bingham, unless it was Winslow Homer or Thomas Eakins, and these men were too serious in their intent, too objective in describing what they saw to be classed with the usual genre painter. Homer, earlier in his life—in the sixties and seventies—had painted pictures like *Prisoners at the Front* and *The Bright Side*, but by 1891 he was living and painting in solitude at Prout's Neck in Maine, no longer interested in popular illustration. Homer St. Gaudens, reflecting on the period, wrote:

> Immediately previous to 1893 the bulk of our painting was so much of the sentimental landscape or story-telling type that the mediocre, unimaginative product might have come from almost any land. Indeed for even a year or two after the Exposition the anecdotal picture remained at its all-time high, with the number of square feet in a canvas still a recognized yard stick's worth.[4]

Thomas Hovenden's *Breaking Home Ties* was the type par excellence of this sentimental genre and won the prize by popular vote at the Chicago Exposition. Yet Winslow Homer's *Fox Hunt*, without emotional overtones but powerful in its simple objectivity, hung in the same exhibit.

Homer's clear rendering of the outdoors was as outside the trend of landscape painting in America as Thomas Eakins's

3. "Art in Philadelphia," *Nation*, February 22, 1912, p. 195.
4. *The American Artist and His Times* (New York: Dodd, Mead and Co., 1941), p. 169.

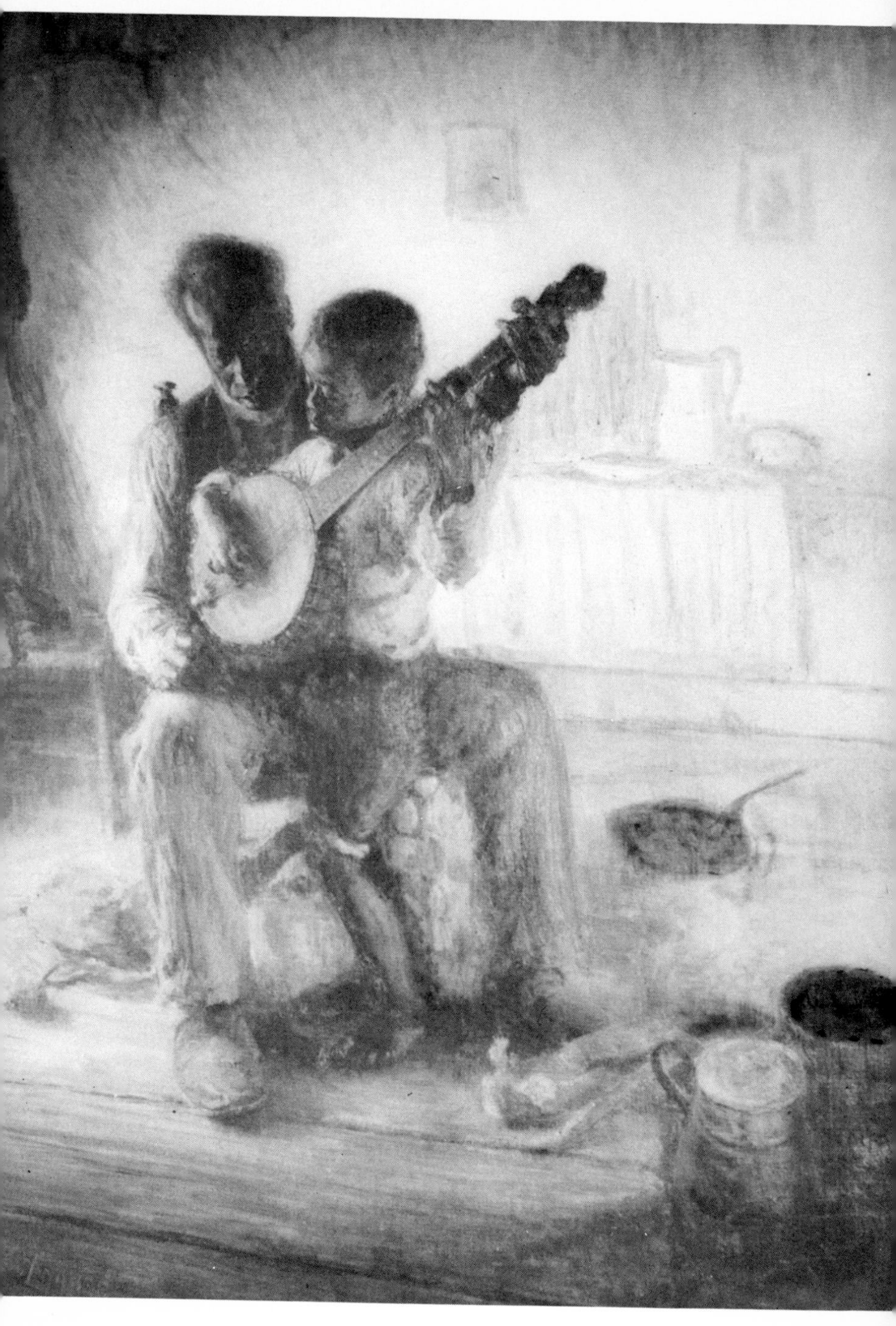

The Banjo Lesson (oil on canvas, 48 inches by 35 inches), c. 1893

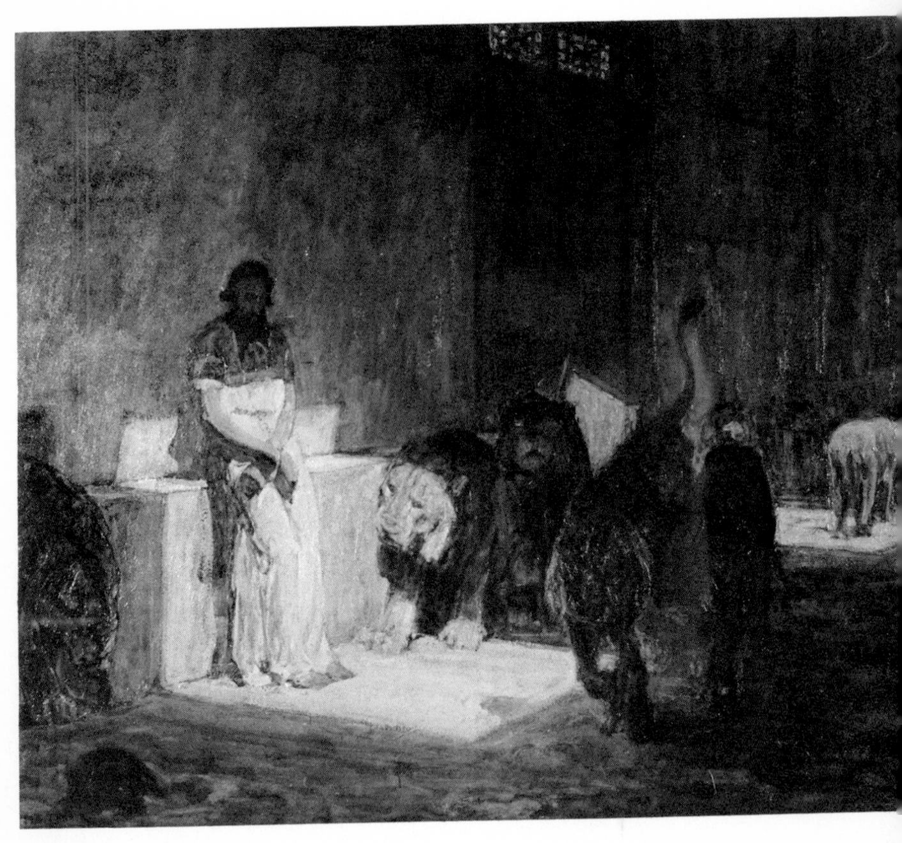

Daniel in the Lions' Den (oil on canvas, 40 inches by 50 inches), 1896

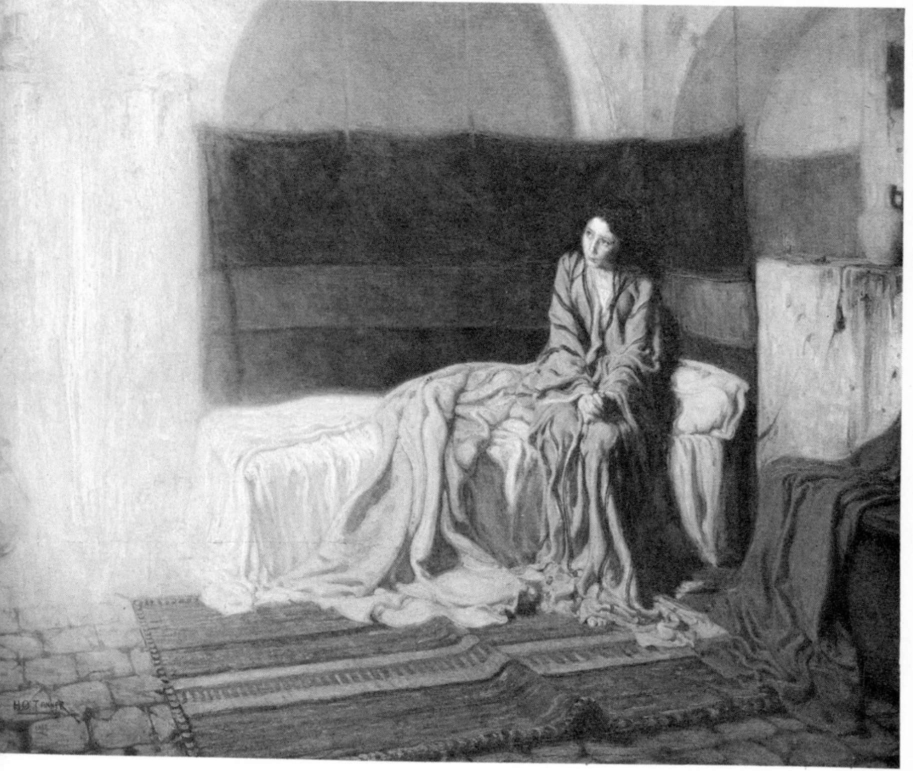

Annunciation (oil on canvas, 57 inches by 71¼ inches), 1898

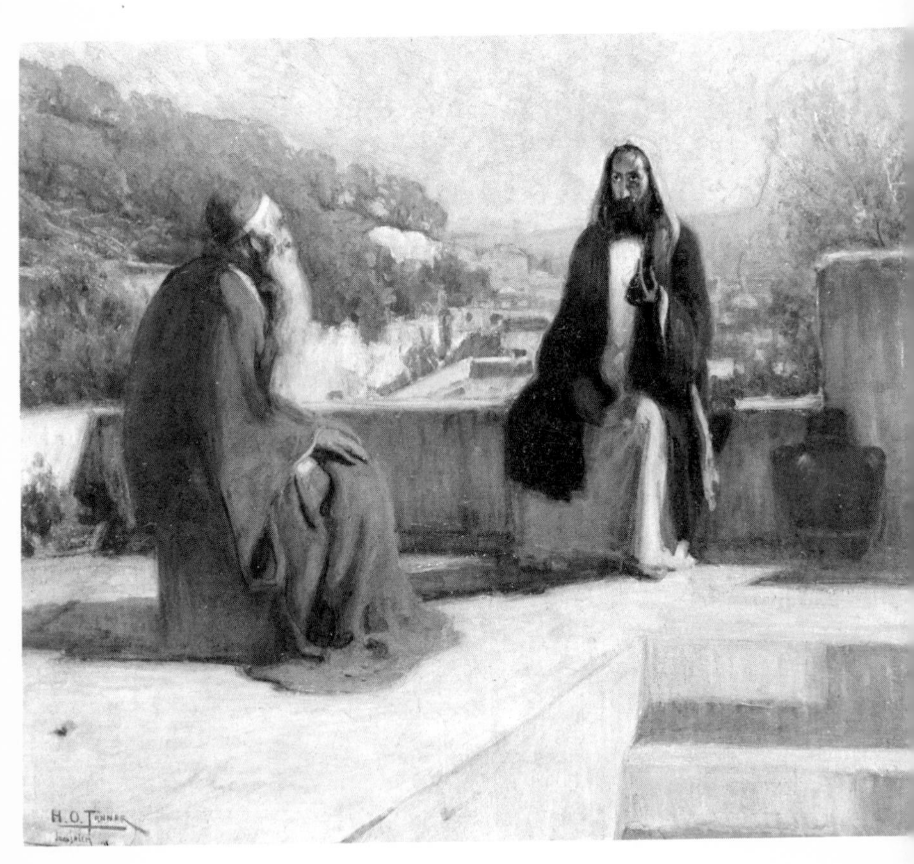

Nicodemus (oil on canvas, 34 inches by 40 inches), 1899

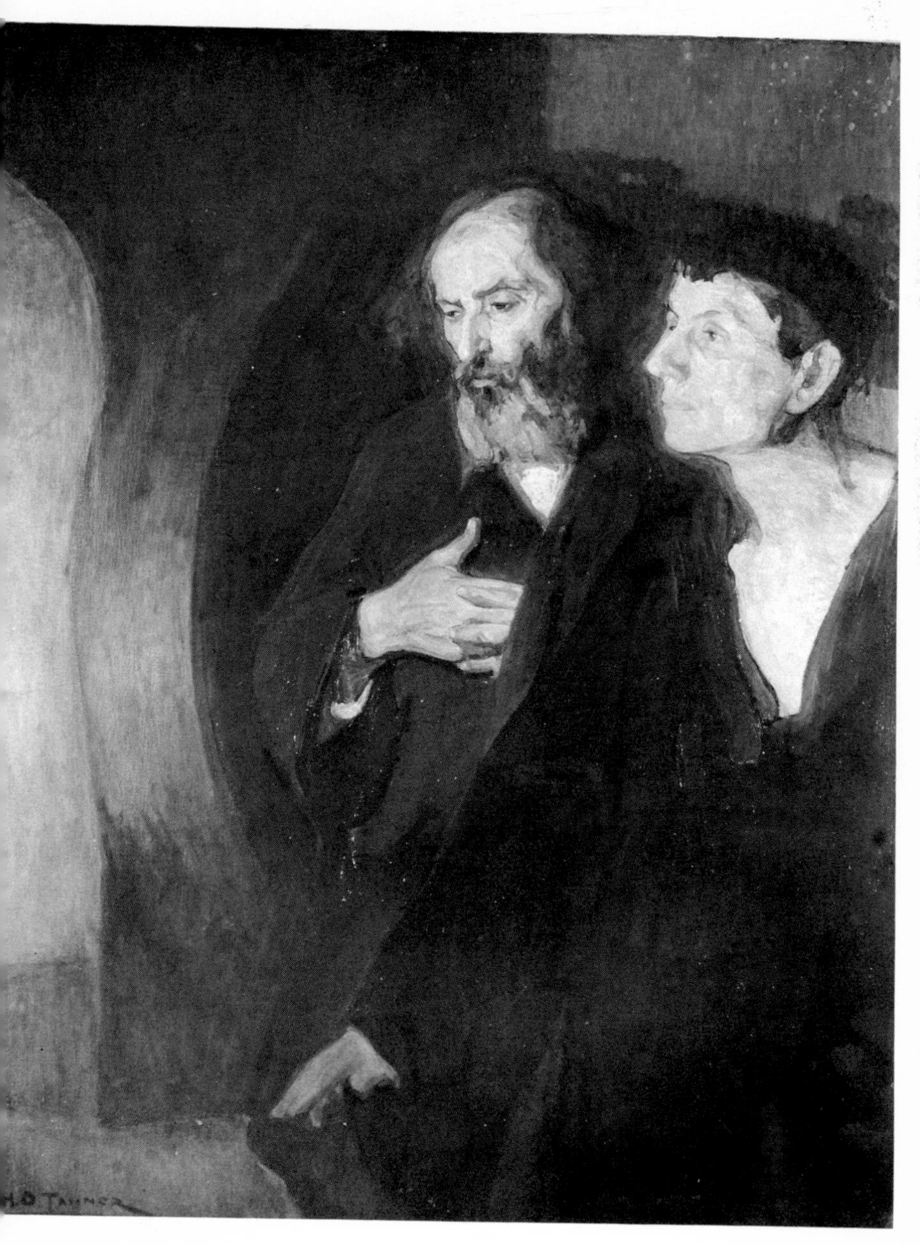

Two Disciples at the Tomb (oil on canvas, 51 inches by 41⅞ inches), 1906

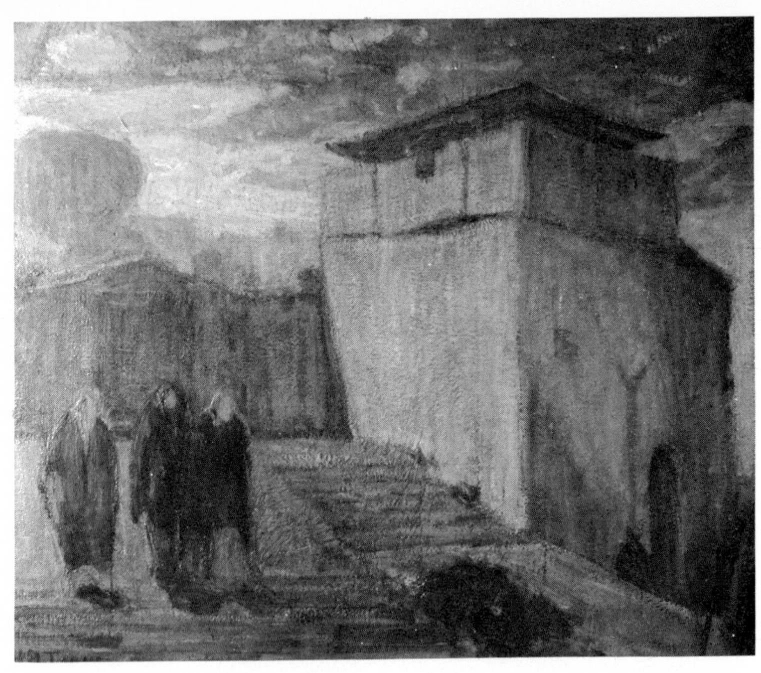

Moonlight, *Hebron* (oil on canvas, $25\frac{11}{16}$ inches by $31\frac{7}{8}$ inches), c. 1912

Sunlight, *Tangiers* (oil on cardboard, $10\frac{5}{8}$ inches by $13\frac{3}{8}$ inches), c. 1912

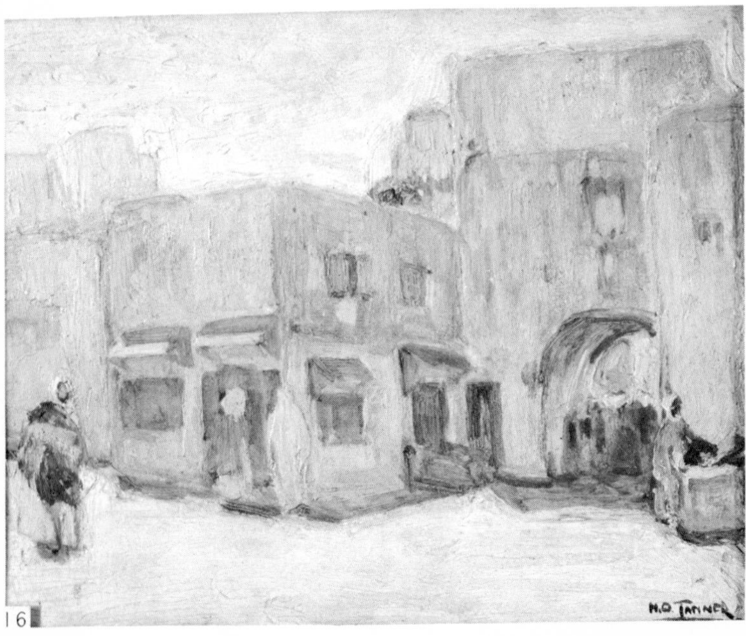

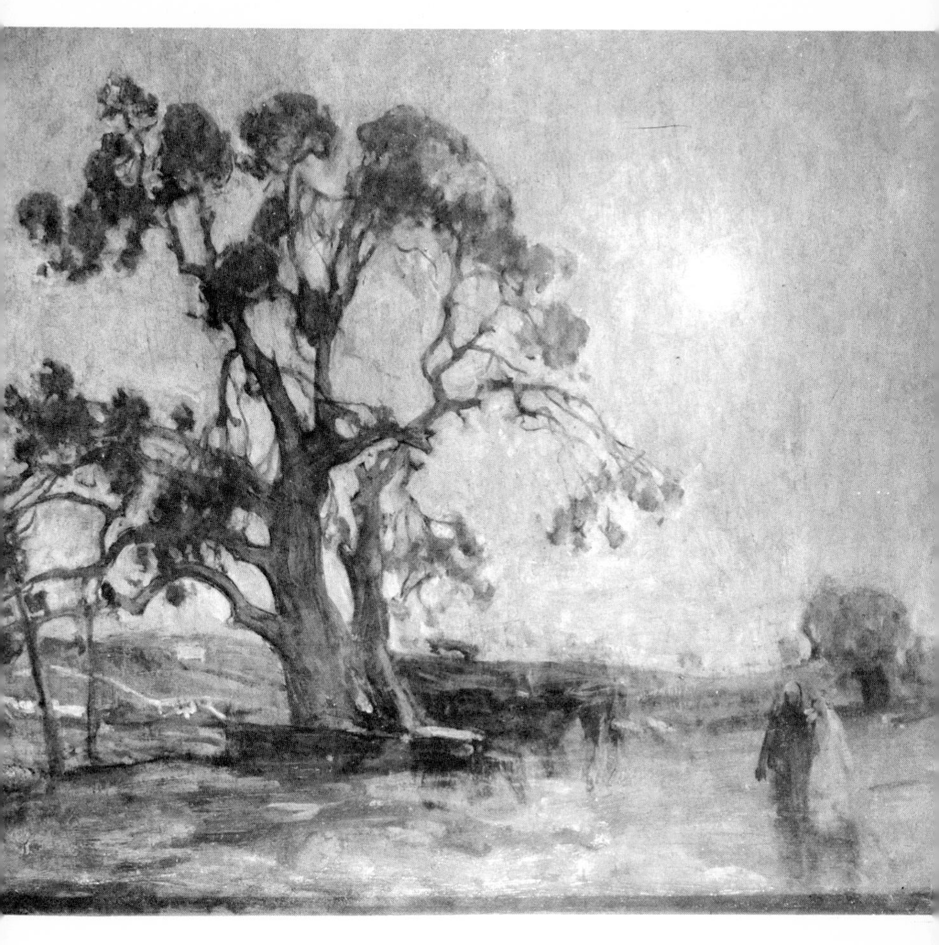

Abraham's Oak (oil on canvas, 29½ inches by 35 inches)

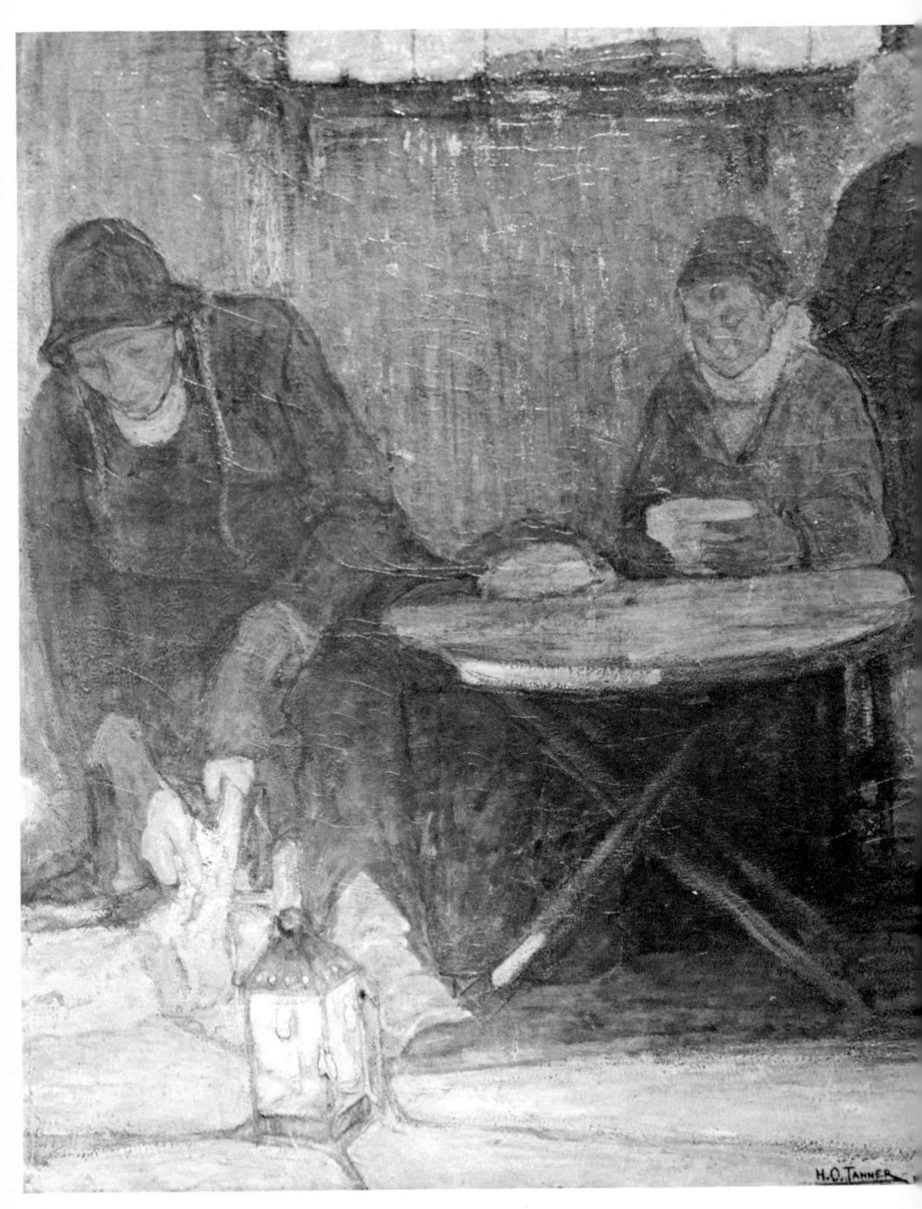

Etaples Fisher Folk (oil and tempera on canvas, 47½ by 37 inches), 1923

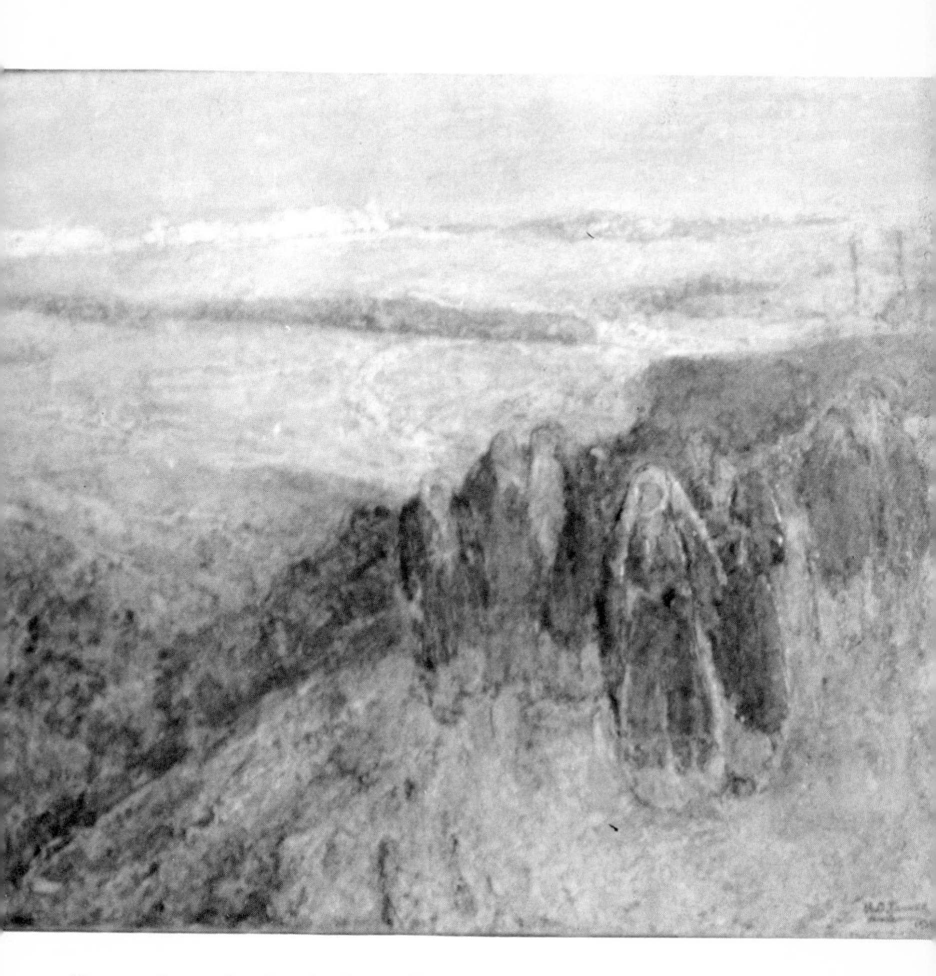

Return from the Crucifixion (oil tempera on board, 18 inches by 23 inches), 1937

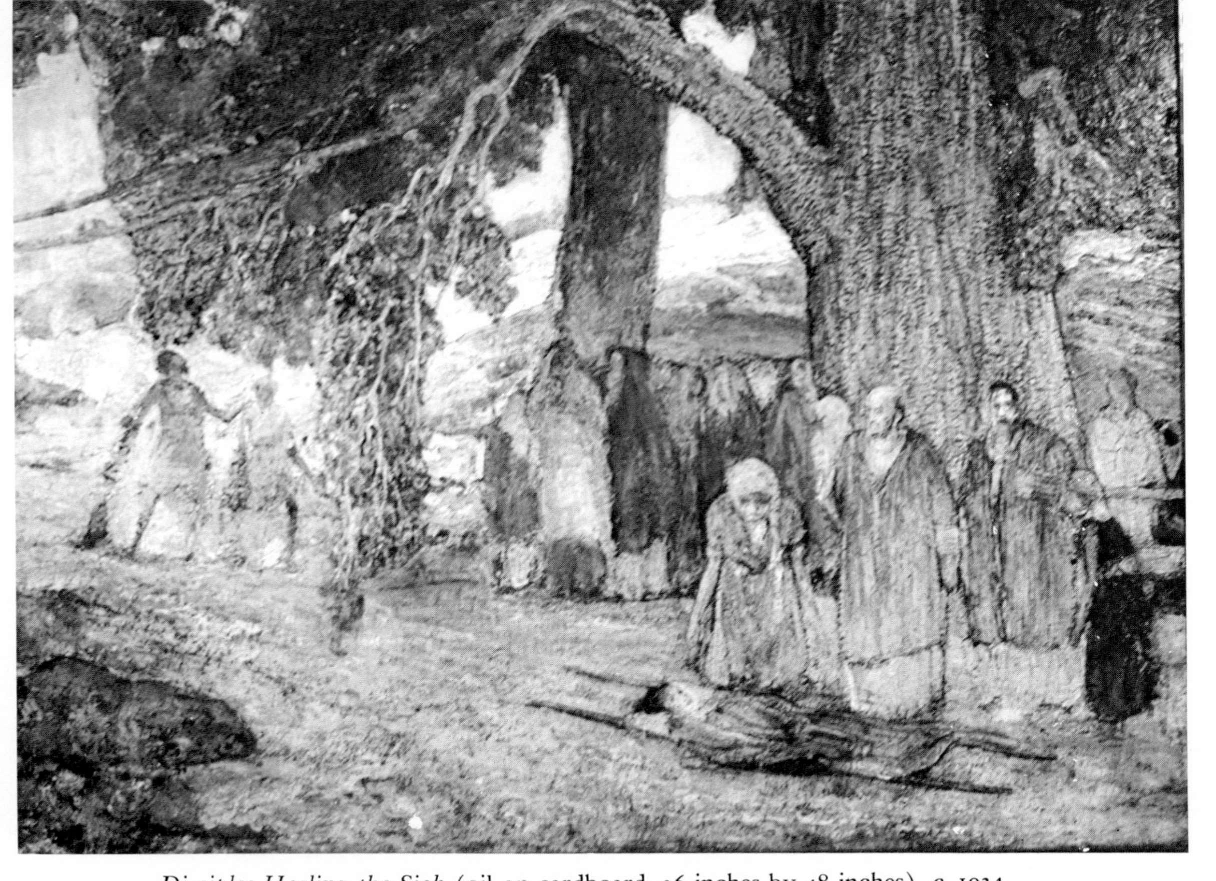

Disciples Healing the Sick (oil on cardboard, 36 inches by 48 inches), c. 1924

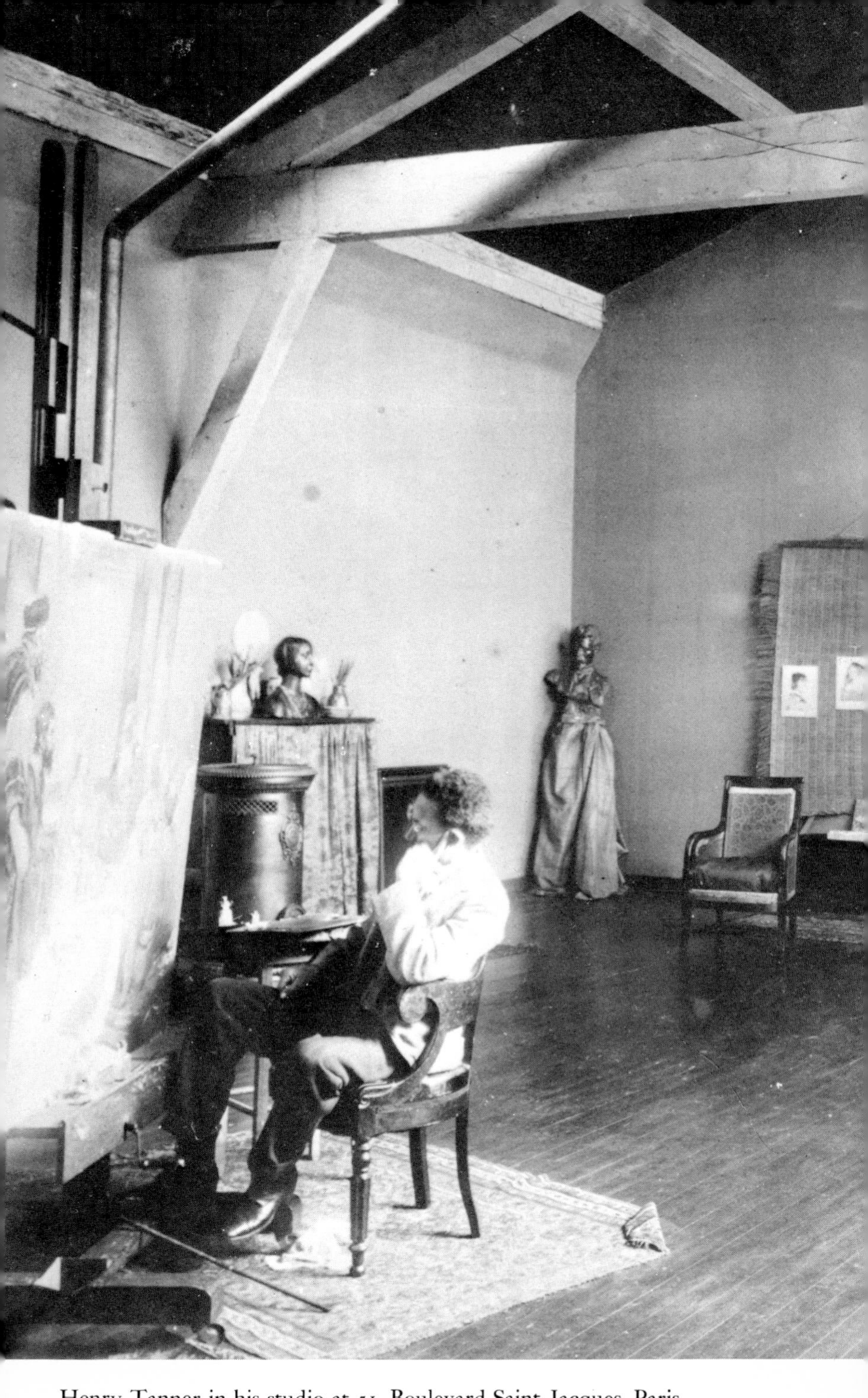

Henry Tanner in his studio at 51, Boulevard Saint-Jacques, Paris

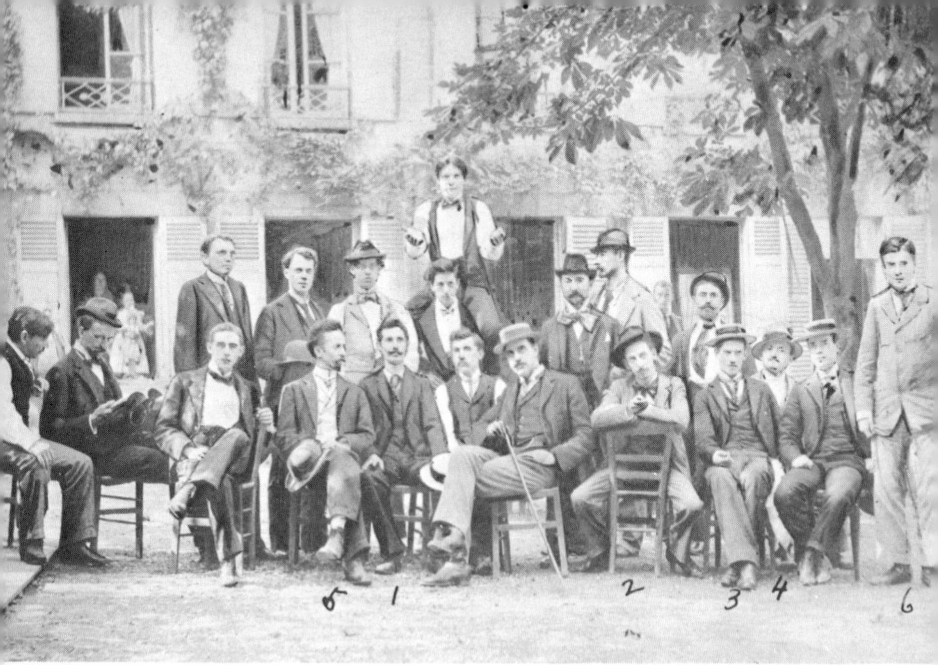

A group of artists in the garden of the American Arts Club on the Boulevard Montparnasse, 1895, including (1) Barlow; (2) Winter; (3) Wood; (4) Landeau; (5) Tanner; and (6) Cucel.

Benjamin Constant, Tanner's professor in Paris

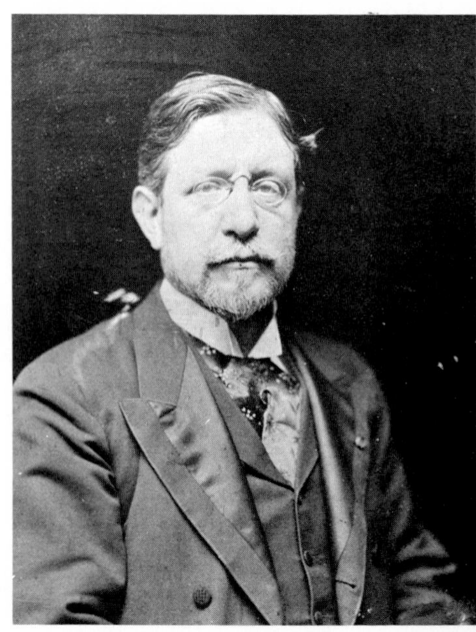

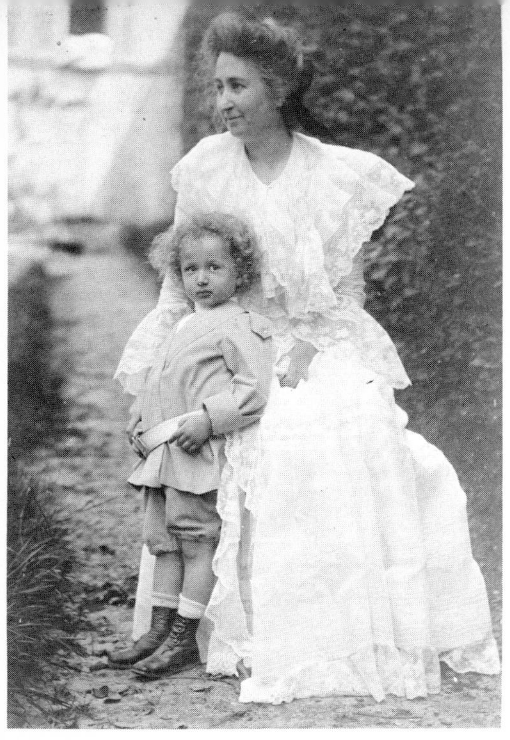

Jessie Tanner and son Jesse at Sceaux, around 1908

Henry Tanner and his son Jesse at their summer home at Trépied, Pas de Calais, around 1910.

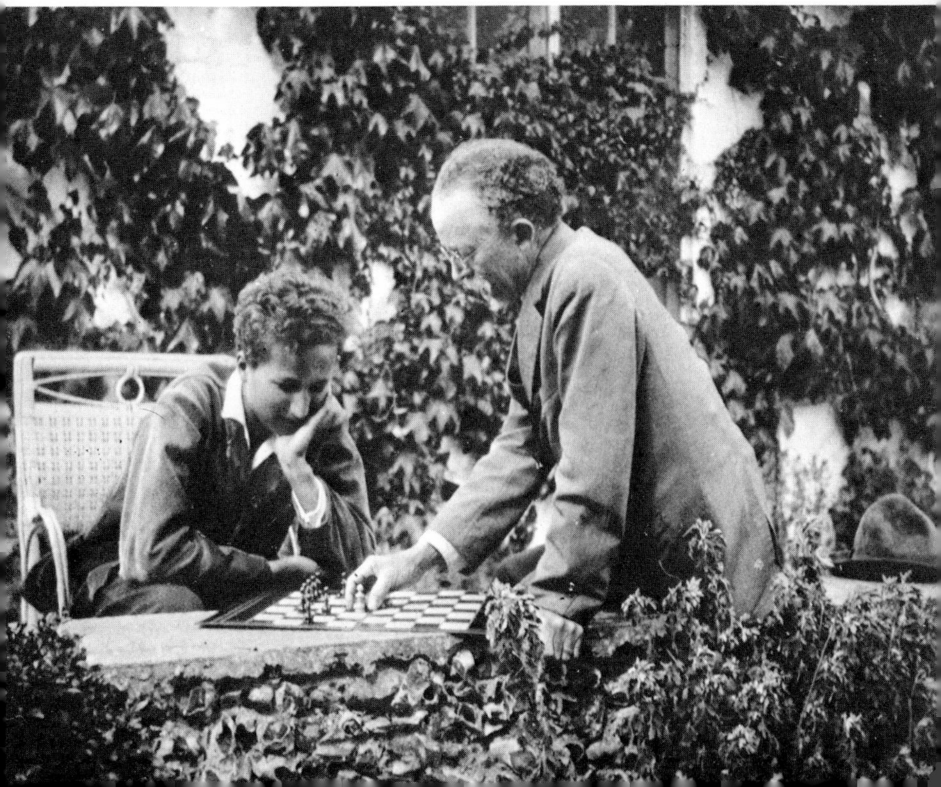

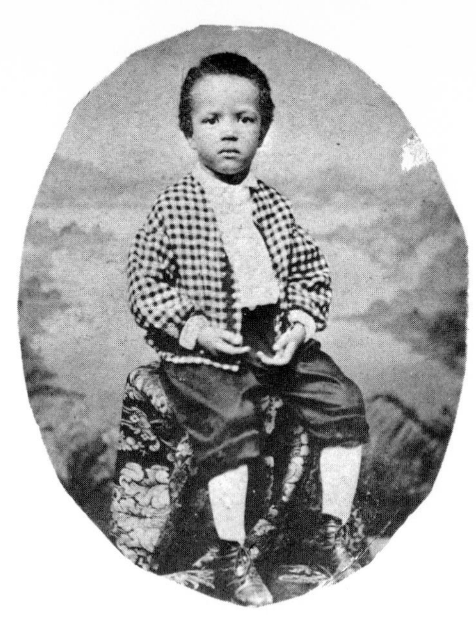

Henry Tanner at age four

Tanner's parents, Bishop Benjamin Tucker Tanner and his wife

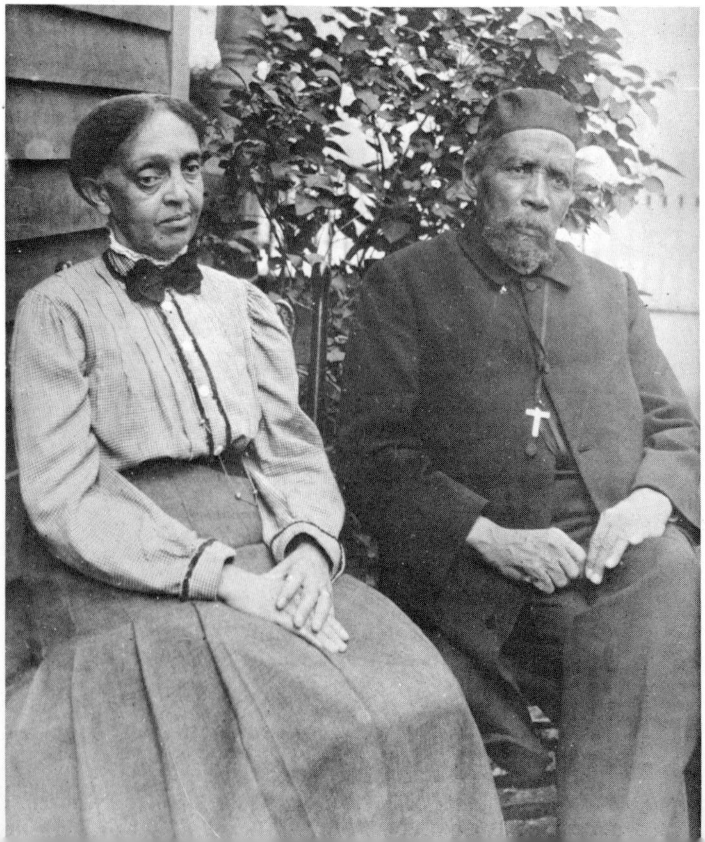

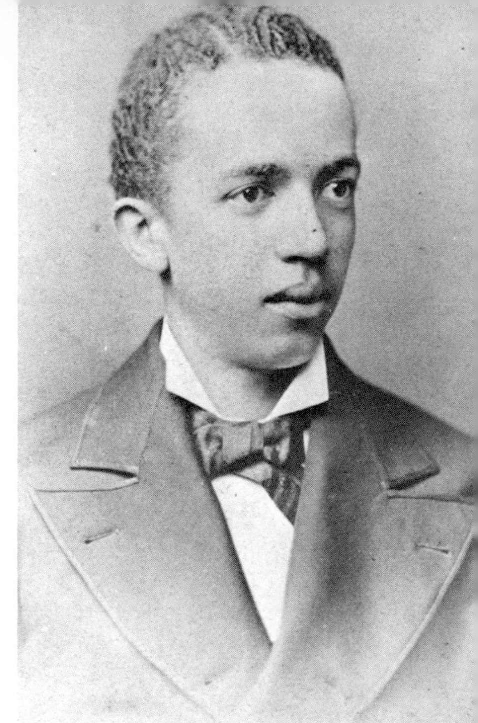

Henry Tanner at age eighteen

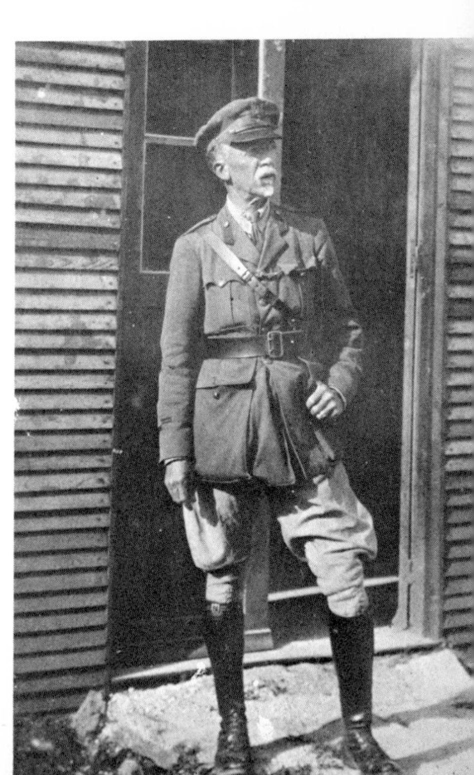

Henry Tanner during World War I

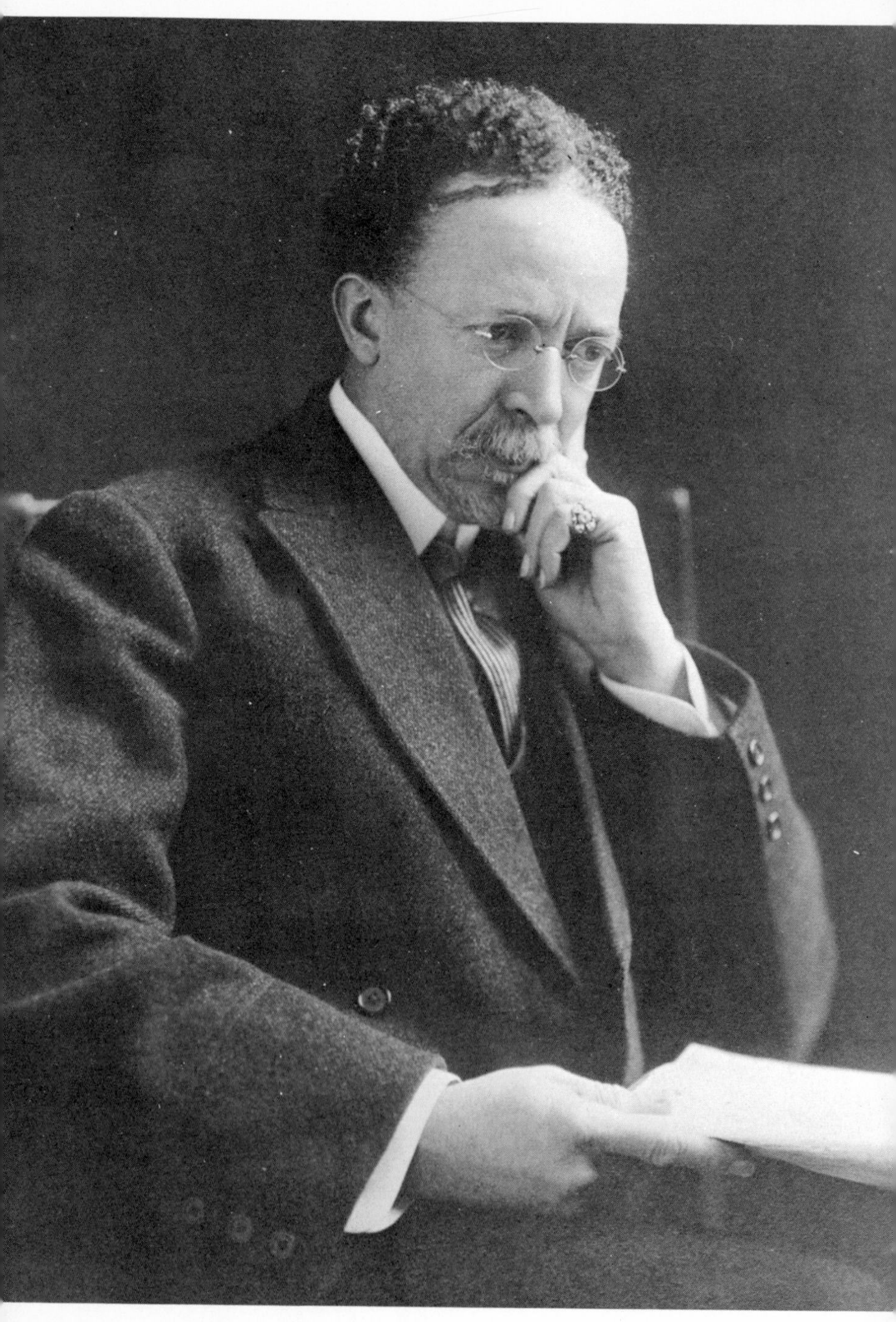

J: Henry Tanner in the early 1920's, at the height of his career

plain-spoken and penetrating character studies were in the field of portraiture. In 1891 there were still a few landscape painters in America faithful to the panoramic views of nature that Thomas Cole in the early part of the century had introduced into American art, but for the most part it was the day of the intimate "mood-inspired" landscape. George Inness, sixty-six years old and finally, after years of struggle, a financial success, expressed the prevailing view when he stated:

> A work of art does not appeal to the intellect. It does not appeal to the moral sense. Its aim is not to instruct, not to edify, but to awaken an emotion. . . . Its real greatness consists in the quality and force of this emotion.[5]

In this attitude the influence of the Barbizon painters is apparent and indeed the *paysages intimes* of Rousseau, Diaz, Harpignies, Millet, were looked upon with something akin to reverence by many American artists. Some of them had lived and worked in close proximity to the onetime French rebels at Fontainebleau and acquired their romantic-realist attitude toward nature firsthand.

Although the influence of the school of Barbizon was dominant, the impact of another French art movement was also apparent in the paintings of American artists. Theodore Robinson in 1884 was among the first to adopt the new impressionist technique of light, air, and broken color. By 1891 illusionistic effects and vivid color were reflected in the work of numerous American painters. The public viewed these innovations with some misgivings, but the trend away from precise drawing and thinly painted surfaces had clearly set in.

William Merritt Chase, Robert Henri, and Frank Duveneck had already introduced into their teaching the broad brush strokes and sketchlike quality of Munich. Chase, more versatile, had given up the rich, dark tones of Munich for the bolder colors of Manet and the textured realism of Velasquez.

5. Ibid., p. 166.

Interiors, still lifes, and portraits were well suited to this free handling of paint, with its emphasis on surface effects, and were often combined in one picture, as in Sargent's *Children of Edward Boit.*

This type of portraiture, done with painterly bravura, seldom revealed the fundamental weaknesses or complexities of a character but rather conveyed the momentary mood, the telling glance, the social milieu, of the sitter. No artist accomplished these tours de force with greater success than John Singer Sargent, the American artist born in Italy and briefly trained in the studio of Carolus-Duran, in Paris. His dexterity with the brush, his sense of color, his skill at catching the fleeting movement, his clever and elegant compositions painted on huge canvasses, brought him a fortune. Thousands of dollars were readily paid for a full-length portrait by Sargent and commissions fell to him like fall leaves during the year 1888–89 that he spent in Boston. But Sargent was a "name"; he had established himself in Europe and except by heritage could scarcely be called American.

In spite of the obscurity in which many American artists lived—Thomas Eakins and Albert Pinkham Ryder, the supreme examples—it was a day of lavish spending on art. Prices had skyrocketed with post-Civil War inflation, and $500, once considered high for a painting, was now a niggardly sum. But the public was whimsical in its tastes. In 1887 at a sale of pictures collected by A. T. Stewart, Meissonier's *1807* was not only given a standing ovation but it sold for between $60,000 and $75,000. Gérôme's *Chariot Race* brought more than $7,000. And a Rembrandt head went for $400.

Since travel had become easy the wealthy could—and most did—purchase their arts works abroad. Dealers had a heyday. Millionaires paid almost any price asked for a Bouguereau or Meissonier or other popular French artist or for an old master that was in demand. There was a passion for Italian Renaissance pictures, and since authenticity was not too carefully scrutinized, many a questionable Titian or Raphael found its way to a rich industrialist's home. So extensive was the importation of foreign works of art that Congress in 1888 put a tax on them. This was not done in the interest of native artists, however, but to increase the budget. The stir created abroad by the unusual procedure was so great that two years later a concession was made and all works of art twenty years old or older were allowed in duty-free, while others were taxed 15 percent of their value.

In spite of the difficulties artists encountered in the United States there was little esprit de corps among them. The fights and rebellions with authority that give drama and excitement to the history of nineteenth-century French art did not exist in America. In 1878 when Walter Shirlaw and William M. Chase led a group away from the Academy of Design in New York to form the Society of American Artists it was not, as they stated—and possibly believed—because of the narrow taste of the academicians but because their pictures had been discriminated against by the hanging committee. According to Homer St. Gaudens, whose father was one of the rebels:

> ... once on their own, in an effort to be broadminded they leaned over backwards so far that they lost the specific aim needed to maintain an enduring vitality.[6]

It is hard to accept this view point since none of the group showed a really open mind in accepting new ideas. Chase thought Cézanne a very inferior painter and expressed shock at the drawings of Rodin. And, six years after the new society was formed, two pictures by Eakins, *Spinning* and *Knitting*, were rejected by the society for their annual exhibition. In 1892—a final blow that led Eakins to resign his membership—they refused to show his *Agnew Clinic*. Yet Eakins himself did not become a partisan of the younger men whose interest was in the new high-key palette of the impressionists.

6. Ibid., p. 167.

John Elliott said in explanation of the situation:

> In order to survive at all, each had to fight so hard for his life that he had little strength or leisure for that cooperation so vital for the success of every calling.[7]

But it is doubtful whether artists had to "fight" for a living any harder in the nineties than they did earlier. In fact, the range of art was wider and offered more opportunities than ever before. The lack of cooperation, the general dissatisfaction, the petty jealousies, were due less to material considerations than to diffused art styles, uncertain values, and selfconscious dependence on the Old World for support. Gone was the sense of identification with American society that the artist had felt in colonial and early republican days. It was a period of nostalgic longings by artists out of sympathy with their national life yet unable to abandon it.

This nostalgia obscured for most of them the creativity they were in the process of developing. For, in spite of what has been said of popular taste and the lack of encouragement given to solid talent, the nineties were years of artistic productivity. Landscape painting, though owing much to foreign influence, was possibly the best that America has ever produced, and portraiture was full of masterful verve. The quality of art produced by such men as Childe Hassam, Alexander Wyant, John H. Twachtman, Maurice Prendergast, J. Alden Weir, George Inness, Homer Martin, Robert Henri, William M. Chase, and Eastman Johnson, compares favorably with all but the leading French artists of the period. And it was in the so-called "barren" years, the last quarter of the nineteenth century, that three of the greatest painters in the history of American art, or of any art, discovered their own aesthetic means of transmuting their personal visions, dependent on no teacher or school.

Of the three artists Thomas Eakins was the only one who

7. Maud Howe Elliott, *John Elliott* (New York: Houghton Mifflin Co., 1930), p. 45.

had undergone a strict régime of study at the Beaux Arts. Albert Pinkham Ryder had worked briefly under William E. Marshall, a former student of Couture's, but academic discipline was something he could do without in constructing his pictorial dreams. Winslow Homer had been abroad twice, but his approach was purely visual; he had found his greatest inspiration not in the Paris studios but in studying the sea, independently, off Tynemouth in England. But Eakins, at twenty-two, had gone to Paris to study under the great Gérôme, inspired no doubt by his Philadelphia teacher Schussele, who had also been trained in Paris, and by an intellectual desire to learn the fundamentals of art, which were inadequately taught at home.

Eakins never regretted his years with Gérôme, for whom he felt a lifelong devotion. His admiration for his teacher was so great that he looked upon him as the greatest artist of the nineteenth century. He also admired Laurens, Bonnat, and Fortuny but closed his eyes to the greatness of Manet and Courbet, with whom his own art was close in spirit if not in style. Once away from Paris, however—in Spain—he was receptive to the lessons of Velasquez and Ribera, lessons that made a far more lasting impression on his painting than those of the Beaux Arts.

When he returned to the United States in 1870 his mind was not filled with a desire to imitate the old masters he had seen or to follow the dogmas of his teachers. He had learned to draw with care and accuracy from the living model, and he had worked out his own philosophy of art. "The painter," he wrote his father from Paris,

> should be faithful to nature but nature seen and understood in the largest way—not slavishly copied but re-created.... He learns what she does with light, the big tool, and then color, then form, and appropriates them to his own use. Then he's got a canoe of his own, smaller than Nature's, but big enough for every purpose.[8]

8. Lloyd Goodrich, *Thomas Eakins* (New York: Whitney Museum of American Art, 1933), p. 17.

When, a few years later, he became a teacher at the Pennsylvania Academy of the Fine Arts it was this independence of vision that Eakins stressed to his pupils. His advice to them was "Get the character of things," and to this end he had them study the structure and anatomical details of dead bodies and the model.

But creative ideas do not necessarily come from intellectual comprehension and a mastery of technique. "They come originally," writes James F. Mathias, "from the artist's conscious and unconscious experience of the world in which he lives."[9]

When Henry Ossawa Tanner left for Europe he carried with him the skills he had learned from Thomas Eakins as well as something of the devout religious atmosphere in which he had been raised. But, more important, he took with him a sense of the dislocations in American life, dislocations that were more deeply felt by him than by most artists. For he not only had to contend with a public unversed and whimsical in matters of art, but with the prejudices of society toward a member of his race.

9. "A View of Creativity in America" (Speech given at Purdue University, Lafayette, Ind.; April 23, 1964), p. 2.

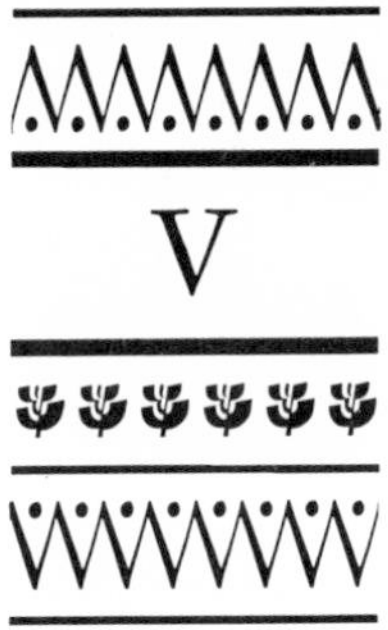

City of Light

HENRY TANNER'S INTRODUCTION TO THE NORTH ATLANTIC IN midwinter was not serene. He wrote that his cabin was located directly over the propeller and that the "demons of the watery plain" waited only for the ship to get out of sight of land before pouncing upon it. When the fourteen-day voyage was finally over he did not linger at Liverpool but took the night train to London, where he found lodgings in a small hotel near St. Paul's. After Atlanta, Georgia, with its segregated society, slow tempo, few paved streets, and numerous wagon yards that accommodated the country people who daily brought their produce to town in mule-driven wagons, the great free city of London with its multitudes, its hansom cabs, its palaces, presented a wonderful and stimulating contrast. Even Philadelphia was a provincial town by comparison.

London was later to become a familiar city to Henry Tanner, but for the moment he viewed it with the eyes of a stranger, hastily scanning its historic attractions, eager to get on to Paris.

It was his intention to remain in Paris only long enough to see the sights and visit the great picture galleries in the Louvre, then proceed to Rome for his studies. Italy was no longer the bright star for artists it had been in the days of Horatio Greenough and Hiram Powers, and there is no explanation for Tanner's decision to reside there. It was, of course, the home of art; and Edmonia Lewis, the outstanding Negro sculptress, had been trained in Rome. Tanner may have thought it would be cheaper to live in Rome than in Paris, or he may have been drawn to the seat of Christianity by a religious bias. He was too serious to have been attracted to Paris by the tales of bohemian life that lured so many American art students. Whatever his reasons for wanting to go to Rome, they were not strong enough to withstand the magic of the City of Light. As Richard Harding Davis wrote:

> On no one class of visitors does Paris lay her spell more heavily than on the American art student. For, no matter where he has studied at home, or under what master, he finds when he reaches Paris so much that is new and beautiful and full of inspiration that he becomes as intolerant as are all recent converts, and so happy in his chosen profession that he looks upon everything else than art with impatience and contempt. . . .[1]

Tanner himself wrote of his "conversion":

> Strange that after having been in Paris a week, I should find conditions so to my liking that I completely forgot when I left New York I had made my plans to study in Rome and was really on my way there when I arrived in Paris.[2]

It was not so strange as Henry Tanner thought, for many

1. *About Paris* (New York: Harper and Bros., 1895), p. 205.
2. Henry Ossawa Tanner, "The Story of an Artist's Life," *World's Work*, 18 (June and July, 1909): 11770.

travellers, before and since, have been held captive by the grace and beauty of Paris. And in 1891 it radiated a warmth and friendliness that were unrivalled. Tanner soon loved every aspect of French life, even

> this little room of mine, with its Empire bed and its heavy hangings, its little washbasin, with pitcher holding scarcely more than a quart, its waxed floor, the linen sheets, so cold to one already half-frozen, and that little fireplace holding a few small sticks and twigs. . . .[3]

Breakfast, that formerly had included beefsteak, mutton chops, fried potatoes, or hot griddle cakes, was for the moment a cup of milk or coffee and a sou's worth of bread eaten in a drafty doorway. Then he learned of a small café where art students were accustomed to stop on their way to Julien's Academy.

> The cafe had across its door (like thousands of others) "English Spoken." It was kept by a sunny-faced middle-aged French woman from Alsace—one of those comfortable kind whose waist-line had long ceased to exist, but whose heart was as warm as the steaming beverages she served. Asked one day who it was that spoke English she so largely advertised, she replied with a merry laugh, "Oh, its you, and you, and you, Messieurs my clients who speak English here."[4]

In spite of the great number of Americans and English on the Left Bank a Negro was not conspicuous. Men of all nationalities and colors lived there, enjoying a camaraderie that Tanner had not known before.

Since foreign art students could not compete for the *Prix de Rome* and were admitted to the ateliers of the Beaux Arts school only on presentation of proper credentials and after passing a stiff examination, most of them attended private academies like Julien's and Colarossi's and the Grande Chaumière.

3. Ibid., p. 11770.
4. Ibid., p. 11770.

But in private studios, as at the Beaux Arts, old traditions had changed. Students were no longer received in patriarchal style, as they had been earlier in the century, by a master who took only the number of pupils he could know personally, and who was privileged to exercise a kind of despotic authority over them since he accepted no payment for his instruction. The change had already set in by the seventies. Carolus-Duran, with whom nineteen-year-old John Singer Sargent studied in 1876, was almost the only teacher in Paris at that time who held to the old personal relations. By 1881 art instruction was so concentrated that a few minutes of criticism once or twice a week was all a student could hope for, and in this brief time it was almost impossible for a teacher to convey his ideas on art or to sense the needs of his students. Pupils no longer felt the personal loyalty and affection for their teachers that had marked earlier relationships, like that between Eakins and Gérôme.

Of the dozens of private academies in Paris Julien's, to which Tanner followed a beaten path, was by far the most popular. Edwin Austin Abbey in 1880 expressed the view of many American students when he wrote to a friend:

> I have about decided to try Paris next winter, if I get a wholesome place to work in. I want to study painting, and, do you know, I have come to the conclusion that Julien's is about my dot.[5]

Julien's was actually not one, but numerous schools located in various parts of Paris, all under the directorship of Monsieur Julien, a former prizefighter from a small village in the south of France who, after studying at the Beaux Arts and enjoying a "*succès de scandale*" along with Manet and Whistler in 1863 at the *Salon des Refusés*, had found his forte in business, first as a promoter of wrestling matches, then, as the novelty of these wore off, as operator of a studio for artists, which he founded in 1868.

5. Edward Verrall Lucas, *Edwin Austin Abbey*, 2 vol. (London: Methuen and Co., 1921), 1: 104.

As he was French, neither his origin nor his eyes for business stood in the way of culture in Fine Arts, far in advance of his opportunities. He was a big, handsome man who never for a moment forgot his position of manager only and held the masters who came to criticize the class in high reverence. Nevertheless, he had an eye on every pupil and would appear unexpectedly in class, a serious and observant figure, decidedly on the watch.[6]

At Julien's, students, for a small sum, paid for the privilege of working—that is, drawing and painting—and receiving criticism once or twice a week from well-known academicians. The students might select the *maître* they wished to work under and they lived in the hope that on his weekly rounds he would look favorably on their art.

Cecilia Beaux gives an account of her first meeting at Julien's with her teacher, Tony Robert-Fleury:

My turn approached. He sat down. I knew only enough French to stammer out that it was my first attempt in Life-Class. He muttered something in a deep voice that sounded like an oath, and plunged me deeper in woe. The class, which understood better, looked around. I began to hear that he was quoting Corneille. He asked me where I had studied, and my story did not seem to account for my drawing. He rose, not having given me any advice, but bent his cavernous eyes on me with a penetrating but very reserved smile and turned to the next. . . .[7]

Abbey, who in 1880 had thought Julien's his "dot," a decade later was less sure that students—except the most determined, and these were not necessarily the most talented—could survive the meager fare of academic training offered under the circumstances. In 1892 he wrote in a letter to Charles Parsons:

6. Cecilia Beaux, *Background with Figures* (New York, Boston: Houghton Mifflin Co., 1930), pp. 119, 120.

7. Ibid., p. 119.

> I think of the dozens and dozens of innocent youths who sit in the schools there [America] all sure that if they could get to Paris for a year all would be well. And some of them do get to Paris . . . and go to swell the hordes of blind kittens who nose and fumble and grope at that very milkless breast—dying their artistic death a little sooner than they would at home maybe, but dying all the same. . . . They seldom get admitted to the Beaux Arts nowadays, and are forced to fall back upon the clap-trap schools—where they breathe foul air and fouler ideas and opinions.[8]

Whether he was referring specifically to Julien's he does not state, but the "foul air" is verified by the account given by George Biddle, in *An American Artist's Story*, of Julien's studio in the rue du Dragon.

> The school was an enormous hangar, a cold, filthy, uninviting firetrap. The walls were plastered from floor to ceiling with the prize-winning academies, in oil and charcoal, of the past thirty or forty years. The atmosphere of the place had changed little since the days of Delacroix, Ingres or David. Three nude girls were posing downstairs. The acrid smell of their bodies and the smell of the students mingled with that of turpentine and oil paint in the overheated, tobacco-laden air. The students grouped their stools and low easels close about the model's feet. While they worked there was pandemonium of songs, catcalls, whistling and recitations, of a highly salacious and bawdy nature.[9]

This was Julien's in 1911, but the description is similar to Tanner's twenty years earlier:

> The Academie Julien! Never had I seen or heard such bedlam—or men waste so much time. Of course, I had come to study at such a cost that every minute seemed precious and not to be frittered away. I had often seen rooms full of tobacco smoke, but not as here in a room never ventilated—or

8. Lucas, *Edwin Austin Abbey*, 1: 254.

9. *An American Artist's Story* (Boston: Little, Brown and Co., 1939), p. 125.

when I say never, I mean not rarely but never, during the five or six months of cold weather. Never were the windows opened. They were nailed fast at the beginning of the cold season. Fifty and sixty men smoking in such a room for two or three hours would make it so that those on the back rows could hardly see the model.[10]

In spite of these unpromising conditions, it was not necessary for M. Julien to advertise his *cours*. Students flocked to them like sheep to a salt lick, anxious for a taste of the exuberant life, the freedom from worldly concerns, the dedication to art that his world represented. Julien himself kept in the background, his presence felt rather than seen. He was a powerful figure and the students knew that a word from him could be the opening wedge that would lead to acceptance by the Salon jury.

Two weekly events gave zest to life at Julien's. One was the visit by the *maître* who came to look over and criticize the students' work. To be passed over without a word by the great man was more damning than severe criticism. To be praised by him sent a student into the skies.

The other event was the weekly *concours*, or competition. Subjects, usually Biblical, were given out at the beginning of the week and compositions illustrating them were done independently. The student whose work was judged best was given the privilege of first choice of place on Monday morning when a new pose was assumed by the model—no small advantage in a crowded studio. If the student was particularly fortunate his picture might be attached to the wall for future classes to contemplate. This was the highest honor he could hope for. There were other *concours*, for which medals and prizes were given, but the weekly composition was the real test of a student's skill.

The students knew how few, if any, of them would ever rival such "names" as Léon Gérôme or Tony Robert-Fleury or

10. Tanner, "Story of an Artist's Life," p. 11770.

Benjamin-Constant, but this did not discourage them. No one knew where luck would fall, and, in the meantime, they were free to hope and to enjoy their *vie de bohême.*

It was a curious new world to Henry Tanner, one that to all outward appearances was not at all his "dot." Raised in a religious home, retiring by nature, and, until now, preoccupied with the necessity of making his way through diligence and conformity, he was not prepared to abandon himself wholeheartedly to a new environment or to cultivate the eccentricities of dress and manner that prevailed in the Latin Quarter of Paris.

What he liked about the unconventional atmosphere was not its license, but the freedom it gave him to be himself—to feel, for the first time in his life, an identification with a world unlimited by color. There was neither nationality nor race in the art that Tanner pursued, and the obstacles that he felt had barred his way to success in America were nonexistent in the cosmopolitan milieu of Paris.

From the outset he occupied a position of ascendancy in his class at Julien's. In the first week's *concours* his picture of the *Deluge* was judged one of the best two in the class and brought him to the immediate attention of his teacher, Benjamin-Constant. The friendship that subsequently developed between him and Constant is indicative of the high regard in which he was held.

Even his naive reactions to certain French customs were amiably accepted by his fellow students. No doubt there were smiles and some raised eyebrows when he canvassed the class to see whether on religious grounds he could get the students to change the day of the weekly *concours* from Sunday to Monday. But there is no evidence that he was subjected because of his attitude to the kind of horseplay students at Julien's were prone to engage in.

It took Henry Tanner some time to wean himself from his strict, Methodist background. He attended the American

Protestant Church regularly during his first years of residence in Paris and maintained moral scruples against the drinking of wine.

> I was afraid I might grow to like it, that there might be lurking somewhere within me an appetite which, once awakened, I could not control—So I began by taking a little for four or five days, and then I would absolutely refuse it for a week and see whether I had any craving for it. I had made up my mind if I discovered the least longing or wish for it I should never touch it again. I confess to quite a feeling of relief when, after a year of such conduct, I found out I did not care whether or no it figured on my bill of fare.[11]

It was not long before Henry Tanner joined the newly-formed American Art Club and through this organization came to know some of the older American artists in Paris. The club had been organized the year before by Mr. A. A. Anderson, with the backing of such prominent Americans as Rodman Wannamaker, who represented the family firm in Paris, and Whitelaw Reid, minister to France. The club was, in a sense, the result of an accident. Mr. Anderson was walking along the Boulevard Montparnasse one day and, coming upon an old wall, peered over it and saw a long, narrow building, abandoned and run down. It had too many windows ever to have been used as a private residence, and its large shaded lawn was covered with weeds and débris. He conceived the idea of having the building converted to use as the headquarters of an art association. Many art clubs had been attempted before in Paris, but none whose purpose was other than to provide a place for gay social affairs.[12]

Through his personal efforts the property—it had formerly been a private school—was obtained and restored, and one night in May, 1890, a group of interested Americans gathered

11. Ibid., p. 11771.

12. E. H. Wuerpel, "American Artists' Association of Paris," *Cosmopolitan*, 20 (February, 1896): 402.

to hear a discussion of the project. Whitelaw Reid described it in the following words:

> It is a movement originating among American artists in Paris, intended for American artists and thought likely to do some service in the development of American art. It presents a plan for enabling a large number of young art students in a strange city to help themselves and increase both their strength and their comfort by associating their efforts and offering them agreeable headquarters.[13]

The clubhouse had a library and reading room, a parlor, a restaurant, an athletic room for boxing and fencing lessons, and a secluded garden. It also had a bulletin board for mail, eagerly watched by the students.

> Here some of us read of the success or failure of our yearly work, our offerings to the Salon. Perhaps, even, we heard of a picture sold at home, or an honor won at some exhibition.[14]

To a young art student like Henry Tanner who lived on very little—his first year he spent no more than $365, including his tuition at Julien's—the American Art Club was not only a pleasant place to spend leisure hours, but one where he could keep au courant of happenings in Paris and meet some important members of the American colony. One of these, Rodman Wannamaker, subsequently had a hand in shaping his career. It may have been at the American Art Club that Henry Tanner met his first studio mate, Hermon MacNeil, who shared a studio with him at 15, Rue de Reine in 1893.

A photograph taken in 1895 in the garden of the club shows Tanner with a group of the younger members, including his longtime friend, Myron Barlow. Another, of later date, shows an older Tanner playing billiards in one of the club rooms with Frederick Frieseke and two other artists. Throughout the club's existence Henry Tanner was one of its staunchest supporters.

13. Ibid., p. 403.
14. Ibid., p. 406.

In addition to his work at Julien's Tanner spent many hours at the Louvre, studying the old masters; and he continued a practice begun in his youth at the Philadelphia Zoo by sketching the animals at the Jardin des Plantes.

As summer approached he learned it was the custom of the art students to spend their vacations in the country, particularly in Normandy and Brittany. Tanner decided to join in the migration and selected Pont Aven, the small fishing village where Gauguin had painted two years before. Here he found a larger colony of English and Americans than he would have liked, since he wished to improve his French, but the board was cheap—$11 a month—so he remained.

It was easy in these picturesque surroundings to forget academic theories and return to the broad view of reality that Thomas Eakins had avocated. And in the simple Breton fisher folk he found subjects, as he had at Highlands, to whom he felt emotionally akin.

Tanner's natural bent was not toward academic art, which demands an intellectual rather than a subjective approach. By 1891, however, "official art" had lost a good deal of its rigidity. There were few artists even among the academicians who painted history to the exclusion of genre, or who did not introduce into their historical compositions a certain semblance of truth based on the observation of nature. The impressionist movement had won full recognition by the elite, if not by the public at large, and its influence was growing. Moreover, it had given an impetus to other artist-adventurers to explore new paths. Three years before, "Vincent," a Dutchman, had hung his sunflowers and other canvases up to dry in a small restaurant, Au Tabourin, in the Boulevard Clichy. Toulouse-Lautrec, a midget, was doing striking posters for Aristide Bruant, keeper of the Chat Noir on Montmartre. And Cézanne, a méridional like Julien, but cast in an entirely different mold, was painting with his "bricklayer's trowel" and selling his largest pictures at Père Tanguy's for $20. There were other artists equally outside the pale of respectable academic art whose work, to bolder eyes, had merit. Curiously, Manet remained on the periphery. When Albert Wolff, art critic for the *Figaro*, was asked how it was that Degas and Whistler and Monet had come into their inheritance while there was still no general recognition of Manet's art, he replied:

> Put that hope aside. The time will never come when people will care for Manet's art.[15]

Paris was the center of lively art squabbles, and what was avant-garde to one artist was moderately conservative to another. What Henry Tanner thought of these squabbles and of the wild experiments engaged in by some artists can easily be imagined. Although he was tolerant by nature, he was conservative in matters of art. While he did not believe in slavishly copying nature, he could not close his eyes to the beauty of the natural world. He would have found little to admire in the vivid colors and distorted forms of such artists as Vincent Van Gogh, Toulouse-Lautrec, and Paul Cézanne.

15. George Moore, "Reminiscences of the Impressionist Painters," *Scribner's Magazine*, 29 (February, 1906): 198.

Salon Success

Henry Tanner's first teacher at Julien's, Jean Joseph Benjamin-Constant, was one of the most highly respected of the academic masters. He occasionally painted sentimental genre, like *Too Late*, the picture of a poet dying just as Fame and Fortune are knocking at the door, but for the most part his reputation rested on his large historical and Oriental, or Biblical, subjects.

Another of Tanner's teachers—there were usually two academicians assigned to each studio—was Jean-Paul Laurens. Laurens had made his debut with classical subjects—*The Death of Cato* (1863) and *The Death of Tiberius* (1864)—then deflected to genre and Biblical scenes, which he painted in the thin manner of Gérôme.

Both of these men were excellent teachers, if not great artists. Like Gérôme, they did not impose either their personal views or their styles on their pupils. To students with talent and imagination who could say to themselves, as did Eakins, "Il faut me décider de ne jamais peindre da la façon du patron,"[1] their careful draftsmanship had much to offer. But the gifted were in the minority. Most of the students at Julien's, even those who claimed to be unsympathetic with academic art, were eager enough to paint "de la façon du patron" in the hope of getting a picture in the Salon. It was their proving ground. An acceptance was the first step toward the momentous day when their picture would be awarded a medal by the jury of selection and, with the greatest of luck, command a speechless crowd of admirers like the one Edwin Austin Abbey described standing before Bastien LePage's *Joan of Arc* at the Salon of 1880.

> There is in the Salon this year the very greatest picture ever painted by anybody since the fifteenth century, a picture before which stood crowds of reverent people every day, too full of the sentiment of the picture to speak of it.[2]

An acceptance, however, held hidden dangers, for too often it raised hopes that were impossible to fulfill. Many students who had a good word said about them were loath to admit thereafter that they lacked the potential to rate with the best. The Left Bank was crowded with these hangers-on, living in their garret studios, talking knowingly of art, unwilling to return to the mundane world of affairs in which their abilities might at least earn them a living.

Even success could be disastrous. Munkácsy, the popular Hungarian artist, was bitter in denouncing to Will Low the débâcle that was, in effect, his artistic career, because of his anxiety to hold on to his Salon reputation.

> You don't live in Paris, you have never known a Salon success; you are fortunate. It is pleasant, everyone praises

1. Lloyd Goodrich, *Thomas Eakins* (New York: Whitney Museum of American Art, 1933), p. 30.

2. Edward Verrall Lucas, *Edwin Austin Abbey*, 2 vol. (London: Methuen and Co., 1921), 1: 103.

> you, it is *cher maitre* here, and *cher maitre* there, and year after year it goes on until it becomes a necessity of your existence. Then they begin to pick flaws; my Hungarian pictures bored them, so I gave them Parisian; and then they called my work upholstery and said that I was a creature of the dealers and incapable of affronting *la grande peinture;* then I did my "Christ Before Pilate," a *vrai succès*. With the public at least, and with the artists, too, though some hung back. And then they began to reproach me with painting dark, and since then there has been no peace. It is like being thrown to the wild beasts. . . .[3]

A few months later Munkácsy was taken to a sanatorium, a victim, as it were, of Salon madness.

It is impossible to exaggerate the importance to Parisians of the Salon—or Salons, since after 1889 there were two: the Old Salon, founded in the eighteenth century, of the Société des Artistes Français, at the Palais d'Industrie, and the recent New Salon of the Société des Artistes Nationales, on the Champs de Mars. Crowds of all kinds, including notables from the stage, literature, and the arts, as well as the social elite and the petite bourgeoisie, poured every spring into these exhibition halls to see the thousands of works of art on display.

Cecilia Beaux gives her impression of the Salon crowds:

> Never had I seen assembled so many men of "parts"—real men, I would have said—so absorbed, so oblivious, greeting each other warmly, and with absolutely no general curiosity; pausing a moment, with great deference, before some quiet lady, or obvious beauty, but really there through profound interest in contemporary art. . . .
>
> Puvis might have been there in his black silk cap, venerated, full of honors, or Jean-Paul Laurens, Raeffaelli or Renoir. . . .
>
> Everyone was there, from the little old man, loved and respected for his lifelong devotion to the *cher métier*, to the young aspirant, long-haired and loose-cravated, and of course

3. Will H. Low, *A Chronicle of Friendships* (New York: Charles Scribner's Sons, 1908), p. 457.

> accompanied by his *petite amie*; and the flamboyant *bel homme*, trying to be satisfied with what he could get of notice. . . .[4]

Each went to admire or revile, to agree or disagree with the judges, to see and to be seen.

Henry Tanner's introduction to the Salon in the spring of 1892 was an exciting experience.

> I had been to Dr. Thurber's Church, and was on my way home when, near the Palais d'Industrie, I saw great crowds making their way into this building, which has now disappeared—such crowds as you might see going into Madison Square Gardens to some great sporting event. To my question, it was *Le Salon* and to see for myself, I joined that good-natured throng.
>
> What a surprise awaited me in the court of that old palais! Hundreds of statues that appeared to me nearly all of them fairer than the "Venus de Milo" and upstairs the paintings—thousands of them—and nearly all of them much more to my taste than were the old masters in the Louvre—not that they were really as fine; but they were more within my range.[5]

His delight over the huge display seems excessive, yet it must be remembered that Thomas Eakins admired Gérôme above all other artists and once said of a picture by Fortuny that it was "la plus belle chose que j'ai jamais vu."[6]

The Salon exhibit opened exciting new vistas to Tanner. Here was an opportunity, at last, to bring his art to the attention of a wide, unbiased, and interested public, and, with good fortune, to establish himself financially. He knew that unless he became self-supporting there was the strong probability that he would have to return to America to live. This he was

4. *Background with Figures* (New York: Houghton Mifflin Co., 1931), pp. 125, 126.

5. Henry Ossawa Tanner, "The Story of an Artist's Life," *World's Work*, 18 (June and July, 1909): 11771.

6. Goodrich, *Thomas Eakins*, p. 19.

not prepared to do. He felt no animosity toward his native land, but he knew that he could not be a productive artist in a country that looked upon his race with reservations, if not contempt. He thought of himself, as did many Americans living in Paris, as a voluntary though reluctant exile, only in his case the reason had to do with racial acceptance far more than with art.

His second summer in France was spent at Concarneau, in Brittany. Again he painted landscapes and genre, but this year he applied himself particularly to a picture of an apple tree that he intended to submit to the next Salon. When the time came, much to his disappointment, it was refused. This refusal at one time would have plunged him into depression, but Tanner was gaining self-confidence. The comments about his work by Constant and others encouraged him to believe it was only a matter of time until his pictures would be accepted.

During his first years in Paris Tanner worked long hours and lived on relatively little, and it is not surprising that his constitution, never very strong, gave in to the strain. During his second year he became ill with what was supposed to be typhoid fever, and he was taken to the Hotel Dieu for treatment. For six francs a day, he had a room to himself.

> I had, when I entered, the usual terror of a hospital that in those days went with them, especially among a class of people who, while poor, rather looked upon it as only a place for "homeless" people, where all sorts of experiments were practised. From my bed I could see a large table with all sorts of highly polished objects upon it. I looked upon it as an operating table and pictured to myself the suffering that must be continually occurring in that building. When I became well enough to walk about, I was surprised that this room of suffering, as I was wont to think of it, was a dining-room. . . .[7]

As soon as he had recovered sufficiently he made plans to return to America to convalesce and to see what he could do

7. Tanner, "Story of an Artist's Life," p. 11772.

to raise funds for continued residence in Paris. He was in Philadelphia by the fall of 1892, and an item in the *Daily Evening Telegraph* indicates that he spent several months there.

> Mr. H. O. Tanner, a graduate of the Pennsylvania Academy of the Fine Arts, having been a student in the Paris schools for several years past and recently returned to America, has opened a studio in this city and proposes to remain here during the coming winter. Mr. Tanner has been known here as a landscape painter, the work he has exhibited at the Academy and elsewhere as well as those sent home from abroad being for the most part plain [*sic*] air studies made directly from Nature. In his more recent pictures he has shown the influence of impressionism, or rather an understanding of what the Impressionists are looking for—namely, the ensemble, the truthful presentation of his subject as a whole, and the right relation of objects seen together in the same light. He has, however, maintained his independence and has not been dominated by the "blue bug" craze so far as to sacrifice his prescription of color, and has kept a place on his palette for other tints besides yellow and purple; and one of his later landscapes painted abroad, a scene near Pont Aven, in Brittany, affords a fair illustration of what may be gained from Impressionistic suggestions without abandoning sanity and disregarding the dictates of experience.[8]

It was at this time that the *Banjo Lesson* was first exhibited at Earle's Galleries. The art critic of the *Daily Evening Telegraph* referred to it as "a new field" for the artist. While the critic assumed a typically American attitude of amused tolerance toward the subject matter, he was nevertheless conscious of the picture's merit.

> An old Uncle Ned, bald and venerable, has a bare-footed little darkey of seven or eight years between his knees, and is earnestly instructing the youngster how to finger the strings of an ancient banjo. The fingers are firmly modelled

8. *Philadelphia Daily Evening Telegraph*, Philadelphia, 1893. Newspaper clipping, Tanner Collection, Archives of American Art, Detroit.

> and well "enveloped," each occupying its own space and place and each bearing the stamp of individuality. The hands are especially well drawn, that of the child being a study Mr. Tanner may well be proud of, and the faces are formed with intelligence and expression.[9]

Tanner was glad to see his family and to renew acquaintances with old friends, but this first trip home convinced him more firmly than ever that Europe was his spiritual home. He held an auction of every one of his pictures he could lay his hands on and realized several hundred dollars. With this money and assurances from his father of further assistance he returned to Paris.

Here, he applied himself in earnest to his "new field." For the Salon of 1894 he submitted a genre painting entitled *The Music Lesson* and, to his delight, it was accepted. Encouraged by this success, the following year he submitted three pictures, two paintings and a pastel, and all three were hung. The pastel was a small landscape of the New Jersey coast by moonlight, and the paintings were a delicately executed Brittany interior and *The Young Sabot Maker*, a genre picture in which he contrasted youth with age, as in the *Banjo Lesson*, though in a more vigorous and lively manner and with less genuine sentiment. The picture represents a young boy working hard on a pair of sabots at a bench in the foreground, while an old workman in the rear turns his head from his work to smile at the youth's energetic performance.

The *New York Times* of April 29, 1894, described Tanner's three pictures very favorably, particularly *The Young Sabot Maker*. It began to look as though Henry Tanner had found his niche in the art world as a painter of genre.

Yet genre painting was not to be the field in which his reputation was won. Almost as soon as the Salon of 1895 was closed he began to plan a large painting of *Daniel in the Lions' Den.* Tanner had painted religious pictures previously but none on

9. Ibid.

the ambitious scale of the *Daniel.* What induced him to forsake genre at this critical period of his career has been variously explained in terms of his early home atmosphere, his father's desire that his son should turn his talent into religious channels, and his own devout nature. While these factors may have contributed to his interest in Biblical painting, it should not be overlooked that in turning to the Bible he was following a well-worn path. The "Orient," as the Near East was called, was a popular theme in nineteenth-century art. Also, there was a prevailing belief that the level of an artist's reputation was in some measure identified with the kind of picture he painted. One of the damning criticisms of Jean-François Millet's pictures had been that his peasant subjects were "low" and "vulgar." Condemnation of Dupré and Rousseau as painters of "realistic" landscapes had led them to cease all attempts to have their pictures shown in the Salon. And Meissonier responded to Lewis Brown's comment that "Monet can only paint from nature" with "Don't talk to me of your Monet and all the gang of the *jeunes.* The other day I saw a picture by someone called Besnard in which there were violet horses."[10]

The artists under whom Tanner studied at Julien's, as well as the successful ones he heard discussed there—Benjamin-Constant, Laurens, Gérôme, Meissonier, Chavannes, Bastien-Lepage—had all won their laurels as painters of history or allegory. If Tanner wished to try his hand at more elevated subjects than Breton fishermen or landscapes, it was logical for him, with his background, to turn to the Bible.

Yet Tanner's interest in the Bible was not impelled solely by practical considerations or a desire to emulate a mode. There is no question that he was deeply religious, though not in the orthodox sense. As a youth he was a steady churchgoer, following a habit instilled in him in early childhood, and he continued the practice of attending services during his first years in Paris,

10. Ambroise Vollard, *Recollections of a Picture Dealer* (Boston: Little Brown and Co., 1936), p. 161.

where he was a faithful attendant of the American Protestant Church. As time passed, however, he lost interest in the formal aspects of religion. For a time, his son says, he even became a Christian Scientist.[11] But this could not last. By nature Henry Tanner was a mystic who found emotional fulfillment in personal communion with God. It was this mystical element in him that gave his art its greatest appeal and that kept him from becoming just another raconteur of sacred anecdotes.

When Tanner died, among his belongings was found a paper on which he had jotted down suggestions for daily meditation. These indicate the kind of faith that guided him safely through experiences that were often frustrating and bitter.

Monday —I am thankful for Thy unfailing bounty
Tuesday —I rejoice in my ability to give blessings to others
Wednesday—I invited the Christ spirit to manifest in me
Thursday —I realize the meaning of Peace on Earth, good will toward men
Friday —I follow the star (high ideal) that leads me to the Christ
Saturday —I am poised. I am not worried or hurried. All my affairs are in order and harmony
Sunday —Joy, peace and plenty are now mine

To prepare himself for his first Salon venture into the religious field Tanner spent the summer of 1895 sketching the lions in the Jardin des Plantes and attending a class conducted by the well-known animal sculptor, Frémiet. Modeling animals was, of course, nothing new to him, as he had done this from early youth.

It was a foregone conclusion to Tanner's friends, observing the work, that his *Daniel in the Lions' Den* would be accepted by the Salon jury. It was. But the hanging committee placed it, to Tanner's dismay, in an obscure location. The placing of a picture on the overloaded walls of the Salon was very im-

11. Jesse O. Tanner to me, May 6, 1966, Archives of American Art, Detroit.

portant to an artist's success or failure. If his picture was hung near the ceiling—"skied"—or in a dark corner, it might go unnoticed no matter how great its merit. Fortunately, Gérôme noted the *Daniel* and insisted on having it rehung. Gérôme did not know Tanner personally, but the *Daniel* was his kind of archaeological art, though Tanner's picture had softer, more harmonious tones than Gérôme was capable of. When the Salon officially opened on April 29, 1896, *Daniel in the Lions' Den* had a conspicuous place right "on the line," the best possible location.

To no one's surprise *Daniel in the Lions' Den* received a coveted honorable mention and Tanner's reputation as a painter of biblical scenes was launched. The United Press correspondent, in writing up the Salon exhibition, had the following to say:

> H. O. Tanner, whose "Young Sabot Maker" elicited so much admiration last year, is again to the front with a large canvas representing "Daniel in the Lions' Den." The prophet is in a large chamber of Assyrian bricks, on whose walls are shown friezes of colored lions. Part of the gallery or balcony dominates the prison from which, supposedly, the king occasionally witnessed the sport provided for his amusement below. Daniel is leaning against a projection which serves to give additional strength to the great walls of the construction. The moonlight enters through a window or trap door over his head, and catches on his folded hands and richly embroidered robe. The upper part of the body is in shadow, with the head turned toward the window above. In the deep shadows are the stark bodies of the lions, walking restlessly up and down, their fiery eyes giving additional terror to the darkness.
>
> One is resting on his haunches, near Daniel, part of his head and paw in the line of the moonlight, while in the background a streak of moonlight catches the back of another lion.[12]

To present-day viewers the oil painting of *Daniel in the Lions' Den*, now located in the Los Angeles County Museum

12. *New York Times*, April 29, 1896.

of Art, is not one of Tanner's finest efforts. Daniel is a posed model, and the lions, whose "fiery eyes" were mentioned by the UP correspondent, are no more terrifying than Landseer's beasts in Trafalgar Square. The merit of the picture does not lie in its narrative appeal but in its deep, harmonious colors, dramatic light and shade, and broad brushwork—qualities that are strikingly absent from the work of his teachers, Benjamin-Constant and Laurens.

Tanner was often to use moonlight effects in his pictures. He liked the semi-obscurity of a moonlight scene, in which he could suppress or soften details, as well as the eerie coloring suggested by it. Even at this early, or archaeological, phase of his religious art, he thought of his pictures first as works of art, then as illustrations.

> It has very often seemed to me that many painters of religious subjects (in our time) seem to forget that their pictures should be as much works of art (regardless of the subject) as are other paintings with less holy subjects. To suppose that the fact of the religious painter having a more elevated subject than his brother artist makes it unnecessary for him to consider his picture as an artistic production, or that he can be less thoughtful about a color harmony, for instance, than he who selects any other subject, simply proves that he is less of an artist than he who gives the subject his best attention. Or for him to suppose that his having such a subject can by any manner of means be construed as an excuse for making a picture in which the literary side shall be its only quality, or in which a so-called religious sentiment will take the place of the qualities loved by artists, thus furnishing an excuse for giving to the world an uninteresting canvas, is equally false.
>
> I believe most sincerely in a religious sentiment in religious pictures but, so far, have never seen it in a canvas which did not possess also artistic qualities. There is no more "bogus" sentiment in poor pictures—pictures in which the artist has tried to convince the world that nothing else was necessary—because he had nothing else to give. . . .[13]

13. Tanner, "Story of an Artist's Life," p. 11775.

It is interesting to note that at the same time *Daniel in the Lions' Den* was attracting attention in the Salon at the Palais d'Industrie there hung in the New Salon on the Champs de Mars, a portrait of Tanner himself,[14] painted by Dudley Murphy, his friend and studio companion.

Tanner was now a well-known and popular member of the American colony in Paris. Rodman Wannamaker was particularly impressed with his talent. Whether it was through Wannamaker or through an earlier contact that Henry Tanner became known to Robert C. Ogden, who was connected with the Wannamaker firm in Philadelphia, is not known, but Ogden was the second of several benefactors who encouraged Tanner materially in his artistic career. A letter dated June 15, 1896, from Ogden indicates the extent of his interest.

My dear Mr. Tanner,

I hasten to congratulate you upon the distinction that your "Daniel" has received from the judges of the Salon. Of the several religious subjects to which you have recently devoted yourself I think the Nicodemus will stand the best chance of popularity, but I understand that at present recognition is more important than a market for your pictures. I am glad that you agree with me that your artistic progress will be best served by continued residence abroad and would be very glad if you would take me into your confidence concerning any plans that you may have for either remaining or returning.

I await the photograph of your "Daniel" with much interest.

Dr. Paden gives me delightful accounts of yourself and your work.

Yours very truly,
Robert C. Ogden

It is interesting that at a time when the Negro was rejected by American society, Henry Tanner found his most devoted

14. This portrait of Tanner was given to the Chicago Art Institute in 1924. See *Bulletin of the Art Institute of Chicago*, 18 (March, 1924): 38.

friends and supporters among white people. It is true that they were "benefactors," but there is not the slightest indication that their benefactions were accompanied by the kind of condescension that Tanner would have been the first to resent. Most were warm and devoted friends whose personal affection for the artist was very genuine.

"Raising of Lazarus"

SO SUCCESSFUL WAS *Daniel in the Lions' Den* THAT HENRY Tanner immediately planned his next Salon picture in the same vein. This time he chose as his subject the *Raising of Lazarus.*

> The only drag was, it had always been, the everlasting question of money. A gentleman who had enabled me to gain a little by writing up art notes in Paris now withdrew this work because he thought I should come to America to paint American subjects. I refused to come home and paint things I was not drawn to, nor did I like the idea of quitting the helpful influences by which I was surrounded.[1]

The year was made possible through Mr. Ogden's and Tanner's parents' generosity. To save money Tanner remained

1. Henry Ossawa Tanner, "The Story of an Artist's Life," *World's Work,* 18 (June and July, 1909): 11772.

in Paris during the summer of 1896, for during the summer months models were not in great demand and were willing to make terms.

As Tanner worked on the *Lazarus* his studio was often crowded with friends wishing to follow the progress of a picture they felt was sure to be a sensation. Tanner was grateful for their interest, but sometimes found the help offered by his friendly critics a severe burden.

> I nearly made a shipwreck trying to follow the advice of a friend who counselled that a canvas that gave as much promise as this small-sized one should be much larger. He prevailed—very likely it flattered my vanity—and I bought a canvas six by ten feet. After working upon it quite a long time, I came to the conclusion that I could only make a very much "watered" edition of the smaller one. I recommenced work upon my "first love," accepting radical criticism with more caution.[2]

News of the picture was bruited about the Art Club and reached the ears of Rodman Wannamaker, who asked to see the picture on its completion. The finishing touches were put on it early in the new year, and Wannamaker was given a showing. He was so impressed with the religious feeling in the picture that he offered to pay Tanner's expenses to the Holy Land for a firsthand look at the setting he felt a painter needed to see if he were to paint Biblical subjects. He is quoted as saying:

> There is Orientalism in the "Lazarus," but it was a fortunate accident. In the Orient the light, both interior and exterior, the mannerisms of the people, the costumes and habits of living, all are vastly different from anything that could be imagined in the West. One should go there every two or three years, at least, to keep in touch with the Oriental spirit.[3]

Tanner gratefully accepted the offer and several months be-

2. Ibid., p. 11772.
3. William R. Lester, "Henry O. Tanner. Exile for Art's Sake," *Alexander's Magazine,* December 15, 1908, p. 72.

fore the opening of the Salon, set forth for Palestine. It was his first trip to the Orient.

In going to the Near East Tanner was following a custom artists had been introduced to many decades before. A love of oriental splendor and color was born with the romantic movement, but the "inventor" of familiar street scenes, landscapes, and historical incidents was the French artist, Alexandre-Gabriel Decamps (1803–60). He was sent to the Eastern Mediterranean as an assistant to the painter Garneray, who was commissioned in 1828 to paint a picture of the Battle of Navarino. While there Decamps visited Smyrna and other Turkish towns and villages, sketching their narrow alleyways and the everyday life of the Asiatic Turks, and when he went back to France he took with him hundreds of sketches and drawings. In the Salon of 1831 his painting *Patrouille Turque* won the favor of both artists and the public, and the Orient, both as a tourist attraction and as an artistic theme, was launched. Pictures of Biblical history began to be enlivened with sites seen by contemporary eyes, and the Bible was brought into sharper focus by a study of Near Eastern types.

In 1832 Eugène Delacroix discovered other picturesque aspects of Mediterranean life in the dark Moorish peoples of North Africa and in the vivid colors, quaint costumes, and classical ruins he found there.

He had gone to Morocco attached as artist to the retinue of Count Charles de Mornay, ambassador extraordinary to the court of the Sultan of Morocco.

Thereafter more and more frequently artists found their way to North Africa, the Nile, Palestine, Turkey, and Greece. Their pictures varied from the "Idylls" of Fromentin to the "official reports" of Gérôme who, in 1854, went to Russia and Turkey and later sailed down the Nile with Bartholdi. Henry Tanner's teacher and sponsor, Benjamin-Constant, went to Morocco in the seventies, also with an embassy, and said of his landing at Tangiers:

> Since that day I have had no other dream than to be a

painter of Oriental scenes; to lead the life pointed out by Marilhat, Delacroix and Henri Regnault.[4]

Henry Tanner was not the first American artist to establish himself as an Orientalist. His contemporaries, Humphrey Moore, Edwin Weeks, and F. A. Bridgman in particular, had scored successes with their pictures of Eastern life. Weeks went as far as India and showed his *Return of the Mogul Emperor from the Grand Mosque of Delhi* at the Salon of 1886. But Americans, like everyone else, had found inspiration in the Bible long before it was thought necessary to give it "realism" through firsthand archaeological and racial studies. Benjamin West had painted a *Raising of Lazarus*—a mammoth production, 8 by 10 feet—in 1780.

In a little notebook Tanner kept a sketchy account of his first journey to the Orient. It is a diary such as a tourist would keep, with costs, dates, and incidents hastily tossed in. It is reproduced here as a sidelight on an artist's tour in the late nineteenth century.

Left Paris 11 o'clock Tuesday Jan 12 1897. 3rd class to Marseilles 42 frcs. 30 kilo of baggage is allowed as we had 10 kilo over paid 4.40 frcs.

Arrived at Valence at Midnight went to Hotel Crois d'Or, will leave D. V. about 12 o'clock. Hotel not cheap (good). Have taken a little stroll around the town but have found little of interest except the bridge which is very picturesque and the remains of an old Roman chateau on noble heights.

Left Valence at 12.19 arrive or will arrive D. V. at Avignon at 2.35. Saw the Palace of the Popes which is now a Barracks—saw soldiers—mounted the town saw the landscape at sunset it was simply charming. The Tower is over 80 metres high—the door of the church is from 14th century and the building the 14th. The palace was of the 14th century also.

4. Clara H. Stranahan, *A History of French Painting* (New York: Charles Scribner's Sons, 1888), p. 326.

15th

Left Marseilles at 4.30 and was soon going along the coast. Ship rolled a good deal during the night—but slept well—got up at daylight and saw the snow capped mountains of Corsica lit by the morning sun—extremely beautiful—we left in the aft. and Sardinia is now to our right—but being cloudy the high mountains are hid and only now and then a glimpse is gotten—

Sea calm—stomach a little squirmish—should be sorry if one had to live on the sea.

Arrived at Hotel de Voyager

Jan 19th Cairo

Had a small walk much pestered by men who wished to take us to see different kinds of show, etc, etc.—can-can and like affairs.

Jan. 20th

Got up and soon off on donkeys the Mosques of Sultan Hasan and mosque Rifarfyeh.

Thence to Citadel built 1166 A.D.

In the Citadel is the beautiful mosque of Mohammed Ali. Also to well of Joseph of which there is a tradition that it is the one in which Joseph was put by his brothers (not likely true) the number of mosques is so great that to remember the names in one day or so is next to impossible. From a picturesque point of view many smaller things pleased me more. Saw the return of the Egyptian soldiers from the Soudan campaign. The street had been nearly barricaded by an enormous crowd of men women and children, suddenly (or rather we arrived at that instant) a line of men marched out of an opening door—they were nearly torn to pieces by their friends each one a centre of a group, such rejoicing I have never seen—I rejoiced with them. But I saw some sad faces standing on the outskirts of the crowd—possibly waiting for sons or husbands who never came. This alone destroyed one's complete happiness—it did seem they would be torn to pieces.

Afternoon went to Old Cairo. Saw old mosque of Gamia or M. of Amon Handsome photo. Copt church in little walled town to itself. Very old and—[illegible]—afterwards a visit to gaze upon the Nile (The Nileometer)! from this place got first view of the Pyramids, saw three. It did not surprise me it seemed I had seen them before possibly because I had seen photos and Paintings before. Coming home saw the Sultan who turned out in great style—a footman with richly embroidered clothes and a sword and runners in white with red jackets with lace barefooted and with a long stick. Saw also the Sultan's brother. Driving a most beautiful black horse.

In Hotel Voyager the rate is 10 frcs per diem but if we stay a month they will take 8 frcs a day. Will settle today or day after. Donkey for morning or afternoon from 6 to 8 piastres.

We were unable to leave Cairo March 2nd as I had just gotten up out of bed with influenza am now much better merci a Dieu.

Arrived Jerusalem March 5th (?) Friday afternoon for dinner.

Fare from Cairo to Port Saide 2nd class 14 shillings 3 pence. From Port Saide to Jaffa by Messagerie Line 2nd class £1 Fare from Jaffa to Jerusalem 1st class 15 frcs. 2nd 5.60 frcs.

Made a trip from Jerusalem to Jericho—Jordan—Dead Sea for 40 frcs. It was with quite a large party otherwise it would have been impossible.

Have taken board at Ahmet House 6 frcs a day.

Left April 4th Fare 2nd class from Jaffa to Alex 55 frcs with board but much the best way is to take 2nd class without board and take lunch as you are in harbor all day Port Saide and Alex.

From Alex to Naples 144 frcs 2nd class—stopping at Messina about 3 or 4 hours.

From Naples to Rome 2nd class on the express 20 frcs.

Got a small room for 1 fr a day not far from the quarter occupied by the American School of Architecture Villa Aurora.

No 7 Via Lombardia—it is in a very high new quarter of Rome.

Arrived April 15

Have visited many churches

"Raising of Lazarus"

St. Marie in Trastevere
St. Cecelia Trastevere
St. Giovanni in Laterano (music)
St. Marie Maggiore
St. Pietrò in Vincoli Built by Eudoxio—contains
St. Peter's chains
M Angelo's Moses
St. Pietro in Carcere
St. Pietro Le grand
St. Orofrio—Tasso

The edifice containing the Scala Santa which are however now covered in wood and can only be ascended on one's knees.

Also St. Paulo where are all the portraits of the popes in mosaic about 300 or 400 a fine old courtyard with columns

Fare from Rome to Pisa 2nd class 29 frcs from Pisa to Florence 3rd class 4.50 frcs.

Saw leaning tower Baptistery—wonderful accoustic propertys—also Campus Santo old burial grounds from the Roman period Cathedral also beautiful.

From Rome to Pisa 6 hours express 3rd class about 11 hours from Pisa to Florence 2 hours.

April 24th, 1897 Florence
Saw tombs of Michelangelo
Dante
Donatello
Galileo
and a couple of Napoleon family
Santa Croce
Visited Fiesole
St. Miniato
Sunday aft. in rain
The last supper by Sodoma

St. Miniato in a cemetery say the old—[illegible] constructed by Michelangelo 1529 for the Republic
also went to pottery

May 3rd Arrived Venice 2nd class 25.50 frcs.

Stopped at Bologna for 1/2 hour saw the leaning tower.

Received an offer from Government (French) to buy my picture—of course I accepted.

Here the diary ends. The matter-of-factness of the last entry gives no indication of the elation that Tanner felt upon receiving the offer of the French government to buy his *Raising of Lazarus.*[5]

Tanner had expected the picture to be accepted by the Salon jury; both of his teachers, especially Benjamin-Constant, had liked it—

. . . so much so that, when I took it to his studio early one morning, he had it taken to the bedroom of one of his sons to show it. I felt this a very high compliment, but we all know what they say—"One swallow does not make a Summer."[6]

But he had not anticipated the government's offer. The letter containing the news had been following Tanner for three weeks before catching up with him in Venice, and he was so fearful that the delay would see the matter dropped that he sent a long telegram of acceptance that he says nearly "broke the bank." In a few days his fears were allayed and letters from friends began to arrive which heightened the wave of happiness on which he was riding. Among them was one from an old friend in Paris who wrote, "Come home, Tanner, to see the crowds before your picture." It was the kind of adulation that all artists dream of but few realize. He wasted no time in arranging his return to Paris.

The permanent acquisition of examples of art by Americans was something relatively new in Paris. Although in the latter half of the nineteenth century deserving foreign works were purchased and shipped to various provincial museums in France, it was not until the Salon of 1882 that an American artist's name appeared among the officially honored. In that

5. The "Raising of Lazarus," for many years on exhibit at the Louvre, now belongs to the Musée d'Art Moderne and has been stored at Compiègne.

6. Tanner, "Story of an Artist's Life," p. 11773.

year Frank Boggs's *Place de la Bastille* was bought by the Ministry of Fine Arts. The next American pictures to be purchased were Henry Mosler's *Return of the Prodigal Son* in 1886 and Walter Gay's *Bénédicité* in 1888. These were followed in 1891 by Whistler's portrait of his mother, which was placed in the small, ill-lighted room in the Luxembourg Museum that was grudgingly set aside for the works of foreigners. Sometime later Sargent's *Carmencita* was purchased for the foreign collection, and slowly other pictures were added.

Back in Paris Henry Tanner found that he was famous. The reception of his picture is described in an account to the *Boston Herald* from their "Special Correspondent."

> One of the serious successes of this year's Salon of the Champs Elysées was a comparatively small canvas representing a biblical scene, the "Raising of Lazarus" and signed H. O. Tanner.
>
> The name meant little to the greater proportion of the vernissage audience; to artists it recalled a young man who has been working for the past seven years at the Julien Academy, turning out such strong school studies that to have a place near his easel was a coveted advantage to a "nouveau"; and to critics and amateurs whose eyes are keenly open to what is excellent among "his Jeunes" the signature brought to memory some four or five paintings exhibited the past few years, each of which was excellent in point of color, tone and style, and possessing as well that magical, sympathetic quality that is akin to that sacred word of *genius.*
>
> I had seen the picture, and felt strongly drawn toward it on the Press day before the opening, and the general verdict among the French critics then was that the honorable mention awarded Mr. Tanner's canvas last year would be followed by a medal this year; yet I was surprised to find on the vernissage, when attention is more given to the presence of celebrities and smart costumes and only canvasses signed by big names or dealing with bizarre or extremely decorative subjects are much noted, that there was a group after group before this quietly beautiful picture. . . .

I met Mr. Tanner by chance on that evening behind the scenes of the Montparnasse theater, where the American Art Association, of which he is a prominent member, was giving its annual entertainment, and to congratulations he could only say that the news of the purchase was as much a surprise to him as to his friends. The picture was voted upon and bought before the opening day of the Salon, but he had only that day returned from his trip through Egypt and Palestine to find the official notice awaiting him in his studio.

It was certainly a pleasant home welcome, and the warm congratulations from his fellow students and the older artists, quite as cordial in their felicitation, made undoubtedly a pleasant epoch in a life that has been sincerely devoted to hard work and study. I doubt if any award given to a comparatively unknown artist has ever met with more genuine and spontaneous acquiescence.

"I am very happy, of course," he said. "I had not seen the picture for several months until today at the Salon. I was a good deal despondent then, for I saw many things in it I should have liked to have done better. But it represented nearly a year's work, and when I had finished it I felt I had done the very best in me."

Mr. Tanner cannot be interviewed, because he has nothing to say; that is, nothing about himself. He has no skill at grasping incidents in his life. He cannot be convinced that the reading public cares a rap about him. . . .

How much proportion of colored blood is in Mr. Tanner's veins I am ignorant for he has one of the faces that shows few of the familiar traits. His skin is as fair as the average descendant of the Latin race, and it is only a second scrutiny that hints of his African descent.

This fact has really nothing to do with his work. Among the charming notices that have been written in the French journals concerning the success of this last picture not one has alighted on this, to Americans, rather picturesque fact, partly because the artist has kept himself so secluded in his studio that few know him personally, and perhaps, too, because in France we are more accustomed to clever men of African descent.[7]

There is no question that the *Raising of Lazarus* was a triumph. It was awarded a medal of the third class before its purchase by the government which, in view of the size of the exhibition at the Palais d'Industrie—3,263 paintings and drawings, representing the work of over 2,000 artists—was a signal honor. All the more so because Tanner resorted to none of the histrionics—size of canvas and flamboyance of style—that artists were prone to use to attract the jury's attention.

Among the religious pictures in the same exhibition were Gérôme's *Fuite en Egypte* and *Entrée de Christ à Jerusalem*, done with the matter-of-fact precision that only he was capable of and that lent itself well to the line engravings that insured his popularity. Other religious pictures were Bouguereau's *Compassion* (a Christ on the Cross) and the *Place des Lamentations, Jerusalem* by G. S. Hunter. None was painted with the perceptive feeling of Henry Tanner. There is no doubt that in his *Lazarus* he established himself as the romantic-realist par excellence of the religious field.

Tanner's version of the familiar theme had none of the shallow sentimentality so often seen in religious pictures on the Salon walls. His picture is a sombre one. Jesus stands above the recumbent figure of Lazarus and stretches out his hand as the dead man begins his struggle back to life. The drama is restrained, the forms solidly modelled, and the colors are rich and dark in tone, with the eerie effect that Tanner was so fond of.

Georges Lafenestre in the *Revue des Deux Mondes* wrote of the "aspect jaunâtre et vieillot" of the picture which, to him, was its only drawback. Like most critics he found the picture remarkable in its tightly constructed composition and fine characterization. He commented, "c'est un début très remar-

7. *Boston Herald*, June 13, 1897.

quable," and added, almost as an afterthought, using the phonetic spelling of Tanner's name, "M. Thaner est Americain."[8]

The year 1897 was a memorable one in the life of Henry Tanner. It not only saw him established as a first-rate painter in Paris—an accomplishment that few American art students ever achieved—but saw his name grow brighter in America. In the August 7 issue of *Harper's Weekly* the *Raising of Lazarus* was reproduced and its importance noted.

Something else occurred toward the end of 1897 that had nothing immediately to do with Tanner's reputation as an artist but that was to have profound influence on his life. This was his meeting with Atherton Curtis.[9] The circumstances under which the two men met will always remain obscure. Mr. Curtis wrote in a letter to Henry Tanner's son, Jesse, on November 22, 1937, a few months after the artist's death:

> I first met him on the 6th of December, 1897, but I really cannot remember what my first relations with him were. I know that he once told me that a little picture that we have at Bourron of the edge of the desert with the Pyramids in the distance was the first painting that we ever bought from him. . . .

8. "Les Salons de 1897," *Revue des Deux Mondes*, 141 (June, 1897): 677.

9. Atherton Curtis and his brother derived their wealth largely from a business in patent medicine, Mrs. Winslow's Soothing Syrup. The trade name was recorded in Maine in 1852 and two years later the firm moved to New York. Neither Atherton nor his brother seem to have taken an active interest in the business. Atherton went to Europe as a young man, became absorbed in the art of the Old World and except for brief periods remained an expatriate. At first he hoped to become an artist but, realising his limitations, became a collector of art instead. When Tanner met him in 1897 Curtis was an avid Egyptologist, but later on he widened his interests and amassed a particularly fine collection of prints, which he ultimately gave to the Biblioteque Nationale. Atherton Curtis assisted several young artists financially, but Henry Tanner was the only one of them who became a close and lasting friend. Curtis died in his eighties in Paris in late 1944, within two days of his wife Ingeborg. Atherton Curtis and the first and second Mrs. Curtises are buried at Vevey, Switzerland.

Atherton Curtis was, like Rodman Wannamaker, an American of inherited wealth who was living in Paris and was interested in art. His interest in Henry Tanner initially was as an artist who was worth encouraging. This interest developed into a lifelong friendship that sustained Tanner, materially and spiritually, over many rough moments and made it possible for him to enjoy a life devoted to his art. There were other people in Tanner's life—the Hartzells, Robert Ogden, and Rodman Wannamaker—whose benefactions helped him to overcome obstacles, but none who could compare with Atherton Curtis for the extent of his help or the affection that went with it. Atherton and his wife Ingeborg[10] became Henry Tanner's dearest and closest friends until he died.

10. Atherton Curtis's second wife, a Danish woman.

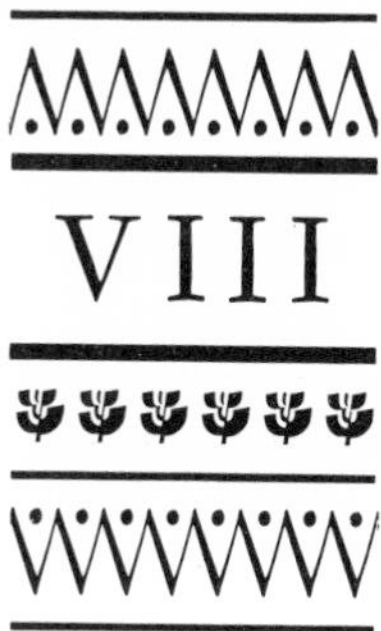

VIII

The Turn of the Century

In 1897 another important event took place in Henry Tanner's life. That year he met Jessie Macauley Olssen, who became his wife and whose companionship and devotion for twenty-six years gave a new and wonderful dimension to his life.

Jessie Olssen was a young white woman fifteen years younger than Tanner. At the time they met she and her sister Elna had been in Germany studying music and were in Paris on a leisurely trip through Europe with their parents. John Olssen, the father, whose profession is listed as "electrician" on Jessie's marriage certificate, was connected with the ship-building industry in San Francisco. He was a Swede by birth. A letter that he wrote to Henry and Jessie in 1901 indicates that he was not well educated, but there is no question that he was able to give his daughters the cultural advantages he himself had missed; both Elna, who played the piano, and Jessie, who sang, mingled easily in any society.

John Olssen's business required his presence in San Francisco, and he returned home, leaving his family in Paris. They went down to Barbizon, and it was here they made the acquaintance of the prominent artist, H. O. Tanner. In a letter written to Ingeborg Atherton in 1909, Tanner refers to this meeting:

> As you will see by the very important printing at head of letter I have left Paris for a few days during the extreme heat. I shall very likely return at the latest Friday, for several reasons. I spent a summer here before 1900 where I met Roy, Avy and lot of the French painters and incidentally Jessie and Elna Olssen were among the party. I doubt not the memories of those days had something to do with my coming back again. Of course I was not so foolish as to expect to live those days over again. . . .

Jessie was tall, attractive, and talented. Her warmth and spontaneity were in contrast to Tanner's gentle reserve, but the difference in their personalities seems to have acted as a magnet between them. That they quickly became friends is evident from the fact that Jessie was the model for his next Salon picture, an *Annunciation*. This was the first of many pictures in which she served as his model.

The *Annunciation* is vaguely reminiscent of the one by Dante Gabriel Rossetti, though Tanner's Mary is somewhat older and less shrinking in attitude. She sits on her bed with hands clasped and looks with an expression of receptive wonder toward the miraculous vision which is conveyed by a shaft of golden light. There is still archaeological interest in the classical arches, dark wall hanging, and stone floor of the peasant's house and in the pattern of the oriental rug that covers a portion of the floor. The bedclothes and folds of Mary's robe are drawn with academic precision, but the warm, glowing tones that give poetic appeal to the picture are unlike anything seen in the conventional Salon *Annunciations* and make it, to this day, one of the most popular paintings in the Philadelphia Museum. It was exhibited at the Old Salon of 1898 and later in Philadelphia, where it was purchased for the Wilstach collection of the Philadelphia Museum.

In the fall of 1898 Rodman Wannamaker suggested that Tanner take another trip to the Holy Land at his expense. The impending and highly controversial visit of the German Emperor to Palestine had been widely discussed in the press, and Wannamaker thought it an excellent opportunity for Tanner to commemorate a contemporary event, using the Biblical setting. However reluctant Tanner may have been to leave Jessie, he was delighted at the opportunity to visit Palestine a second time. With an artist friend he sailed from Brindisi for Jaffa by way of Alexandria and reached Jerusalem just one week before the Emperor's arrival on October 25. But the pictures he had hoped to make of the Emperor's entry into the city did not materialize. Police regulations were so severe, the crowds so great, and the entry made so hastily—"on the double"—that even sketches were out of the question. Nevertheless, Tanner's second stay in Palestine was much more productive than the first.

> We spent six months painting around Jerusalem and the Dead Sea, and this gave me an insight into the country and the character of the people that my shorter visit had only whetted my appetite for.
>
> It was here that I made a study of the Mount of Temptation from which I afterward painted "Moses and the Burning Bush." I also commenced a picture, "The Scapegoat," which still languishes in a dark closet of unfinished efforts.
>
> "Christ and Nicodemus," exhibited first in the Paris Salon (1899) and afterward at the Pennsylvania Academy of Fine Arts, where it was awarded the Lippincott prize and purchased for the Temple Collection in 1900, was made during this trip. I still remember with pleasure the fine head of the old Yemenite Jew who posed for Nicodemus. "A Flight into Egypt" and several smaller canvases were the result of this

trip. Never shall I forget the magnificence of two Persian Jews whom I once saw at Rachel's Tomb; what a magnificent "Abraham" either one of them would have made. Nor do I forget a ride one stormy Christmas night to Bethlehem. Dark clouds swept the moonlit skies and it took little imagination to close one's eyes to the flight of time and see in those hurrying travelers the crowds that hurried Bethlehemward on the memorable night of the Nativity, or to transpose the scene and see in each hurrying group a "Flight into Egypt." . . . Nor do I forget the deep pathos of the "Jews' Wailing Place"—those tremendous foundation stones of that glorious temple that stood upon Mt. Moriah, worn smooth by the loving touch of tearful and devout worshippers from all over the world. . . .[1]

The painting of greatest merit that resulted from this second trip to Palestine was his *Christ and Nicodemus*. In this picture Tanner shows greater independence of vision than in any of his previous religious paintings. He eliminates all archaeological details and makes no attempt to "tell a story." The picture represents a moonlit scene with the young Christ and aged Nicodemus, in the foreground, seated on a terrace overlooking the country around Jerusalem. The drama of the picture lies in the juxtaposition of youth with age, as well as in the skillful contrast of light and dark. It was impossible for Tanner not to react physically to light and color. The following passage from his autobiography reveals the extent to which his art was affected by his emotions:

> One evening, while riding in a jiggling ill-lighted omnibus in Paris, I was struck with the beauty of the effect around me. Inside, the figures dimly lighted with a rich cadmium; outside the cool night with here and there a touch of moonlight. I did not want to paint the interior of an omnibus—so "Judas Covenanting with the High Priest" is the result. I have a very clear recollection that in my childhood days the sky

1. Henry Ossawa Tanner, "The Story of an Artist's Life," *World's Work*, 18 (June and July, 1909): 11773.

and fields were never so beautiful as when by some illness I was confined to the house. In after years it has often seemed to me that, when bowed by some sorrow, nature seemed more radiant than ever before. This apparent fact influenced largely "The Return of the Holy Women." The moon has risen, a shepherd returns with his flock, all unconscious of the terrible tragedy of the morning, or the sorrowing figures, one of them, Mary, supported by John, in front of him. All is tranquility and loveliness, only within the souls of that sorrowing mother and those loving disciples is there turmoil and sorrow.[2]

During the months that Henry Tanner spent in Palestine he did not forget Jessie Olssen, nor did she forget him. If anything, the separation convinced them both how dependent they had become on each other. A telegram from Jessie addressed to Tanner at Olivet House, Jerusalem, Syria, dated February 25, 1899, reads "Come to me." It was the final straw that broke down Henry's resistance, if there was any, to an engagement. The marriage took place the following December 14 at Saint Giles-in-the-Fields, Bloomsbury, London. The witnesses to the ceremony were Jessie's sister Elna, who had remained in Paris to continue her studies, and a Dutch friend by the name of Gerhoodt C. Mars.

Although Jessie's parents were not present, the marriage had their blessing, as it had that of Bishop and Mrs. Tanner. The Tanners knew that their son Henry moved in a world where color did not matter. His marriage to a white woman was of less consequence to them than it might have been to the Olssens, but there is no indication that either John or Bessie Macauley Olssen—she was born in Glasgow, Scotland—felt anything but the warmest affection for their son-in-law. In a letter that Mr. Olssen wrote to Henry and Jessie in 1901 from San Francisco he made the comment, "Well, our relations I never see, since they treated you and Henry so bad." In what

2. Ibid., p. 11774.

way they were treated badly is not known, nor does he say who the relations were. Some years later two of Jessie's San Francisco cousins, Jessie and Ella Bateman, came to Paris and met Henry Tanner. They became as fond of him as was Elna and, later on, her husband Charles Tough. Mrs. Olssen was devoted to her son-in-law, as may be seen by the following note written from Paris in 1902, when Jessie and Henry were living in America for a brief period.

MY DEAR HENRY,

I must have a word to say to you today on your birthday. May you enjoy many of them with good health and happiness and last though not least good luck and prosperity dear one, my blessing to you both this sunny day and that the good Lord may watch over you and your dear self Henry live to enjoy many Happy Years.

Lovingly,
MOTHER OLSSEN

After a honeymoon at Martigues, Bouches-du-Rhône, Jessie and Henry returned to Paris and took an apartment on the Rue d'Assas, overlooking the Luxembourg Gardens. Tanner shortly began work on a large canvas, *Christ Before the Doctors*. He had a studio in the same building on the Boulevard St. Jacques where he and Dudley Murphy had shared one. It was here that he was interviewed for an article Vance Thompson was writing on "American Artists in Paris" for *Cosmopolitan*.

It was a gray day, bleak and windy weather. The broad and dreary Boulevard St. Jacques was deserted. I had not known that in all Paris there was a corner quite so desolate. At No. 51 there is a pair of iron gates. An old man, who was warming himself at a charcoal brazier, admitted me into the court.

At the head of the first pair of stairs a youngish looking man came to meet me. He was rather slight, not very tall, with a small beard and mustache, and a mass of fluffy hair brushed up from his forehead. He looked startlingly like Henry Rochefort—but a young Rochefort who should have had negro blood in him. There is no American artist in Paris more talked about than Mr. H. O. Tanner. Perhaps this is because he is a mulatto and, in spite of the example of Dumas and De Heredia, we are still a trifle surprised when the artist reveals himself under a dark skin. And then there may be another reason: Mr. Tanner is not only a Biblical painter—not only a Philadelphian—but, as well, he has brought to modern art a new spirit. His is not quite the simple realism of M. Tissot, of Munkaczy [*sic*] and Verestchagin. He has not been content to translate the Ghetto into terms of biblical history. There is in him too much of the Orient for this naive irreverence. He is a mystic, but a mystic who has read Renan and studied with Benjamin-Constant.

I was very much surprised in his artist's career. To him it seemed very simple. His early struggles, his fight against an environment which you may imagine, have left no impress on him. He likes to date his artistic life from the time he entered Aikens' [*sic*] studio in Philadelphia. . . .

I daresay you remember that the French Government bought one of his pictures for the Luxembourg; that another—an "Annunciation"—is in the Wilstach Collection of Philadelphia, and that last year his "Christ and Nicodemus" was in the Salon.

The painter wheels the big canvas forward into the light. Not an extraordinary composition—simple, rather, and inevitable. Christ is in the center of the picture, the learned men are grouped to left and right. The color scheme is rich and somber. There is more of the Orient in it than in any other painting by this artist that I have seen.

The picture, of course, was far from finished when I saw it. The dark winter days have held it back, and then, Mr. Tanner, like some one in a parable, has just married. But you will see it in the Salon. A strange personnage, this young mulatto—the product of Philadelphia and the Latin Quarter and Bethlehem—who is destined, I like to think, to give the world a new conception, at once reverent, critical and visionary, of the scenes of the Bible.[3]

3. Vance Thompson, "American Artists in Paris," *Cosmopolitan*, 29 (May, 1900): 18, 19, 20.

Chapter Eight

Christ Before the Doctors was exhibited at the Salon of the Société des Artistes Français in the spring of 1900 and was greatly admired. One of its greatest admirers, however, was not present. This was Robert C. Ogden, whose financial assistance to Tanner has been previously noted. The following letter, dated July 12, 1900, was sent from Philadelphia:

My Dear Mr. Tanner,

The photograph of your last Salon picture is now before me, and has interested me intensely. The interest increases under the light of your letter of the 1st inst., which gives me some glimpse of the inspiration and of the plans that are moving in your mind. Allow me to caution you against overwork. Your art draws heavily upon your sympathies, and such work is always, both mentally and physically, exhausting. "If you want to get there quick go slow." This is one of the wise maxims of Josh Billings.

I have only to say that, in case you should find it desirable to ask my co-operation in anything that you may desire to do, I shall be very glad to receive your suggestions. Of course, my only assistance can be financial. I am not in position to do that on any large scale; but I do so clearly recognize the importance of your mission in art, and am so interested in your career, that I shall esteem it a privilege to co-operate in any way agreeable to yourself that is within my power.

I like the idea of the production of a collection that may be suggested by subjects that you may find in Palestine. It strikes me that, if the number of pictures is sufficiently large to command general interest, it would be a very great success. The Tissot pictures when first exhibited in this country, were welcomed by crowds of intelligent people. Of course, they were greatly advertised in advance, but some of the wisdom of this world may be applied to the development of your idea.

With kind wishes for Mrs. Tanner I am
Very sincerely yours,
Robert C. Ogden

The letter suggests that Henry Tanner had in mind an exhibit of his Biblical paintings in the United States. This plan was not to be realized for several years.

While the spring Salon was going on, another artistic event of even wider interest was also in full swing. This was the Universal Exposition, that opened in Paris in April. The Palais d'Industrie, on the Champs-Elysées, which had housed the Old Salon, had been torn down the year before to make way for the Grand and Petit Palais, where the Universal Exposition was held. For a time it had appeared the Old Salon would have no place for its yearly show, but the Société Hippique came to the rescue of the homeless artists and offered them their hall on the Avenue de Breteuil as well as funds to help defray the cost of the show. This rescue by the horsemen of Paris was especially fortunate for American artists as the space given the American section in the Universal Exposition was a niggardly 600 feet on the line, space enough for about one tenth of the pictures representing American art. When Whistler and Sargent were informed of the situation they refused to exhibit with the Americans, choosing to place their pictures in the British section.

The Universal Exhibition was more interesting for the comprehensive view it gave of nineteenth-century art than for its suggestions of future art trends. *The Corn Sifters* by Courbet, *The Man with the Hoe*, by Millet, and *Breakfast on the Grass*, by Manet, which had been absent from the last Universal Exhibition in 1889, were shown, but the impressionists, who had given such an impulse to art, were treated in a perfunctory manner.

> In a far-off gallery altogether, where the Exhibition of the Century commences, I have found modest and small Pissaros and Claude Monets, which, where they are, look for all the world like poor relations who have had their seats allotted them at the lower end of the table.[4]

4. Armand Dayot, "The French Pictures (1890–1900) in the Grand Palais," *Art Journal*, 1900, p. 40.

The names of the impressionists were on everyone's lips, and many pictures, especially the landscapes, showed their influence. There was some justification for Munkácsy's plaintive comment, "Non, non faire claire, il n'y a que ça."[5] But Tanner's picture, which won a silver medal, did not conform to this credo. It was an older picture, his *Daniel in the Lions' Den*, which had received acclaim at the Salon of 1896.

In spite of its reduced size, the American section was considered one of the best in the exhibition. M. Jules Comte, in his review, stated that it was possible to foresee the time when American painting, entirely free and independent, would become an active element in world art.[6] The *International Studio* went a step further and claimed that the exposition proved there already was such a thing as American art.[7] This was due, in part, to the fact that Americans were represented whose work had not been properly shown in Europe before. Among them was Thomas Eakins. His *Man with Violoncello* and *Boxing Match* attracted attention by their straightforward and vigorous truthfulness and led to a guarded statement by "N. N.," critic for the *Nation*:

> The work of American artists who stay at home I know less well and yet to it one must look for the development of any purely American characteristics, though it must be remembered that great art is not to be produced because a man chooses to live within the boundaries of our glorious Imperial Republic, much as some of our law-givers would like to make American artists, residing temporarily abroad, believe it.[8]

5. Will H. Low, *A Chronicle of Friendships* (New York: Charles Scribner's Sons, 1908), p. 454.

6. *L'Art de l'Exposition Universelle* (Paris: Librairie de l'Art Ancien et Moderne, 1900), p. 195.

7. Clark H. Caffin, "Pictures Exhibited at the Pan-American Exhibition", *International Studio,* 14 1901, p. xiii.

8. "The Paris Exposition—American Section," *Nation,* 71 (August 2, 1900): 88, 89.

Few, if any, American artists living abroad gave a thought to painting pictures that might be called "American." Edwin Austin Abbey, who lived in England, voiced their attitude toward nationality in art in a letter to his future wife when writing her about the Lord Mayor's dinner of January 26, 1889:

> I sat near Frederic Harrison and Sargent—Leighton [afterwards Lord Leighton] harped on the tiresome old string about the efforts of men still seeking to express themselves in forms which do not yet bear the stamp of their national characteristics. I cannot understand a man so clever as L. is, taking this narrow view of art, not recognizing the fact that artists who can do so will gravitate towards what seems to them the artistic field in which they will be best able to do justice to, or display their ability. I cannot think the quality of this ability is a matter of nationality.[9]

By 1900 there was a growing criticism in the United States of this attitude. Sadakichi Hartmann, in his *History of American Art*, published in 1901, wrote:

> There are in Europe, particularly in Munich and Paris, a number of American artists, who, by remarkable work, have won fame before the European public and who with perfect right would be considered our strongest men if they still deserved to be called Americans. . . .
>
> Anybody who has a serious interest in the welfare of American art can feel but little sympathy for these Franco and Teuto-Americans, however one may admire their works.[10]

Will H. Low, a former expatriate himself, discussed the question of American artists at home and abroad in *A Chronicle of Friendships*.

> As the greatest artists of the past, as Raphael, Rubens, and

9. Edward Verrall Lucas, *Edwin Austin Abbey*, 2 vol. (London: Methuen and Co., 1921), 1: 185.

10. *A History of American Art*, rev. ed. (New York: Tudor Publishing Co., 1934), p. 160.

Velasquez, were men of the world about them, so is it the birthright of the modern artist to take his place in his environment and his share in the shaping of events.

The American artist abroad, however, would be ill-advised if he openly demanded this right in the republic of arts, and consequently such little influence as he is permitted to exercise is by favor only, and too often by favor purchased at too dear a cost. Therefore the privilege to live in an atmosphere where art, where the continuous effort at perfection of technical expression, is recognized and honored, is the chief recompense which falls to the lot of the American artist in Europe; and is one which, from the point of view of one who loves his craft, is by no means to be disdained. The men of my generation who from circumstance or choice have been called upon to work at home, have had by way of compensation an abiding sense that they were aiding to implant a standard of art hitherto unknown upon these shores. This our exiled brethren abroad have missed, and to this foundation of a future American school of art the humblest worker in our ranks here at home has been privileged to do his part.[11]

Nevertheless, the average merit of the American artists in Europe was exceptionally high. Their peasant girls, provincial bourgeois, humble interiors, landscapes, and portraits, painted without extravagance and often with great sensitivity, were generally excellent examples of their kind. Lionel Weldon, William T. Dannat, Humphrey Johnston, Walter McEwan, Alexander Harrison, Frederick Frieseke, Max Bohm, and Walter Gay are but a few of the Americans whose names were seen regularly in the Paris Salons at the turn of the century. Tanner also was a "Salon painter," but in his ability to translate traditional themes in terms of poetic significance he was far above the usual *salonnier*.

It is interesting that while *Daniel in the Lions' Den* and *Christ Before the Doctors* were on exhibit in Paris, a different type of Tanner was seen in America at the Twelfth Annual Exhibition of the Philadelphia Art Club.

11. *Chronicle of Friendships*, p. 117.

A modest little canvas that might be overlooked is the work of H. O. Tanner, that poetic painter of African blood. It bears the title of "Night Scene," and though hardly more than a sketch, is a thing of beauty, full of artistic merit.[12]

This picture—a group of men sitting about a lamp-lit table out of doors with a white house for a background—is of special interest, as it was one of Tanner's early and little-known sketches, which he frequently did as models for larger pictures and which, in spontaneity and depth of expression, are often more effective than his "finished" productions.

It was Tanner's biblical pictures, however, that commanded the public's attention, as well as that of Edward Bok, a prominent Philadelphian who, in his capacity as editor of the *Ladies Home Journal*, conceived the idea of reproducing a series of *Mothers of the Bible*, for his magazine. He may have been motivated by the *Raising of Lazarus*, which had appeared in *Harper's Weekly* in 1897. But paintings were expensive and difficult to reproduce at the turn of the century and his correspondence with Tanner about the project is written on a note of businesslike caution.

Dear Mr. Tanner,

I have read very carefully your letter of November 14, in which you give a more detailed outline of the six Biblical pictures. But I find, as I feared, that the outline really gives a meagre and inadequate idea of what the final result will be. Of course, I get your general trend of mind better but, after all, the final adjudgment must be made upon the pictures.

Hence, I can only thank you for writing to me so fully, and simply express the hope that the paintings themselves may be all that we hope for them.

Believe me, with best wishes for your success in this work.

Very sincerely yours,
Edward Bok

12. Philadelphia newspaper clipping, 1900, Tanner Collection, Archives of American Art, Detroit.

CHAPTER EIGHT

On July 23, 1901, Bok acknowledged the receipt of Tanner's first three paintings and on September 9, wrote a letter in a different vein.

MY DEAR MR. TANNER,

Your letter of August twenty-eighth pleases me very much indeed for it meets the unfortunate issue so squarely that there is nothing for me to do but to express my appreciation to an artist who has the unusual gift of a practical side to his nature. This does not often occur.

Indeed I do realize the serious effort you have made with the paintings, and the results you have obtained, and upon these I congratulate you. Don't mistake me, however, I do not mean to say that these paintings are absolutely incapable of reproduction. I say they are almost *so, and while we may succeed in reproducing them, the attendant expense will be so great that we are forced to consider it. We will go ahead and reproduce one and see where we come out with it, and we will make the strongest endeavor possible to get an adequate reproduction. To do this well and carefully we shall take plenty of time and spare no pains or expense in getting everything out of the painting that can possibly be shown in a reproduction.*

That was quite a slip of the tongue in speaking of the Rachel and Jacob picture as portraying Rebekah and Isaac. I knew better, of course.

Considering the work you have put upon the next painting —that of Sarah—we will, of course, accept it and pay you therefor. It is pleasant, however, to have you release me, as you do in your letter, from the fifth and sixth pictures. This makes it more possible for us to go to the expense of producing the four, but even this I cannot promise at this moment. We will simply go ahead with one and see where we come out.

Thank you for your promise to send me the two hundred and fifty words of description for each picture, and I shall be glad to have these from you. In the meantime, I will have a remittance made to you for the three pictures in hand.

Thanking you again for the way you have met my letter, and once more regretting the circumstances, believe me

Very sincerely yours,
EDWARD BOK

The four paintings—*Sarah*, *Hagar*, *Rachel*, and *Mary*—were successively reproduced in the September, October, November, and December issues of the *Ladies' Home Journal* for 1902. In spite of the care with which the work was done, the technical problems were great and the reproductions do not do justice to Tanner's art. Nevertheless, the reproduction of his four paintings in the most widely circulated of the women's magazines brought Tanner's name to the attention of many people, most of whom did not know he was a Negro. But those Negroes who knew of Tanner were grateful to him for establishing their right to compete for honors in a field few of them had previously entered. In 1900 the Negro artist in America was still an isolated and exceptional figure. The ordinary young Negro who attempted a career in art met with constant discouragement, if not rigid barriers. The usual channels for exhibiting his work were denied him. There were no Negro art associations and the state fairs were almost exclusively the sole outlets for his art. A Negro, like Tanner, who had been able to break the barriers of prejudice was viewed as a pioneer whose success blazed a trail that others might hope to follow.

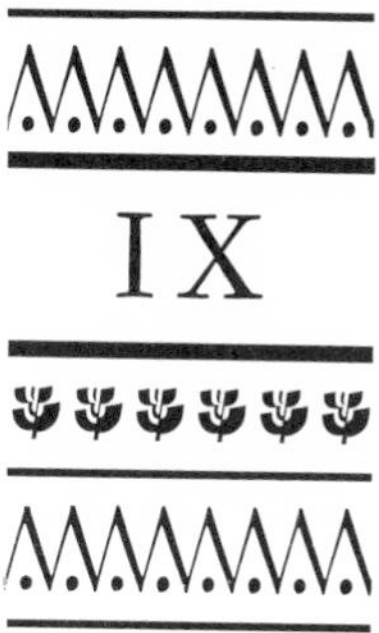

Changing Scenes

In 1900 Henry Tanner was uncertain whether he would remain permanently in France, move to England, or return to the United States to live. At one time he would not have considered this last alternative, but professional success had opened many doors, and in spite of the racial difficulties he had encountered in America, he had never lost affection for his own country. His parents and other relatives lived there, and in November, 1900, his friend Atherton Curtis moved back to the United States and settled at Mt. Kisco, just outside of New York City.

But Tanner was not immediately ready to follow. In January, 1901, he wrote his old colleague, Professor Crogman, at Clark University in Atlanta, that he and Jessie were going to the south of France for a few months. Nothing is known of this journey except that they were back in Paris by May, for in that month John Olssen wrote his daughter from San Francisco:

> I heard that you and Henry would perhaps go to England to live. Now, don't go there. England is on the downfall. The Boars [*sic*] have ruined her finances and before they are done with the Boars they will be bankrupt. But time will tell better than I, and if we have good health all will come out well, I hope. Thanking you and Henry for your kindness when I was in Paris, hoping this will find you both well, as I am.
>
> JOHN OLSSEN

How seriously Henry and Jessie considered the matter of moving to England is not known, but the idea could not have been of long duration. Bishop Tanner went to London the summer of 1901 to attend a church conference and later visited a friend in Somerset. A letter from the friend, Mr. Impey, to Jessie Tanner in October makes no mention of the projected move. It does, however, give a picture of Henry Tanner's father, vigorous and alert at sixty-six.

> Our dear old friend Bp. Tanner left on Friday morn. I went as far as Bristol with him to see him into a through train for Liverpool and he wrote me thence that he had had a very enjoyable journey and was met on arrival by Bp. Derrick. He certainly seemed more strong and vigorous—more his old self before he left us than when he arrived so I hope country life benefited him. On the Wed. previous we drove about 12 miles to meet about 100 other lovers of antiquities—at the spot where Alfred the Great lived during the great crisis of his life when the Danish army had nearly destroyed his people and country. Some interesting historical papers were read and we had a delightful climb to the summit of his camp and a glorious view in almost every direction from it as the mount rises steeply in the center of a plain (in those days a vast swamp or inland tidal sea).
>
> Bp. T. so longed for "Henry" to see it and paint the scene....

We had several social functions while Bp. Tanner was here—going to tea with friends, others coming here, etc., etc., the last evening about 30 preachers (lay and professional) gathered here to listen to the reading of the paper he had read previously at the Conference in London. A good deal of interesting talk followed. . . .

My affectionate regard to you both.

Yours very sincerely,
C. IMPEY

We do hope to have a nice quiet visit from you both next year.

By the next year, however, Jessie and Henry were in America. William E. Barton, an American clergyman, wrote an article for the *Advance* in 1913 in which he described a meeting with Tanner in 1902 and attested to his intention at that time of returning to the United States. Mr. Barton was in Paris to learn what he could of the painters who were introducing modern interpretations of Christ in art. He wrote:

> I remember how I came to meet Mr. Tanner on a Sunday night in the Latin Quarter. I had preached that morning in the American Church in the Rue de Berry, and was invited to preach again in the evening at a service held for American students. This meeting combined religious and social features. There was a violin solo, I remember, and refreshments were served after the benedictions. The studio in which we met was a great loft and nothing was done by way of clearing it, except to move the easels back and hang the sketches on the wall to protect the paint. After the sermon I met a large number of young people from America. There may have been 150 to 200 of them, and many of them were lonely and glad of a word from home.
>
> Announcement of this service had been made at the American Church in the morning, and a number of people were present who were members of that congregation. As Major Williams and I climbed to the top of an omnibus, making our way homeward, I found myself sitting next to an artist to

whom I already had been introduced, Mr. Henry Ossawa Tanner. I talked with him as we rode on top of the omnibus about the art of Paris as he knew it, and we discussed some of the men whose pictures I had seen. He told me a little of his own struggles and of his determination to win recognition and return to his own land. Mr. Tanner is the son of Bishop Tanner, of the African Methodist Church. In Paris his color never counted against him in the least, and he and his wife, who was with him on top of the omnibus that night, moved freely in such society as they chose. It was not quite so in America but he intended to win fame and return to his native land.[1]

It seems more likely that it was Atherton Curtis who influenced Henry in returning to America. It was Atherton's desire to form a small, congenial colony of people at Mount Kisco, and for the purpose he built four houses, one of which he offered to the Tanners.

Henry and Jessie arrived at Mount Kisco on June 23, 1902. It was Henry's first visit home since he had become famous. He remained only six months. Whether it was his original intention to stay longer is not clear. According to Atherton's diary, the Tanners left Mount Kisco on December 31, 1902, for Boston and sailed from there to Spain. In a letter to Jesse Tanner after his father's death Atherton makes the statement:

> I know that he had been to Spain before his trip in 1902, but I know nothing about the dates of his visit.

It is likely that the first trip was made two winters before, at the time Henry and Jessie went to the south of France, though there is no evidence for this. Nor are there firsthand accounts of the second and longer visit to Spain, though Jesse Tanner recalls his father's description of the house he occupied there.[2] It was located on the ramparts of Granada and had a small door that led outside the city, by which a person could

1. William E. Barton, "An American Painter of the Resurrection," *Advance*, March 20, 1913, p. 2011.

2. Jesse O. Tanner to me, May 9, 1966, Archives of American Art, Detroit.

enter or leave the city without passing through the city gates. Tanner was surprised at the low rental of the house and after moving in discovered the reason—the small door was used by smugglers passing bales of merchandise into the city. The police, noting that Tanner locked the door one night, asked him to please keep it open for their "friends." He kindly obliged.

Life on the ramparts could hardly have compared in comfort with that at Mount Kisco, and for Jessie Tanner at this particular time it may have been rigorous, for she was pregnant. It is unlikely that she knew of her condition when she and Henry left Boston, for they had not been in Spain many months before they decided to return to America. Atherton Curtis wrote:

> . . . I do not seem to have any record in my diary as to when they returned to Mt. Kisco. At all events they were there in the winter of 1903–4 because on the 5th of January 1904 we had 28 below zero Fahrenheit and as your father often referred to that afterwards I know that he was there at that time.

As a matter of fact they were there by September 25, 1903, for on that date their son and only child, Jesse Ossawa Tanner was born in New York City. It was an event joyfully welcomed and one that was to give Henry and Jessie the greatest happiness of their lives. The following letter was written to Jessie by her husband shortly after the baby's birth:

Monday 9 p.m.
(Sept. 1903)

Dear Jessie,

I arrived safely and met Atherton on the train. When I arrived at the door who should be looking out the window but baby in nurse's arms, baby blue eyes bright as stars. He is simply looking fine and his colic is not near so severe as formerly. Miss Risdin puts hot water in his bottle and a few sucks brings up the gas and he is happy again. The hot water works like a charm. We expect (DV) to weigh him tomorrow morning.

He is getting much more color than when he first came and his eyes are larger. His bowels are now all right. Hope you passed a good night. All inquired after you and were happy to know you were so *much better.*

Be happy in the knowledge that you have one of the handsomest babies going and we will hope and pray that he may grow up to be a good and strong man.

With love,
HENRY

Tuesday morning

Our little treasure is fine this morning, as bright as a new dollar.

May the good Lord bless you and keep you.

Your loving husband,
HENRY

There is no mention by Atherton Curtis of any racial problems connected with Henry Tanner's residence at Mount Kisco. Probably few people in the area knew of his Negro blood, living, as he did, in a small colony surrounded by congenial friends and protected by his friendship with a man of wealth and distinction. Atherton Curtis described to Jesse Tanner his parents' life at Mount Kisco in these words: "Your father painted and your mother kept house for him and that is practically what their life was while there." Nevertheless, there can be little doubt that Tanner's race presented certain difficulties to him in America. His relatives were Negro, his wife a white woman, and his child completely Caucasian in appearance yet reckoned, by blood, a Negro. It was a complex situation in a country that did not readily accept mixed marriages.

Aside from the racial problems it is doubtful whether, after living for years in the artistic hub of the world, the cultural resources of New York seemed very inspiring to either Henry Tanner or Atherton Curtis, and it is not surprising that after a while Paris began to cast its lure. The 28-degree-below-zero weather may also have added weight to the argument for returning to France. Whatever the determining factors, Atherton and Henry both decided they had had enough of America and that they would go back to Paris. Once their minds were made up, they immediately set about their preparations. Henry and Jessie were to go on ahead and find an apartment sufficiently large for the Curtises, as well as living quarters for themselves.

On April 18, 1904, Henry and Jessie and baby Jesse sailed from New York for France. Letters from Atherton in May and June indicate something of the problems involved in moving a wealthy ménage, as well as his confidence in Henry's judgment:

May 6, 1904

Dear Henry,

We are all wondering now how you got on with your ocean trip and how His Majesty stood it. No doubt we shall get a letter before long telling us about the trip. But whatever its inconveniences, you are now in Paris pleasantly hunting apartments and all your cares are over. Well, Paris is Paris, after all, and one can stand a little trouble for the sake of being there. I wonder how you are getting on with your apartment hunting. By the way, I don't think we gave you absolutely precise ideas as to what we wanted. Supposing that you came upon apartments with rooms about the size of our sitting room here. Then we should need two rooms for books, one for storing works of art, one for prints making four in all. These could be in a separate apartment from the living apartment and need not be even on the same floor though they ought not to be below the third on account of dampness. In addition to this we need an apartment with kitchen, sitting room, one double bedroom and two single bedrooms. Then we need a room for a store-room. This can be in either apart-

ment. And finally we need somewhere to place Marie and Joseph. A small apartment in the court would do for them and temporarily even one room would be enough for them. Then we want a balcony to one of the rooms of the living apartment and we do not object to balconies scattered about among any of the other rooms. We want water and gas and the stair-way must be wide enough in the turns for the orchestrelle to pass, which as you know is very much larger than a piano. These I think are the full extent of our simple requirements, excepting that we should like a pleasant outlook if possible and we must have the morning sun.

Things here are about as usual. I am expecting the packers Monday. They hope to finish in a week. So do I but I don't expect to be done inside of two weeks. This packing business is not amusing. I wonder how soon after getting settled in Paris we shall have to do it all over again. What queer people we are! How I envy the people who get into one apartment and stay there for years with all their belongings. One may move about one self as much as one pleases. Traveling is a good thing and broadens one as nothing else can but this traveling with a museum full of works of art and a library of books is overestimated by anyone who thinks there is any value in it mentally or morally speaking.

The Ivanowskis have been here about ten days. Ivanowski has a craze about the pianola and plays it some three hours a day to the neglect of his family and everything.

The weather was cold here until the first of this month and in fact is not particularly warm even now. The trees are only beginning to show signs of green. Everything is very backward. But the grass is green and we are really having spring even if things are behindhand and this is something at least after the severe winter.

Louise[3] *joins me in love to you both. Please give our most profound and humble respects to His Majesty.*

Sincerely your friend,
Atherton Curtis

3. The first Mrs. Atherton Curtis, who died after their return to France.

Mrs. B. says please to send her love too.

In regard to apartments, it is not necessary that the rooms be divided exactly as I have indicated. The print room or the room for works of art could be in the living apartment for instance.

May 20, 1904

Dear Henry,

I went to the city yesterday and had a procuration *made out and duly certified by the French Consul. I enclose it herein and hope it will be what is wanted. I thought it best not to wait until hearing from you. I suppose you are sending me the form required, by mail. If the one I am enclosing does not suit, you can cable me to sign the one you are sending, that is supposing you have sent me one to sign. The word "sign" will be enough and I shall understand that I am to sign and send you the one you have sent.*

I sent you a cheque for 2250 francs on the 17th to pay the rent. You may say to the concierge that he need not worry about his denier à Dieu *as this will be given to him. I don't know how much I ought to give him for an apartment of this price and have written to ask Bing as he must pay about the same rent. Perhaps you have some idea yourself. At any rate, you can assure the concierge that it will be all right, if you have not paid it already. After everything is settled, if any money is left over you may keep it until we arrive or if you prefer you may deposit it to my credit at Munroes, in which case please let me know how much you deposit so that I can enter it in my book.*

We are ever and ever so much obliged to you for all the trouble you have taken. I cannot tell you how much of a relief it is to feel that we know where we are going to be located in Paris. I am sure that you have found us exactly the place we want.

All our things are packed now and are waiting for the American Express Co. to tell us when they will be wanted for shipment. Including the 57 cases of prints we have 170 cases, so you can see that our moving is not easy.

I received the cheque for the furnace and thought I had written you so. Please excuse my neglect.

You must not worry about your overdrawn cheque. I understood exactly how it was even before you explained it. It did not bother me in the least and Kohn understood the situation too. I do not understand the steamship company's letting a cheque remain uncashed for ten days.

I must close now, as it is nearly time for Joe to leave.

Love to you both from us both.

Ever sincerely yours,
ATHERTON CURTIS

June 9, 1904

DEAR HENRY,

Your cable message came this morning asking if we would take the apartment for six years and I telegraphed back to take it for that term. We are glad to have it for six years if it is what we want, as I am sure it is, we do not like to go to the expense of putting it in order with the chance of being put out at the end of only three years. Six years is a long period and many things may turn up by that time, so that we shall feel comparatively safe in going ahead with what we want to do.

I do not want to bother you any more than possible with the house, for you have had no end of trouble with it already; but your suggestion that the rooms upstairs might be cleaned and papered for Marie and Joseph is a good one as it would let them move in as soon as we could get them a bed and they could then be on hand to help in getting the rest of the house in order. I have written them to be in Paris about the 15th of August. But I do not want you to go to much trouble in the matter and if you find you are to be bothered you must let it go until our arrival. The rest of the apartment can wait as to paper and paint until we arrive.

I have received a letter from Bing in answer to mine, saying that he thought 100 francs was about the right amount to give the concierge. This is the amount I had already thought of myself and so I think it about right. Will you therefore be kind enough to give the concierge a hundred francs for me and tell him that I asked you to give it to him (or her—perhaps it's a she.)

We are greatly excited about that apartment and garden and have planned out the arrangement of all the rooms already although we do not really know enough about them to make plans that will not have to be changed. Well, we shall be there before a great while, I hope.

I cannot express to you in writing how much we appreciate everything you have done for us. You have taken a great load off of us but you have put one on yourself. You have been very, very kind and we are extremely grateful.

Most of our things have left for Paris. We are not sending everything at once as the American Express is willing to divide the shipments for the same price, 38 cents a cubic foot—a price they made us on account of the size of the shipment. There is about 1400 cubic feet of stuff not counting the prints and when all is done we shall have sent about 180 cases which will give me some little amusement in Paris—perhaps even more than they have here. Everything will have left here in about ten days more.

Miss Flinch is going with us.

Here is a great deal of love from us both to you all.

Sincerely,

ATHERTON CURTIS

June 23, 1904

yesterday but I could not answer it as I was in the city. Now, I have only a few minutes to send you a few necessary lines before Joe leaves.

Your letter with plans and drawings of the house came

DEAR HENRY,

Thank you very much for your offer to attend to the painting for us; but we really cannot tell what colors we want until we have seen the apartment. You see we do not even know what rooms we want to use for what until we have seen them.

Everything that you have done has been perfectly satisfactory. We can arrange the six years lease when we arrive. We will let you know from London the exact day we expect to reach Paris. I am sorry that there will be a delay in our getting in the apartment on account of the painting but I don't see how we can avoid it, not knowing exactly what we want to do.

I am telegraphing you today to take the pavillion in the the garden. We think we ought to have this; but the apartment that will be for rent in October we think best to wait for until we have seen it. We do not need it and do not care to add 1700 francs to the rent just yet.

I think if the cleaning could be done before we arrive, time would be saved, so perhaps you would not mind having this done. I have said very little in my letters by way of thanking you for what you have done because I really cannot express our gratitude. We realise fully all the trouble you have been to and we appreciate your kindness even if we do not seem to show our appreciation in writing.

We are getting more and more anxious to reach Paris. All our things have gone now—even the orchestrelle and the pianola and the music to go with them. We finally reached a total of exactly 180 cases. I don't think I could stand another moving. Two of them are about my limit. Well, whatever fool things we may do in the future, I don't think we shall be likely to move over here again.

I must close now. Here is love from us both for you all. Mrs. B. is in Hampden or would send love too.

Sincerely,

Atherton Curtis

The house that Henry found, in which the Curtises' apartment was located, was part of what had formerly been an old convent and covered a half block in the Latin Quarter. One side of it faced the Rue Notre-Dame-des-Champs, another the Rue de Fleurus, and a walled garden that belonged to the property ran along the Boulevard Raspail. A few years later Curtis bought the entire property.

The Tanners' domestic needs had changed since their last residence in Paris, and for a while after their return they did not live in the familiar Latin Quarter. John Olssen had retired, and, since neither he nor his wife had deep roots in the United States, it was arranged for them to live with Jessie and Henry. For the enlarged household Henry found a house with a garden at Sceaux, a pleasant little town in the southern suburbs of Paris, and for two years, until Bessie Olssen's death in 1906, they lived there, a happy *ménage à quatre*. After Mother Olssen's death the Tanners returned to Paris and Henry rented a studio apartment near Atherton Curtis at 70 *bis* Rue Notre-Dame-des-Champs. John Olssen remained with them until he died in 1921 except for the war years and during the brief visits to his daughter Elna, who had married and was living in New York City.

The studio on Notre-Dame-des-Champs was very spacious—twenty-two feet high, with a balcony all around it. Gérôme had once rented it, and Sarah Bernhardt had come to see him there. Tanner kept it until 1912, when he returned to his old studio at 51 Boulevard Saint-Jacques. The last few years of his life he lived at 43 Rue de Fleurus, in a small apartment in the block of buildings owned by Atherton Curtis.

After the Mount Kisco experience Tanner seems not to have contemplated living anywhere but France. The cosmopolitan atmosphere of Paris discouraged racial prejudice; and his success as an artist, his light complexion, his marriage to a cultivated white woman, lowered whatever barriers might have been raised against him by Americans not yet completely emancipated from New World attitudes. The majority of his friends and associates were exiles, like himself—members of the largest American colony in Europe. While each individual American found a focal point around which his or her particular clique, or set, revolved, the dividing line between the wealthy, leisurely class and those with artistic or literary leanings was the Seine; though all Americans were drawn together by their common nationality and a love of France.

Paris was, in many ways, more American than French. Since 1891, when Tanner had first arrived, the number of well-to-do Americans with homes in Paris had grown tremendously, and during the late spring and early summer, when the tide of tourists reached its peak, the predominant language heard in the vicinity of the French Opera House was English spoken with an American accent.

The presence of America, however, was felt in almost every part of the French capital. Two Yankee concerns supplied light and electric power to Paris. Electric cars took tourists over Paris on rails and equipment brought over from the United States. Marble, quarried in America, was used in the building of new, fine homes. The newer hotels were all advertised as "American." Radiators of American make heated the great new apartment buildings. Automatic elevators were introduced and the newest office furniture was machine-made in America. American newspaper buildings and offices dominated the chief sites of Paris, and the Avenue de l'Opéra was as American as French with its Yankee dental parlors, shoe stores, Tiffany's, New York Life Insurance Company, and Great Atlantic and Pacific Tea Company. On the Left Bank the appearance of things American was less apparent, but all Americans felt the impact of their homeland. The best of two worlds literally converged in Paris.

The life that Henry and Jessie Tanner lived in this cosmopolis was a relatively quiet and simple one. Although Henry got over his dislike, or fear, of alcohol, he never really liked to drink in the social sense. Nor did he like to keep late hours. He found his pleasure in his home, his close friends, and in his art, at which he worked hard. In a pencil "jotting" written in 1909 he explains this by saying:

> Making money never seemed my strong point, and yet I will not believe that I was stupid or that I had less ability than some who did make it. In painting I know it came from never knowing what the popular taste was. Among my fellow painters I have known some who always felt what should be done to please and did it more or less instinctively. Their "pot boilers" always sold—mine usually remained on my hands and I was worse off than before—so that at the commencement at least of my career I deserve little credit for doing my level best, for nothing else received the slightest attention, but this meant long effort and extremely small pay and so it has continued.

Though Tanner was never to be a rich man in material assets, he was wealthy in intangibles. Sometimes this meant money for him, as in the case of Atherton Curtis. Shortly after Tanner and Curtis returned to Paris, an arrangement was made between them whereby Atherton was to pay Henry a certain sum each month, and in return Henry was to paint for him a picture—or more than one, depending on its size and value—in the course of the year. The arrangement was not particularly feasible as far as Atherton was concerned since he had only a small collection of paintings, and, as he wrote Jesse Tanner after his father's death, "a considerable number by one artist would have overwhelmed it." Nevertheless, he kept to his agreement, believing in Tanner and wishing to relieve him, insofar as it was within his power, of all worries that would impede his creativity.

Not long after the Tanners returned to Paris from Mt. Kisco they bought a long, one story peasant house at Trépied, near Etaples, in the Pas de Calais, and here Henry and his family lived during the summer months. The area was a popular artists' retreat. Dieppe, not many miles from Trépied, had attracted artists since the time of Delacroix. Tanner's charming, white-walled, old house, surrounded by a garden where poppies bloomed in late spring and early summer, became the very center of the art colony at Trépied. The artist or student from Etaples, or Le Touquet, Paris-Plage, was always sure of a warm welcome at "Les Charmes," the Tanner home. Max Bohm and Myron Barlow, prominent American artists, were among the members of the colony.

The years following Tanner's return from America until the war began in 1914 were probably the happiest of his life. He was one of the most outstanding American artists in Paris and considered by many the leading biblical painter of his day. His friendship with Atherton Curtis, his activities with the American Art Association in Paris and with the art group at Trépied all contributed to a pleasant, active life. But the greatest source of his happiness was Jessie, his wife, who adored him. She had given up all thought of a musical career when she married and was a lovely, popular hostess at the informal gatherings in their home. She was also a devoted mother. That Jesse Ossawa Tanner remembers his childhood as "supremely happy"[4] is indicative of the pleasant atmosphere that permeated the home. In regard to Jesse, Atherton Curtis again proved his friendship. When the boy was seven years old he sent him to Hillcrest School, at Folkestone, in England. Tanner had succeeded far beyond his fondest dreams not only in his profession but in his personal life as well.

4. Jesse O. Tanner to me, May 6, 1966, Archives of American Art, Detroit.

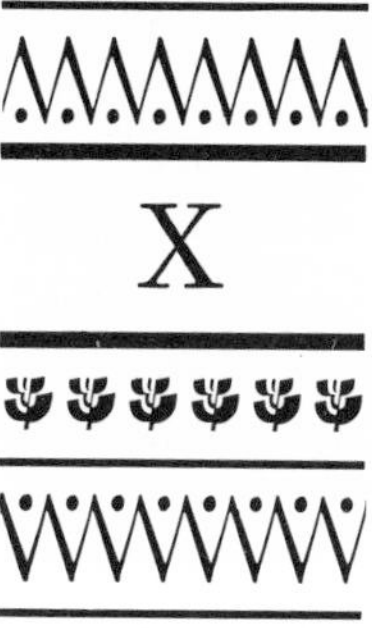

X

Happy Years

THE FIRST DECADE OF THE NEW CENTURY, WHICH SAW Tanner's name in the forefront of American artists, were years of rapid change in the art climate of Paris. It is doubtful whether Tanner was completely aware of the significance of this change, but few Americans were. Leo and Gertrude Stein and their group were exceptional in their enthusiastic approach to the new art trends.

As the century progressed the Salons of the Société des Artistes Français and the Société Nationale des Beaux Arts began to lose their importance. The Salon des Artistes Independents, founded in 1884 and long derided by the critics, had introduced to the public new ideas and new personalities that later became a force to be reckoned with in French art. As the years passed the importance of this Salon grew and other Salons came on the scene, the most famous of which was the Salon d'Automne. Started in 1903 by the architect François

Jourdain, with the assistance of Bonnard, Marquet, and Matisse, it marked the public's rising interest in the new styles of painting. The first Salon d'Automne, with its great Gauguin show, was held in the basement of the Petit Palais and attracted little attention. But the second, at the Grand Palais, was a different story. Parisians flocked to it, as they did to the Salon of 1905, another important date in the history of French painting. At this Salon a retrospective Cézanne exhibition was shown, as well as the works of a new group of painters centering around Henri Matisse and called by a derisive critic "Les Fauves," or wild beasts. With each succeeding year the Salon d'Automne became more and more *the* Salon, as new artists became recognized and discussed.

Art dealers Vollard, Durand-Ruel, and Bernheim Jeune, had set a precedent some years before for one-man shows. Now these shows multiplied and, with the new Salons, took away a good deal of the glamour that had attended the time-honored spring Salons. Curiosity about an artist's work tended to abate when his pictures had been seen on display elsewhere. The two Salons continued to attract their yearly throngs, but they were no longer the chief arbiters of style.

Academic art steadily declined in popularity during these years, and painting became characterized by a great diversity of styles. Guillaume Apollinaire, the critic and friend of the "moderns," summed up the situation in 1914 when he wrote:

> There are so many artistic schools today that they no longer have any importance as particular schools. One can say that, in truth, there are no schools today, only painters of diverse temperaments and talents. . . .[1]

In spite of the varied forms to select from, the public was loath to change loyalties. The new art was exciting to see and talk about, particularly that of the cubists, futurists, and expressionists, but only the reckless investor or farsighted critic

1. *Chroniques d'Art* (Paris: Gallimard, 1960), p. 397.

would risk his money on a Picasso, Duchamp, or Munch when he could afford a Bonnat or Carolus-Duran. It was difficult for many people to believe that the insurgents, who were occupying more and more space on exhibition walls, could exert sufficient force on the mainstream of art to direct it permanently into new channels. John Singer Sargent expressed the prevailing view when he wrote apropos of the postimpressionist exhibition at the Grafton Galleries in London in 1911:

> I am absolutely skeptical of their having any claim to being works of art with the exception of some of the pictures by Gauguin that strike me as admirable in color and in color only.[2]

Tanner felt much the same. Although he believed that impressionism "lifted up the color scheme" and induced greater individuality and freedom in painting, he was never converted to the movement as a whole and postimpressionism he considered "anarchic" in its disregard of law and order.[3]

Yet Tanner's art, during the decade prior to 1914, shows technical changes that were affected, consciously or unconsciously, by the new movements. The warm, brown tones of his early paintings gradually lightened, and his tonality grew closer to the blues and blue-greens of Monet. He also began to experiment with pigments and developed a technique similar to that used by Albert Ryder, painting by means of oil glazes. By the beginning of the First World War he was using this method almost exclusively.

A change in Tanner's art may be noted as early as 1902 in a picture painted before he left Paris to join Atherton Curtis at Mount Kisco. In style and technique it is curiously unlike any that he painted before or after. When it was shown at the Salon of 1902 it no doubt caused spirited conversation

2. Quoted in Jerome Millquist, *The Emergence of American Art* (New York: Charles Scribner's Sons, 1942), p. 57.

3. Clara T. MacChesney, "A Poet-Painter of Palestine," *International Studio*, 50 (July, 1913): xii.

among the Salon habitués who had come to think of Tanner in terms of religious art. The *New York Herald* of April 30 describes the picture in the following words:

> Here is a surprise, a wildly incredible thing. A painter, an American, has tried to revolutionize manner and shed his personality. It is Mr. Tanner, who used to concoct estimable works in a dark brown medium, and now astonishes us with a large painting, "Chamber Music," in which one sees a lady playing the cello. The quaint grace and amusing color of this large canvas make it one of the attractions of the Salon.

The model for the lady in evening dress playing the cello is Jessie Tanner, her piano accompanist is her sister, Elna, and the gentleman with the pointed beard standing in shadow by the piano is Tanner himself. The picture has the elegance and something of the flourish of a Sargent and shows what Henry Tanner could do in the realm of secular art. But he gave no repeat performance.

After Tanner's return from America his Salon paintings were again religious in theme. In 1905 he exhibited *The Good Samaritan* and *Christ Washing the Disciples' Feet*, pictures singled out by the critic of *L'Eclair* as examples of the few biblical paintings in the Salon that year showing real religious sentiment. In these pictures Tanner's tonality is warm, his *pâte* thick, his color effects vibrant and spontaneous. The critic of *L'Eclair* comments:

> I imagine that the youthful school of American painters are proud to possess a comrade who, like M. Tanner, has moved steadily up the slippery incline of success with such masterful skill.[4]

The year 1906 was another landmark in Tanner's career, for in that year the French government purchased a second of his Salon pictures, *The Disciples at Emmaus*,[5] for a price four

4. *L'Eclair*, April 29, 1905.

5. *The Disciples at Emmaus* was, for many years, in the Louvre. According to the Ministère des Affaires Culturelles it disappeared about the time of World War II and cannot be located.

times that given for *Raising of Lazarus.* As a result of the award Tanner's stock went flying, and for a time his canvases were in such demand that they were sold as soon as they were finished, sometimes before.

In 1908—Tanner did not exhibit in 1907—his *Wise and Foolish Virgins* was given a place in the Salon d'Honneur second in importance only to that of *Le Chant du Départ* by Edouard Détaille. It was a large canvas, 15 by 20 feet, with a half-dozen draped female figures, nearly life size, sweeping across a dimly lighted hall. In one corner of the picture the night sky is visible and, with the yellow flares of the lighted lamps, reveals the artist's skillful and subtle handling of tone.

The Salon that year was a gala affair. On the day preceding the vernissage itself Vance Thompson sent a long item to the *New York American:*

> All that is worth while in Paris flocked today to "Varnishing Day" of the annual Salon of French artists. Ambassadors and their wives, actresses and their dressmakers, paraded for hours through the huge halls, which have been newly decorated with coffee-colored carpets and mouse-colored hangings. . . .
>
> Looking down from the balconies on the great court where the military band played and fashionable folks breakfasted at little tables among the palms and statues, it was evident that the women this year have gone in for various shades of green. Madame Bernhardt wore an arsenic-colored gown. Both Bartlet and Mary Garden were in blue and black.
>
> Almost the entire American aristocracy was present at some time during the day, including the Countess Adhemar, Baroness Eynard, and Ambassador and Mrs. White. By 3 o'clock the crowd was so dense it was impossible to see any pictures, save those on the skyline, or to find acquaintances in the rush.[6]

Tanner's picture was acclaimed by the French press in the highest terms. The *Journal des Débats* wrote that *The Wise and Foolish Virgins* was Tanner's masterpiece; the *Liberté* that

6. *New York American,* May 1, 1908.

M. Henri Tanner interpreted the parable in pure, classical style; the *Revue des Deux Mondes* that Tanner's painting, though influenced by his master, Jean-Paul Laurens, exceeded in merit the work of that excellent artist.

As a result of the success of his picture Tanner was invited to attend a dinner given by the president of the republic at the Elysées Palace. A note from Robert MacCameron indicates the esteem in which Henry Tanner was held by his fellow artists.

MY DEAR TANNER,

Delighted! Call for me, please, any time after nine Saturday evening, for the President's reception.

Let me thank you for your kind note of congratulations on my second medal. There is no painter living whose judgment I value more, and the influence of your superb colour in every canvas you paint has had a good influence on my work.

Until Saturday night then
Very sincerely yours,
ROBERT MACCAMERON

During his years of ascending popularity in Paris Tanner's reputation was also growing in America. In 1905 his painting of *Christ Covenanting wtih the High Priests* was shown at the Carnegie Exhibition. He was the only "colored painter" represented. The following year the Carnegie Institute of Art acquired his *Christ at the Home of Mary and Martha* for its permanent collection. In 1906 *Christ Washing the Feet of the Disciples* was exhibited at the yearly show of the Pennsylvania Academy of the Fine Arts, and his *Two Disciples at the Tomb*, first shown at the Art Club in Paris in the winter of 1905, received the Harris Prize of $500 for "the most impressive and distinguished work of art of the season" at the annual Chicago Exhibition and was acquired for the Robert Alexander collection of the Chicago Art Institute.

The *Two Disciples at the Tomb* still shows a lingering preference by Tanner for warm tones, though the picture has a grandeur and simplicity of composition that is lacking even in his *Christ and Nicodemus.* Light is focused upon the faces of the disciples, who stand in quiet meditation before the door of the tomb. The contrast of youth with age, which Tanner so often used, is seen in the troubled bearded face of the old disciple and the youthful clean-shaven face of the younger one, whose eyes stare hopefully beyond the tomb into a world of their own imagining. There is something of Thomas Eakins in the firm, authoritative modelling of the two figures, and in the subdued color. But the rhythm, fluidity and sensitivity of line are those of Henry Tanner.

The purchase of the *Two Disciples at the Tomb* by the Chicago Art Institute and the earlier acquisitions by the Philadelphia Museum, the Pennsylvania Academy of the Fine Arts, and the Carnegie Institute of Art, were only some of the honors Tanner received in America. He won a silver medal at the Pan-American Exposition at Buffalo in 1901 and another at the St. Louis Exposition of 1904. His paintings were seen regularly at the Pennsylvania Academy of the Fine Arts. Yet, in spite of the recognition of his art, there is no question that his race had a limiting effect upon his reputation in America. Seldom was his art mentioned without the qualifying term "Negro" attached to it. Newspaper headlines like "Art Prize Won by Negro," or "Negro Artist Wins Prize," placed Tanner in the forefront of Negro artists but did not, in the minds of the general public, assert his position in the mainstream of American art. This kind of discrimination, unconscious though it may have been, was noted in an issue of *Current Literature,* in 1908:

> For several years past the art world of Paris has shown steadily increasing interest in the work of Henry O. Tanner, a young American painter who has done much toward strengthening that high position in contemporary art which was won for us by Sargent and Whistler. In American pub-

lic recognition of Tanner's genius has been somewhat retarded by the fact that he is a negro, and our publications have persistently spoken of him as the greatest negro painter. It has pleased them to slight his art in the exploitation of his race.[7]

William R. Lester expressed some of the Negroes' bitterness toward this slight:

> Commanding in stature, easy yet dignified in manner, genial and affable in conversation, fortunate in his chosen career and happy in his home life, Mr. Tanner is a notable example of the genius of American art, a brilliant product of the New World's creative and heterogeneous civilization. Yet the art world of his own country has but scant knowledge of him or of his art creations, so highly regarded and appreciated in critical Europe.[8]

In their pride of Tanner's accomplishments Negroes sometimes unconsciously detracted from his reputation by identifying with him. Booker T. Washington wrote:

> Tanner is proud of his race. He feels deeply that as the representative of his people he is on trial to establish their right to be taken seriously in the world of art.[9]

Tanner never disclaimed his heritage and was always sincerely interested in the Negroes as a people but there is no evidence that he felt he was "on trial" as a representative of his race. Living in France, secure in his home and friends, most of whom were white, he lived for his work and in this alone felt he was "on trial." Throughout his career he avoided racial entanglements and was careful to deny there was a distinction between a white and a Negro artist. When his assistance was sought by young Negroes wishing a career in art, as in the

7. "An Afro-American Painter Who Has Become Famous in Paris," *Current Literature*, 45 (October, 1908): 45.

8. "Henry O. Tanner, Exile for Art's Sake," *Alexander's Magazine*, (December 15, 1908), p. 80.

9. Quoted in "Afro-American Painter," p. 45.

case of William A. Harper, a young Negro whose pictures were highly commended at the Chicago Exhibition of 1906 and who died in 1910, he gave it gladly, but on the basis of talent, not race.

Henry Tanner was too intent on his work and too absorbed in his activities in France to be concerned with the petty details of publicity in America. He probably gave it no thought. But the idea that he had expressed to Robert Ogden in 1899, of having a one-man show of his biblical paintings in America, was finally realized. On December 3, 1908, a news item appeared in the *New York Herald:*

> Mr. Henry O. Tanner, an American artist, who returned to this country a few days ago after an absence of five years, is to give an exhibition of his religious paintings in the American Art Galleries. It will begin on December 12 and continue two weeks. Many of the canvasses portray scenes in the life of Christ, and for this reason the display is regarded as appropriate to the approaching celebration of Christmas. . . .
>
> Mr. Tanner will lease a temporary studio and remain in New York until May.

Henry Tanner brought his wife and young Jesse with him. Jessie's sister Elna had married an American, Charles Tough, and was now living in New York, and Tanner's parents that year were celebrating their golden wedding anniversary. The visit was a happy one for all concerned, but for no one more than Bishop or Mrs. Tanner. With the exception of Sara, their youngest child who had died in 1900, all of their children were with them to celebrate their fiftieth wedding anniversary. It was truly a remarkable family.

In Carlton, Bishop Tanner had realized his ambition of seeing a son enter the church. Carlie, after graduating from the Institute for Colored Youth, had attended the Episcopal Divinity School in Philadelphia and was now a successful minister.

Hallie, the oldest daughter, had studied medicine at the

Women's Medical College of Pennsylvania and established the Nurses' School at Tuskegee Institute. She was married to a minister, John Q. Johnson.

Isabella was active in religious and educational work in Pittsburgh and was also married to a minister.

Mary, the daughter born in 1865, was married to A. A. Mossell of Philadelphia and was the mother of three children, one of whom—Sadie—was to become the first Negro woman graduate of the University of Pennsylvania Law School and the first one admitted to practice in the state of Pennsylvania. Mary was always Henry's favorite sister. She had the same sweet voice and frail health as her mother, as well as her warm and understanding nature.

The exhibition at the American Art Galleries was a great success. His work was not generally known in New York, for New York at that time was not an exhibiting center compared to Philadelphia and Chicago and Pittsburgh. In spite of its greater number of resident artists and art auctions there was a dearth of space in New York's exhibition galleries, and the American Academy of Design "invited" few pictures and did not send or appoint agents abroad to obtain the work of American artists in Europe as did exhibiting institutions like the Pennsylvania Academy of the Fine Arts and the Carnegie Institute.

Of the thirty-three paintings on exhibit at the American Art Galleries only two of his most famous were absent—the two pictures hanging in the Luxembourg Gallery. Others were loaned by American museums and by private owners, including Rodman Wannamaker, Atherton Curtis, the Reverend William B. Will, and Mr. Daniel O'Day. Among the notable canvases were *Christ at the Home of Mary and Martha*, *Christ and Nicodemus*, *The Return of the Holy Women*, *On the Road to Emmaus*, *He Vanished Out of Their Sight*, and *Behold! The Bridegroom Cometh*. This last was his salon picture of the year before, *The Wise and Foolish Virgins,* renamed.

The following, taken from a review in the *New York Tribune*, is a sample of reaction to Tanner's art:

> His first and most obvious quality is that of a kind of realism which needs to be carefully distinguished from the realism practised by divers modern artists who nominally share the same mood. Over and over again in Europe men have sought to interpret the Scriptures in paintings based largely on the aspect of life at the present time. Whether, like Von Uhde, they placed the Saviour among peasants, or, like Béraud, have introduced Him into a company of fashionable Parisians, they have left the impression of somehow forcing the note, of building up their scenes in a fictitious manner. Even the undeniable sincerity of Von Uhde has failed to efface from his work a certain faint suggestion of sensationalism. Here is where Mr. Tanner has, from the start, enjoyed a distinct advantage. There is an almost artless simplicity about his work. He seems to have been able to project himself back into the past and to paint religious subjects realistically without a trace of that archaeological reconstruction of Tissot. He does not adapt a Scriptural theme to latter-day conditions. He simply makes his appeal on broad human grounds, painting his sacred figures simply as men and women moving against their natural background. He does this, too, without offering any violence to the high associations of his material. There is no want of dignity in his work. He states the truth in a large if not precisely noble manner. Looking at his pictures, you feel that thus indeed may this or that Biblical episode have occurred, made impressive by the nature of the action involved and illuminated by no supernatural rays, but just the familiar light of Palestine. Rarely, in anything that he has done, is there a hint of shrewd stage management.[10]

The *New York Times* noted one aspect of Tanner's art

10. *New York Tribune,* December 19, 1908.

that had often been overlooked, and that deserves greater notice, even today—the importance of landscape in creating emotional mood in his pictures.

> They are settings for the episodes and persons described in the Bible, but in many instances these are frankly subordinate, and the character of the landscape itself is felt to be the important matter. . . .
>
> Mr. Tanner is interested not only in telling once more the story of the Christian religion, but in the mysterious qualities of nature as she appears to the human vision.[11]

Only the *New York Evening Mail* found in Tanner's race the clue to his greatness.

> As a painter of religious subjects, Mr. Tanner is all the better for having a little of the blood of Africa in his veins. Religious emotion is part and parcel of the life of Africa. Mr. Tanner has infinitely honored this element in his blood by the eminence which he has attained; and the beauty and real greatness of his work have made him an honor of the country of his birth.[12]

At the same time that Henry Tanner's pictures were on display at the American Art Galleries, an exhibition of paintings by Childe Hassam was shown at the Montross Gallery. Comparison between the artists was inevitable.

> What more violent leap into a veritable Armida's garden of art can be taken than a visit to the Montross Gallery (372 Fifth avenue), there to see the Childe Hassams after the misty Orientalisms of Tanner. Naturally it would be absurd to make comparisons. Each man seeks his own chimera. The visions of Tanner often o'erweigh his capacity of expression; while the too fluent, too brilliant Hassam has expressed with a pantheistic fulness the glories of earth and sky, not until recently greatly concerning himself with a Beyond. . . .[13]

11. *New York Times,* December 19, 1908.
12. *New York Evening Mail,* December 16, 1908.
13. *New York Sun,* December 18, 1908.

During the spring of 1908, before leaving for America, Henry Tanner had been represented at the yearly exhibition of the Carnegie Institute by his picture entitled *Ox-Cart*. He had selected it from among his early paintings, possibly because he was preparing the larger exhibition and had no Biblical scenes available that season. It is simply the picture of a country road, with woods beyond and two Negroes standing near an oxcart.

> Although rather uninteresting as a painting, this canvas shows the early manner of a man who has since adapted quite a different character of subjects, whose ability has won him honor and recognition.[14]

Not only had Tanner adapted a new style since the *Ox-Cart* was painted, but he himself had grown away from his early ties with American Negro life. Although he was devoted to his parents and especially to his younger sister Mary, the closed society in which he had been raised was a world he no longer identified with. To Henry and Jessie, Paris and the lovely cottage at Trépied were now home. The visit they made to America during the winter and spring of 1908–09 was the last of any length they were to make to the land of their birth. In the future Tanner's trips to America were brief and governed by expediency, for though his personal ties to the United States became less binding, his professional ties were the basis for most of his sales. His election in April, 1909, as an associate member of the National Academy of Design, along with Mary Cassatt and Frederick Waugh, gave his name an added distinction.

14. *Pittsburgh Dispatch,* May 17, 1908.

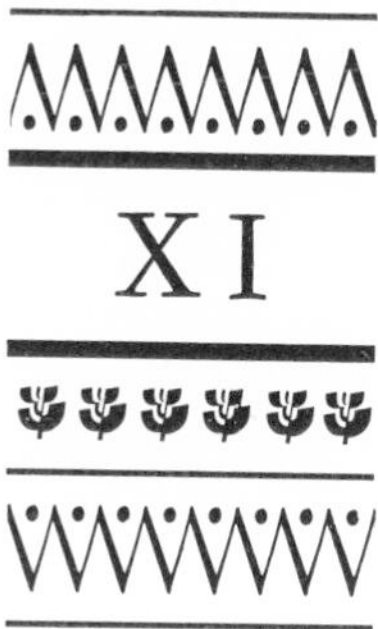

The Years Immediately Preceding World War I

THE UNITED STATES THAT HENRY TANNER SAILED FROM IN 1909 was a different place, for an art student, from the one he had left in 1891. European training was no longer considered a necessity. The number of art schools had increased, art instruction had improved, and scholarships—unknown in Tanner's student days—were now available at most art schools. Conditions were also better for artists wishing to earn a living by their art.

The young artist returning from his studies abroad today finds more sympathetic conditions awaiting him, for interest in our art has grown with its progress. If we still lack the full recognition of art as a factor of life, which has grown through centuries of effort in the Old World, the present affords some recompense to the generation that has worked for these better conditions, and the future smiles encouragingly upon the aspirants to come.[1]

The atmosphere conducive to these changes had been created, as Will Low stated, by those artists who brought back from abroad new standards for the teaching of art. It had also been created by the expatriates who had established the right of America to be taken seriously in the sophisticated art circles of Europe—expatriates like James McNeill Whistler, John Singer Sargent, and Mary Cassatt, as well as others less well known. Through their individual triumphs abroad they had given Americans new pride and self-confidence in their own artistic accomplishments. As it has been noted, there had always been a group of artists in the United States who championed the idea of a native art that portrayed the life and scenes of the New World, but formerly they had been a minority. Now it was a more or less accepted view that American artists who prolonged their stay in Europe once their student days were over were shirking their duty. Art was not designed to be international, but to express the life of a people. Even Thomas Eakins, who at one time had felt the importance of Europe to an artist, said in 1914:

> It would be far better for American art students and painters to study their own country and portray its life and types. To do that they must remain free from any foreign superficialities. Of course, it is well to go abroad and see the work of the old masters, but Americans must branch out into their own fields as they are doing. They must strike out for themselves and only by doing this will we create a great and distinctly American art.[2]

The February before Henry Tanner arrived in New York for the opening of his American Art Galleries exhibition, an

1. Will H. Low, *A Chronicle of Friendships* (New York: Charles Scribner's Sons, 1908), p. 233.

2. Lloyd Goodrich, *Thomas Eakins* (New York: Whitney Museum of American Art, 1933), p. 139.

impressive "strike" had been made by a group of eight American artists, the leader of whom had once been a student at the Pennsylvania Academy of the Fine Arts and later at Julien's —Robert Henri. The "Eight,"[3] as they subsequently became known, all felt a need to break away from the imitativeness seen on exhibition walls and to express their individual views of America.

There is no doubt that Henry Tanner heard repercussions of this exhibit, held in the Macbeth Gallery on Fifth Avenue, for the "shocking" realism of the ashcan school was the subject of wide discussion in New York. Few critics had written favorably of the show and most were openly hostile.

> Vulgarity smites one in the face at this exhibition, and I defy you to find anyone in a healthy frame of mind who, for instance, wants to hang Luk's posteriors of pigs, or Glacken's *At Moquin's*, or John Sloan's *Hairdresser's Window* in his living rooms or gallery, and not get disgusted two days later. . . .[4]

Vulgarity of subject matter, as it was then interpreted, was not in Tanner's repertory, and it is unlikely that he would have defended the Eight, yet as a colorist he would have seen much to admire, especially in the landscapes of Maurice Prendergast.

But the expatriates also were interested in the question of Americanism in art. Was there a quality, undefinable perhaps, that made an artist's paintings, regardless of subject matter, truly *American?* Many of them believed there was. Tanner himself said of the Paris Salons:

> It is not difficult to pass through the galleries and pick out the work of American artists. I have done it myself,

3. The Eight were: Robert Henri, Arthur Davies, William Glackens, Everett Shinn, John Sloan, George Luks, Ernest Lawson, Maurice Prendergast.

4. Quoted in Bennard B. Perlman, *The Immortal Eight* (New York: Exposition Press, 1962), p. 179.

saying, That is an American—and that—and that—with hardly a possibility of error.[5]

It has been questioned whether Tanner's own paintings possess this quality. Many present-day critics believe that once he divorced himself from the realities of American Negro life, so feelingly portrayed in his early *Banjo Lesson*, there ceased to be anything American in his art. On the other hand, there are others who believe that his religious paintings show the American Negro's deep and abiding faith in the Bible and in this sense *are* American. There is little doubt that Henry Tanner would have discounted both views. Art, to him, was the sum total of an artist's personality, in which heritage, environment, and circumstances all played a part. Neither his Negro blood nor his religious background were sufficiently strong in his mind to account for his art. Of the latter he wrote:

> I have no doubt an inheritance of religious feeling and for this I am glad, but I have also a decided and I hope intelligent religious faith not due to inheritance but to my own convictions.

His attitude toward his Negro heritage is indicated in the following letter to Eunice Tietjens, who sent him from Chicago the copy of an article on "H. O. Tanner" that she intended to submit to John Lane of the *International Studio*.

May 25, 1914

DEAR MRS. TIETJENS,

Your good note and very appreciative article to hand. I have read it and except it is more than I deserve, it is exceptionally good. What you say is what I am trying to do and in a smaller way am doing (I hope).

The only thing I take exception to is the inference in your last paragraph—and while I know it is the dictum in

5. William R. Lester, "Henry O. Tanner, Exile for Art's Sake," *Alexander's Magazine*, December 15, 1908, p. 72.

the States it is not any more true for that reason. You say "In his personal life Mr. T. has had many things to contend with. Ill-health, poverty and race prejudice, always strong against a negro." Now am I a Negro. Does not the ¾ of English blood in my veins, which when it flowed in "pure" Anglo-Saxon men and which has done in the past *effective and distinguished work in the U.S.—does not this count for anything? Does the ¼ or ⅛ of "pure" Negro blood, in my veins count for all? I believe it, the Negro blood, counts and counts to my advantage—though it has caused me at times a life of great humiliation and sorrow but that it is the source of all my talents (if I have any) I do not believe, any more than I believe it all comes from my English ancestors.*

I suppose, according to the distorted way things are seen in the States my blond curly-headed little boy would be "Negro" - - -

True—this condition has driven me out of the country, but still the best friends I have are "white" Americans and while I cannot sing our National Hymn, "Land of Liberty," etc., still deep down in my heart I love it and am sometimes sad that I cannot live where my heart is. . . .

There was no bitterness in Henry Tanner as there was in Mary Cassatt, who never ceased to resent having been ostracized by American society for taking art seriously at a time when it was not considered a proper profession for a wellborn lady. Through the years, though he did not choose to live there, he retained an affection for his native land and never ceased to think of himself as an American. If this Americanism can be found in his art, it is in his unsentimental yet poetic approach to traditional themes, an approach that never attained the epic grandeur of Albert Pinkham Ryder but led to a lyric beauty that in its way is as individual and, perhaps, just as American.

The Paris that Henry Tanner returned to in 1909 was the same enchanting city it had always been. It was gay and beautiful and full of a kind of spiritual irridescence, very different from the materialism he had seen in New York. He was in a position to enjoy it. He was comfortably fixed, his art widely appreciated, and his position in the American colony firmly established. His friendship with the Curtises and with the artists at the American Art Club—since the spring of 1909 in new quarters on the Boulevard Raspail—as well as with members of the Paris Society of American Artists and of the Société Artistique de Picardie, gave Henry and Jessie pleasant and stimulating contacts.

The artistic atmosphere that Tanner shared with American artists like Walter Griffin, Frederick Frieseke, Walter MacEwan, and Myron Barlow was relatively conservative, although these men were not blind to the art movements that followed one another in Paris in such rapid succession. Fauvism, cubism, expressionism, and all of the other avant-garde movements that were represented with ever-increasing frequency on exhibition walls before the 1914 war brought on some interesting debates at the Art Club. Tanner and his artist friends were not converts. Of all the movements, cubism, originated by Pablo Picasso, a young Spaniard who had come to Paris in 1900, was, in their minds, the most questionable. Tanner had met this young artist and seen some of his work in which blue and pink tones predominated, and he had found in it great sensitivity and feeling. But he thought that in his cubist pictures Picasso was merely making fun of the public, possibly because of their rejection of his previous work.

The number of new art movements was so great that it was difficult to keep up with them all. José Belon, in the *Revue des Beaux Arts*, expressed the general attitude of the press:

> And so, why have certain Gentlemen once again the effrontery to inflict upon us the empty drivelling of nincompoops and loathsome daubers, whose whole originality consists of a terrific impudence, of a cynicism for the good-

for-nothing father's boy safely sheltered from the vicissitudes of fortune?[6]

It did not occur to Henry Tanner, or any of the established American artists on the Left Bank, that "nincompoops" like Maurice Vlaminck, Emile Braque, or Francis Picabia would someday have pictures in the National Museum of France or that their kind of art would be a motivating force to artists throughout the twentieth century. Nor, for that matter, did even a forward-looking critic like Guillaume Apollinaire accept all of the new art. When a large exhibition of the works of Georges Rouault was held at the Galerie Druet in 1910 he wrote for *l'Intransigeant:*

> I am perturbed by the recklessness of M. Rouault in exhibiting this collection of his nightmares at the Galerie Druet. It is the work of a hack and sad stuff at that.[7]

Henry and Jessie travelled a good deal during the years 1909–14. Little Jesse was in school at Folkstone, and they made several trips to England. Tanner's address book of this period is full of the names of English friends, many of them artists who owned homes in the Pas de Calais.

In 1910 the Tanners made a visit of several months to Morocco, where Henry painted the streets and alleys of Tangiers and, by muleback, visited Tetuan, an ancient Moorish city in the interior. From Morocco they travelled to the Near East. In Egypt Tanner painted a portrait of Prince Mohammed Ali on horseback and was honored with a reception by the Sultan.

The pictures that he painted during this period show a greater interest in bright color harmony, influenced by the clarity of light and vivid colors that he saw in Africa. At the Salon of 1910 the critic for the *Siècle* thought this color in-

6. "Les Râtés Célébrés," *Revue des Beaux Arts*, cited in Bernard Dorival, *The School of Paris* (London: Thames & Hudson, 1962), p. 41.

7. Quoted in Dorival, *School of Paris*, p. 49.

terest destroyed the religious character of his *Three Marys* and *Flight Into Egypt.*

> What have these marvellous color harmonies to do with religion? Their subjects are borrowed from the Bible as others are from history or legend, but that is all. There is in them no religious inspiration whatsoever. . . .[8]

This new use of color was also noted by Harriet Monroe in Tanner's next large American exhibition, which was composed almost entirely of pictures painted about this time. The exhibition was held in February, 1911, at Thurber's Gallery in Chicago. Miss Monroe, who wrote for the *Chicago Daily Tribune,* was an appreciative critic of Tanner's art.

> An exhibition of eighteen paintings by Henry O. Tanner opened yesterday at Thurber's Gallery. The artist, who recently arrived in New York from Paris, accompanies his pictures and will remain in town for a few days.
>
> The present exhibition is the first he has given in Chicago, and the pictures, with one exception, are recent works now shown for the first time. Most of the subjects are Biblical, as is customary with this painter, who has studied his scenes and human types in Palestine. He is usually styled a religious painter, and sometimes his pictures achieve this quality, while others, even though bearing a Biblical title, have little or no religious feeling. In the present group, "The Holy Family" and "Christ Walking on the Sea" seem infused with this quality of spiritual mystery and poetry, while "Mary Visiting Elizabeth" and "Christ Learning to Read" are far less religious in their suggestion than some of the landscapes.
>
> More important from the artistic point of view than the sacredness of the titles is the beauty of color, the clarity of light and shade, and the serene and lofty poetic feeling which the best of these pictures attain. These qualities are noticeable especially in "The Holy Family," an interior remarkable for the grace of its composition and for the soft richness and depth of its shadowy greenish tone crossed by

8. *Siècle,* April 10, 1913.

a streak of yellow light, and in that wonderfully transparent blue moonlight scene called "Morocco," which shows a group of oriental figures outside the dim white walls of a town.

"Hebron," another view of moonlit walls with cloaked figures is a poetic little picture, and the large landscape called "Hills Near Jerusalem" has a stern simplicity and grandeur.[9]

Two years later many of these same pictures were shown in an exhibition at Knoedler's Gallery in New York City. Tanner's new use of color, which had impressed Harriet Monroe, was especially striking to those critics who had seen his exhibition at the American Art Galleries in 1908. The critic of the *New York Tribune* commented:

> The last time that Mr. Henry O. Tanner appeared in a N.Y. exhibition there was in his pictures a good deal of the "brown sauce" which savors more of a Parisian studio than of life observed at close quarters. His religious subjects were enveloped in a queer penumbra, which was effective in its way, but not, on the whole, very satisfactory. Now all that is changed, and in his show at the Knoedler Gallery of Moorish and French subjects he demonstrates that he can exploit to some advantage an infinitely lighter key. Here he is all for pure white tones, or delicate greens and piercing red. The result is capital and should convince Mr. Tanner that his old method is best left utterly behind him.[10]

The critic of the *New York American* made a closer study of Tanner's colors:

> If you examine his canvases closely, you will find that the blue is threaded through with strokes of purple, gray and pinkish mauve, and more sparingly with pale, creamy yellow. On the other hand, where the "local" color is creamy, it is found to be dragged over with threads of pink, pale mauve and green.

9. *Chicago Daily Tribune*, February 2, 1911.
10. *New York Tribune,* April 13, 1913.

> It is this way that Tanner introduces chromatic relations into the dark and light colors of his canvas and so draws them into a unity of vibrating and resonant harmony.[11]

The "vibrating and resonant harmony" was produced in part by Tanner's use of white underpainting. During the summer of 1913 Clara MacChesney, herself an artist, visited Trépied and described for the *International Studio* Tanner's method of painting.

> His work is never direct, but obtained by a series of glazes. As his manipulation is process work he usually has fifteen or twenty canvases on hand at once, in different stages of completion. . . . He finds that his results are made more permanent, when working slowly, thus giving each glaze layer sufficient time to dry and harden.[12]

This method, which produced some of his most beautiful effects, was one that took Tanner some years to perfect. Either because of an inadequate knowledge of the drying properties of varnishes, or because of impatience, some of Tanner's earlier paintings done by means of glazes have had an unfortunate tendency to flake, exposing the white underpainting. But the damage in most cases has been slight and easily repaired.

Miss MacChesney also described Tanner's studio at "Les Charmes" which, except for a less elaborate use of props—furniture, décor, etc.,—was similar to that used by many historical and genre painters of the period. He had purchased many of his accessories from the estate of the painter Munkácsy, who died in 1900.

> His studio is an ideal workroom, being high-ceilinged, spacious and having the least possible furniture, utterly free from masses of useless studio stuff and paraphernalia. The walls are of a light gray and at one end hangs a fine tapestry. Oriental carved wooden screens are at the doors and win-

11. *New York American,* April 14, 1913.

12. "A Poet-Painter of Palestine," *International Studio,* 50 (July, 1913): xii.

> dows. Leading out of it is a small room having a domed ceiling, and picturesque high windows. In this simply furnished room he often poses his models, painting himself in the large studio, the sliding door between being a small one. He can often make use of lamplight effects, the daylight in the large room not interfering.[13]

At the time of Miss MacChesney's visit Tanner was at work on his next Salon pictures, a *Christ at the Home of Lazarus* and a picture of a seated female figure with a lighted taper in her hand that he called *Mary*.

Tanner also was actively engaged in arranging the yearly exhibition of the Société Artistique de Picardie, of which he was president. The Société Artistique de Picardie was an institution in the Pas de Calais. It had seen its first exhibition in 1904 under the presidency of Max Bohm and was composed of artists living in the area around Etaples. For the yearly show held in late summer, other artists were also invited to submit their pictures. In 1913 many prominent names, including those of Albert Besnard and Alfred Maurer, figured in the catalogue.

Trépied was the heart of the art colony whose members had founded the society. It was a small community of about twenty-five houses and adjoined the growing pleasure resort of Paris-Plage. Henry and Jessie had gone there since shortly after their return from Mt. Kisco in 1904 and were popular leaders of the art group. They were also popular with the farm people who lived in the vicinity, who liked them not only for their friendliness and consideration in personal and business dealings, but also for their active interest in community affairs. One of Tanner's most appreciated contributions to civic life was his organization of a fire brigade at Trépied. The uniformed *pompiers*, though seldom needed, were a matter of local pride.

In April, 1914, Tanner's paintings of *Christ at the Home of Lazarus* and *Mary* were exhibited at the Old Salon, the 132d

13. Ibid., p. xi.

of the Société des Artistes Français. An Associated Press dispatch stated that they were two of the best paintings he had done for many years.[14]

The summer of 1914 Tanner was again with his family at Trépied, secure in the belief that, aside from minor annoyances like a stretch of bad weather, all was well with the world.

Not quite "all," for Henry's mother had suffered a paralytic stroke and was seriously ill in America. In July he received a letter from his sister Mary saying she was growing weaker every day.

> We have the advice of three doctors, all agree there is absolutely nothing can be done.... We keep a day and night nurse, good trained nurses . . . she so often speaks of Jessie's last letter and has us read it, she says it was so beautiful.

Fortunately, Henry had much to preoccupy him that summer. He was still president of the Société Artistique de Picardie and working hard, as he had done the year before, to make the late summer exhibition a success. There were also many questions under discussion by the members. One was whether an etching press should be purchased for the use of the artists. A long letter to Tanner from Henry Boddington goes into the pros and cons of this purchase—whether enough of the members would be interested, how much to charge for the use of the press, whether a notice should be put up advising members to leave the press, blankets, etc., in good order when they were finished with their work.

At the meetings of the société there were the usual conversations about art and, almost certainly, discussions of the Anglo-American exhibition that opened in June at Shepherd's Bush in London. This was the first representative exhibition of American art ever seen in England, and many of the members of the art colony, including H. O. Tanner, had pictures in it.

14. *New York Journal of Commerce*, April 30, 1914. Clipping in Tanner Collection, Archives of American Art, Detroit.

But time was running out for the artists of Trépied. In two short months their pleasant meetings under the tall pines, in "the big studio," or at their cheerful homes would come to an end. The First World War, a disaster of phenomenal proportions, was about to shatter not only the tranquillity of Trépied, but of the world as they knew it.

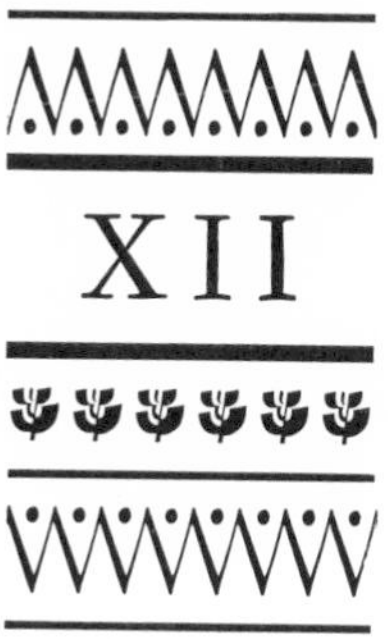

The War

War came like a thunderclap. Most Americans made a frantic effort to leave France by the first ship, but longtime residents, like the Tanners, did not feel this compulsion. France was their home. They loved it and identified with it, and it was their belief, as it was that of most Frenchmen, that the war would end quickly or, at least, be fought on German soil.

But art was no longer discussed by the artists at Trépied, and the exhibition at Le Touquet, which had taken so much time and work to arrange, was closed by the local authorities after five days and the building converted to use for war refugees.

Throughout the month of August each day brought graver news to Picardy. One by one the summer residents left—for Paris, for the United States, for Switzerland and England. By late August it appeared that the village of Trépied was on the line of enemy march, and even "permanent residents" like the Tanners had to think of leaving. Henry Tanner's "jottings" include a description of their hasty departure.

> 25 August
> Tuesday night—Noble came while we were at supper with word that all who wished to leave had better leave at once—I went and told Leonard and McKay. The next morning the Sennconys and Nobles left. We heard grumbling of cannon firing all day.
> Wed. 26
> All day packing—a sad time.
> We left with the idea of staying a day or so at Boulogne as last of news at Etaples was trying.
> Thursday Aug 27th
> Left our home about 8 a.m. Train about 2½ hours late. German prisoners at Etaples station. Arrived at Boulogne about 3 o/clock. Great excitement. Wounded. Town full of officers and Belgians from the Front.
> 28th Aug
> Friday left Boulogne on 11.30 boat. Small no. of passengers as train did not arrive from Paris. On boat was wounded aviator being brought back to Engl. Arrived at Rye 4 o/clock—long search for rooms. Finally located. We were very, very tired.

There were several reasons for Henry's selection of Rye as a place of refuge. It was less crowded and expensive than London and was one of the more picturesque towns in southern England. Nevertheless, it was his and Jessie's intention to return to France as soon as possible.

Rye was the home of Henry James, and during their brief stay there, the Tanners were invited to his home for tea. Jesse Tanner, who was eleven, remembers the event.

> The tea was served against a garden wall, that protected us from the sea breeze. There were roses and good alleys, a round tea table. . . .
>
> The conversation was jovial and relaxed. I seem to remember a rather slim man in not very good health, speaking

in a quiet voice. My mother and father seemed very pleased to have seen Henry James.[1]

Atherton Curtis, back in France, was worried about the Tanners. The following letter was written to Henry by his secretary:

17 rue Notre-Dame-des-Champs
Paris

September 15, 1914

Dear Mr. Tanner,

Mr. Curtis wants to send you some more money but does not like to do so until he is sure whether you are still at Rye or whether you have returned to Trépied. Would you be good enough to let him know where you would like to have it sent? It could be sent to you if still in England by an ordinary mandat but if you have any means of cashing a New York cheque Mr. Curtis thinks that this would probably be the safest way of sending it as if lost it could not be used by anyone else. Very likely though at Rye it might be difficult to cash such a cheque unless you have friends in London who would do it for you. If you prefer it can wait until your return to Trépied, if you are not already there. On account of the fatigue of the past month Mr. Curtis has been ill, not seriously but just tired and used up and in bed for about a week, and that is one of the reasons why he has not written to you. Also during part of the time the mail system of Paris was a good deal disorganized and still is to some extent. He is better now. He has received your letters but very much behind time. Mrs. Tanner's two letters from Trépied saying that you were thinking of leaving arrived only yesterday but he knew that you were in Rye because the letter from Rye arrived with only a few days delay.

With kind regards
Sincerely,
Amy Oliver

1. Jesse O. Tanner to me, May 9, 1966, Archives of American Art, Detroit.

Chapter Twelve

A rough unfinished draft of a letter that Tanner wrote about this time was probably designed for Atherton Curtis.

Sept. 14th 1914

Today the news is better—better yesterday than the day before and so it has been for the last 4 days. The Germans are on the retreat, Amiens evacuated, etc.—soon you can work say some of my friends—but how can I? What right have I to do that which I like to do, what right to be comfortable? In London I saw some of the Canadian contingent and many volunteers, fine, handsome, intelligent men going out to fight, to suffer and to die for principles which I believe in as strongly as they and sit down to paint a little picture, and thus make myself happy—No it cannot be done. Not after what I saw in London.

A distinguished old English lady and her daughter came to the American Ambassadors to ask if they could telegraph to Berlin to find out if her son whom she knew had been wounded was among the wounded or prisoners or dead—a comrade who had returned had seen him seriously wounded but the "War Office" had no other news than "missing." If one could see the dry anguish of that loving mother and sister without being moved to try and aid or being made to feel the terrible suffering the war brings in its train. It makes one feel a little like I felt when I saw a haggard Belgian soldier at Boulogne. I felt like some of the old Patriarchs must have felt when we read about them "cursing" an enemy—I never felt so much like cursing the man whose fault this terrible war is as then, a curse, a malediction with all its 13c weight of evil. I felt that the originator of the war deserved it.

One reads the papers all day—but only once in a while, thank God, does one realize the suffering and despair that is contained—a sentence like 40 killed, 400 killed, 4000 missing, 40,000 losses. How many loving, carefully raised sons in that number, how many fathers, how many lonely wives, mothers, children, sweethearts, waiting for the return that never comes. This waiting—how hard it is—how much harder than action, waiting, waiting, with less light each day until despair puts all out all light of life—and this is why I cannot work. Jesse said this morning, "Now Father that the news is better you can work."

Henry and Jessie returned to France as soon as the German tide was turned back. They placed Jesse as a boarder in "Mr. Denny's" school in Paris and went to Trépied to look after their possessions. The house was intact, as was their fine collection of pewter they had buried in the garden, but the garden and the orchard, stripped of its fruit, were in a sad state, as was the country generally. Henry did what he could to salvage the belongings of his friends, but the artists had departed in such haste that their studios were left pretty much to the mercy of marauders and German soldiers. Some of their art works, left at this time, were never recovered.

Even though the war news was better, Henry Tanner found it difficult to paint. The atmosphere of war was not conducive to creative work, for art was of no interest to people who lived in daily apprehension of death. Many French artists turned to poster work as a means of helping the war effort, but the quiet sentiment of Tanner's paintings seemed ill-suited to war propaganda.

The first two years of the war were possibly the hardest for Tanner, for everything that he believed in seemed in danger of destruction. Jessie was a source of moral support during these dark months, but it was Atherton Curtis who encouraged Henry to see meaning in his life. The following letter from Atherton appears to have been written in answer to a particularly despondent one by Henry.

MONTIGNY-SUR-LOIRE
SEINE-ET-MARNE
July 29, 1916

DEAR HENRY:

Everyone has moments of discouragement in life and at those times we all have the feeling that our life has been a failure, that we might have done more, that we might have done otherwise, that in some other line of work, in some other sphere of activity we might have accomplished something worth while or at any rate something better, something more useful than we did. It is natural that we should have such moments if we take life seriously. How could we do otherwise? The wonder is that we are not in a discouraged mood all the time; for who can say that he has accomplished all that he would have liked to accomplish or that he has even done more than a small, very small, part of what he would wish to have done? Our ideals, if they amount to anything, are necessarily very far beyond our results. After all, it is our ideals that count. Is it Emerson or who is it that says —He loves his friends not for what they have done but for their aspirations? Of course, everyone likes to see some little result to give him some satisfaction and encouragement. In moments of discouragement it is easy to see only the failures; but the life of a person who is serious in his aspirations is not all failure. Scarcely anyone's life is all failure. Perhaps no one's life is really a complete failure. To be a complete failure it would have to be without a single good impulse, without a single moment of ideal and such a life seems almost impossible. That moment of ideal in itself constitutes a success and is therefore an encouragement.

In your own work, you have always set your standard high. You cannot hope to attain all that you have wished to attain. No one does or can. You have painted faithfully and you have done good work. You have produced some beautiful pictures, some very beautiful ones. You have also produced some that have been failures, complete or partial. Some of your pictures, I have not liked at all. There are many Rembrandts that I do not like. An artist must be judged by his best work and not by his failures; and your own best work is good. It is worth while to have made many failures to produce it. That best work will be appreciated some day. I cannot say when. No one can say when. You can only do what you can and wait. Perhaps you will never see your works appreciated and recognized by the public, even the artistic public; but the works are there for those who love beautiful colours and other beautiful qualities. I know that your work has not brought you money success. It is unfortunate that this is as it is. We need to eat, the more is the pity, and we like therefore to see some money come in as a result of our effort. It is good when one's work can produce this result; but unfortunately it has generally been the less good works of art that have had the greatest money success. When Milton sold "Paradise Lost" for £5, he cannot have thought that his years of work were very well paid. But "Paradise Lost" was no less one of the great masterpieces of world literature. The artistic side and the money side are two different things and we cannot make them otherwise. I imagine that this was so way back there in the days of those old Egyptians that we love so much.

As to judging your own work, I do not find anything strange in your discovering that what you thought was coming on all right was in reality coming on wrong. The sudden discovery that you have been misjudging your work, discourages you; but you know from experience that this is so. You know that it is true in the case of all artists; that they all have such results at times and very often. When one is in the heat of production one often loses sight of the ensemble; or of some part of the work, because of concentration of mind on other parts. When time has passed over, the point of view is different and then comes a different judgment—very often better, though not always. Then, too, in your special case today you must remember that you are living in times that are not conducive to artistic production. Do what one will, one cannot get rid of the awful war. You have been trying in these two years of awful anxiety and awful world suffering to produce a work of art. It is not strange that at such a time, even more than in ordinary times, your judgment should find itself at fault on your looking back on what you have done. It is naturally discouraging to be stopped suddenly this way. You will have to try to encourage yourself by thinking of the beautiful things done in the past by you and start again for the future. It is easy for me to write this, I know. It is always easy to preach; especially to others.

I am sorry for your having to go to America again next winter. It is very unpleasant, I know. I wish that it could be otherwise; that you might spend your time quietly in Trépied and Paris and keep away from a country whose love of liberty and fair play is not so extraordinary as it tries to make the world believe.

This is an awfully long letter but I cannot help writing what I feel. I appreciate greatly the free way in which you write to me. It is so that it should be between friends. I wish that I could do more to encourage you. I think that you ought to take into account not only that we are living in times when artistic production is difficult for all who have any feeling but that you have been living in the very midst of the war and that artistic production is doubly difficult in your case.

Ingeborg joins me in love to you all.

Affectionately,
ATHERTON

The Tanners moved about a good deal during the first two years of the war. Henry's passport shows that he made another brief trip to England in the summer of 1915, returning by Boulogne to Etaples in June. In November, 1916, he obtained permission to go to the United States, the trip alluded to no doubt in Atherton's letter, but there is no evidence that he made the journey. These years were spent principally in Paris and at Trépied, though in 1916 the Tanners were also at Vittel, a health resort in the Vosges. Jessie's passport discloses that on May 21, 1916, she was given permission by the French government to leave Vittel and to return to her home, "Les Charmes," at Trépied, in the "zone les Armées." She remained at Trépied more or less permanently from then until the end of the war, when conditions forced her to leave. It was a difficult time for Jessie—one that took its toll on her strength and may well have shortened her life.

As the war progressed Henry Tanner felt that the only

way he could overcome his feeling of despondency would be to serve actively in the war effort. He was excluded by his age and training—in 1917 he was fifty-eight—from entering the armed forces, but after the United States declared war on Germany he developed an idea that had come to him during his stay at Vittel, where there was a base hospital. He believed his plan would not only help the morale of the wounded soldiers but would assist the army in a practical sense. This plan was to utilize the unused lands around hospitals and base depots to raise fresh vegetables and to organize the convalescent soldiers as a working force for the project. In November, 1917, he made a trip to England to enlist support for his plan from Walter Hines Page. He returned with the following letter for the American ambassador to France.

EMBASSY OF THE UNITED STATES
OF AMERICA
LONDON
November 26, 1917

MY DEAR COLLEAGUE,

This introduces to you Mr. H. O. Tanner, an American whom I have long known, a painter of great distinction, and a man of philanthropic impulses and activities. He will explain to you an interesting scheme that he wishes to further in connection with convalescent hospitals.

Very sincerely yours,
(signed) WALTER H. PAGE

His Excellency,
The Honorable William G. Sharp,
American Ambassador Paris

The plan interested Mr. Sharp, and he presented it to the Red Cross authorities in Paris. As a result, the following month Henry Tanner was attached to the American Red Cross as a lieutenant in the Farm Service Bureau and his plan put into effect. Although there were problems involved in the new and untried project, on the whole it turned out to be a success. An account book that Tanner kept shows the extent of his work. He not only raised vegetables, but sold livestock and hay as well. The following letter, written by his superior officer about the time he left the project, suggests something of the nature of his work:

HOTEL REGINA
2, PLACE DE RIVOLI
PARIS
October 17, 1918

October 17, 1918 from WM. GILLESPIE, *Capt. ARC*
Chief Hosp. Farm and Garden Section
to MR. H. O. TANNER, *Lieutenant ARC, Am. Red Cross—Chantiers-Martiers, Neufchateau*
Subject: Garden at Base Hospital No. 66

Your letter of October 14th just to hand. I am very pleased indeed that the potato crop at this Hospital is going to be so satisfactory. I shall write Lieut. Cobb about it and ask him to let me know exactly how many bushels or tons of potatoes he has been able to raise.

I note that you have been at La Fauché and that part of the land is being taken by buildings. I sincerely trust that they will not destroy altogether the garden that has been so well prepared.

Your expense accounts were sent by the Comptroller's Dept. to Vittel on October 7th and no doubt are waiting there for you.

I am glad to hear that you have started on your own work, and rest assured that you have my very best wishes for entire success.

In all probability I shall have left this Service at the end of this month. I am not yet sure who will take my place but I think it will be Lieut. Frost.

CAPT. WM. GILLESPIE, *Chief*
Hospital Farm and Garden Section
Home and Hospital Bureau

While Henry was stationed near Vittel working for the Red Cross, Jessie was alone at Trépied, trying to work the garden and keep the house together. Jesse was with her only during his holidays, but in April, 1918, he was at home sick with the flu. It was at this time that the enemy spring offensive got underway, bringing the war for a second time close to Trépied. The following letters are descriptive of their experiences:

[*From Jessie to Henry*]

Trepied, April 11, 1918

MY DEAR HENRY—

Yours of Monday with Helga Hawkins' letter and postal from Trouffant arrived OK yesterday.

I at once had the letter sent over to Nelson and of course he is delighted and hopes to get the field plowed at once and get the spuds planted. He has sent several men over to spade up our grass plot, and Alice and I planted about half of it in Early Rose spuds. You remember you especially selected some yourself and they were put into the cave. Nearly a sack full. Those we planted—the rest of the plot I will put in late carrots. Our potatoes are about all planted at the other place.

Asparagus is beginning to come. Alice and I weeded it all today.

Mr. Nelson is to buy all the seed potatoes I will let him have. I have sold already 6 boisseau to people around here. He is to give me 21 frc for 100 lbs. Not so bad, is it? I really do not know how many sacks there will be.

Our Jesse is up and is getting to feel and look better. He hasn't been out as yet, but, if tomorow is as fine a day as today I will let him go out and sit in a well sheltered spot for a little while. This is his second day up.

I trust you have received my letter to Vittel O.K.

Your letters are coming up more quickly, but I fear mine take days and days to reach you. So funny I wrote you about Jesse the day after you left here—you seemed not to have received it.

Chapter Twelve

Do try and get another can of that delicious syrup. *We are sweetening our tea and coffee with it. That bit of sugar I keep hidden as it would disappear if Alice had anything to do with it in a very short time. So I keep it when J. and I are alone. All for now.*

Love from us both,
Yours,
JESSIE

May 14, 1918

MY DEAR HENRY,

Yours to hand of May 9th. I suppose by now you are near our base. I trust all goes OK with you and that the "Flu" has not left you with any weakness, as it did me for several weeks—

Jesse's extras came rather high this last term but, of course, he had to have the eggs—He has them now you bet, freshly laid that same day.

You would hardly know the Kid, he has really grown quite stout and rosy.

Jesse has his tea nearly every day with his soldier friends near us. I give them potatoes as their rations in potatoes are not enough, and they are delighted so in that way I repay them for what they give Jesse—and he does enjoy being with them as they are a very nice lot of men, well educated, his English will not suffer. . . .

We had last night the first really big lot of asparagus this season—it was fine and such a feast—all we wanted and that is saying a lot when Jesse is here. We are eating our own salad too. . . .

TREPIED *Tuesday*
May 21st

MY DEAR HENRY,

Just a line to let you know (if by any chance you have heard) that we are all OK. We had a terrible air raid Sunday night that lasted 24 hours and 10 minutes. Bombs fell all over the place. On the hospitals, in the camp, 50 yards from us, a 120 in all. E. is in a terrible state. Nurses and Drs. killed and many many soldiers and people.

Luckily for us we are just far enough away to be out of the zone that is the bridge and railroad. Two or three Gothas were brought near us at St. J.

I think I am not doing wrong in writing you this, as you are in the American War Zone; and I feared you might hear and worry. I think I will try and have a dugout made under our sand dune at one other place. I have given my guest room over to a dear English nurse for no one is sleeping in E. during this full moon. All nurses are put into dugouts. Jesse and I were in one until 1 a.m. last night, and will be again tonight near our A.S.C. friends 40 ft. deep. A wonderful place, then they drive us home when all danger is over and the moon is quite low. The German aviators regret very much about the hospitals NoI can. and NoF can.—badly done in.

I had my first few hours sleep last night and feel better this morning. Jesse is still sleeping.

With love,
JESSIE

Happily for us friends happened to be here last Sun. night so we had company. All laid flat on the floor for 2 hours.

May 23, 1918

MY DEAR HENRY,

Your first letter from Vittel to hand, dated May 19th but post marked May 21st, so it has come very quickly.

I would like very much to come up to Paris and be with you those few days, but under the circumstances of my last letter—I cannot leave Jesse here alone. It is too great a risk. How I wish Denny would move his school to Brittany. I do so hope you will be able to come up for a vacation in July as you say.

My pass expires May 31 but I think I can have it renewed. I have not been to the bank yet, nor to the Notaire, as we have all been so tired no one has done anything but what has been necessary and I will until this offensive is over hold on to that money you sent for other purposes. . . .

We are turning day into night during this moonlit weather. We get to bed at 4:30 or 5 sleep until 12 and 1 (noon) last night came up stormy and we got home at 1:30 so have had more sleep than usual.

May 24, 1918

DEAR HENRY,

I think that after all it will be better for Jesse to go back to school for the ½ term. He cannot do much in his studies here and as the long gun has stopped he is not in such great danger there than he is here—He is good and strong now too.

He gave me your letter to read after I told him I wanted him to return. He said he wanted to go very much so I decided then and there that he should. He wants to play all the time and when I asked him to help Alice to weed he did not want to.

All for now,
JESSIE

[*From Jessie to Ingeborg*]

May 27, '18

MY DEAR INGEBORG,

Many thanks for your thoughtfulness in having Miss Oliver send me that egg preserving powder. If eggs were not so expensive up here at present—10 frcs for 26 (they haven't been lower than 8 fcs for 26 this spring) I would put up several hundred—and as things are up here for the moment I really do not know from one day to another if we can remain on. I can assure you I want to hang on if possible but one's nerves cannot stand but a certain amount and then they go. It would really make me feel very badly if I had to leave my home and garden, and everything is just going so well in the garden too, and the fine season coming. I have to think of course of our safety, especially Jesse being here. He is a real "brick" and can sleep dear kiddie, when I cannot. I am so glad he can.

I hope to have a good dugout made in our dunes this week.

I trust you are all in best of health and get enough sleep to keep you going.

Our fondest love for Atherton from Jesse and me

Your loving friend,

JESSIE

[*From Jesse to his father*]

DEAR FATHER,

I am writing to answer your long letter which I received yesterday, and a lot more with it.

As you know by now we had a big raid, the size of which, the killed can be counted in 100 dead, and the bombs 3 times 50 while two Gothas were brought down.

We had 7 bombs go off 100 yards from our house.

Now as you can understand this has upset mother a good deal, it scared me badly but luckily I haven't many nerves.

The next day they attacked Boulogne and Abbeville causing frightful damage and only throwing 7 bombs in our vicinity. Think of it bombs near the train line, bombs all along Carmier road, everywhere on the night of the big raid we had a few people over, 3 or four officers and several ladies.

These officers invited us to spend the next night with them in a dugout 50 feet deep and apparently safe. So on all moonlight nights we run over to them in a wagon which they send for us.

Now since the big-raid night and the following night we have had no raid, but mother as I said before has been badly shaken so that if another big raid was to happen I don't know what would happen.

On the other hand mother is very loathe to leave the place on account of the impossibility of coming back for a rather indefinite time, and on account of the garden.

Again on the other hand these officers may leave and so leave us without a dugout, which is a help to mother, as she feels among friends.

Unfortunately it (the dugout) is near the railway station, and as I do not fear the bombs, as it is a big chance for one to hit you, but rather the effect of one falling near and giving mother a shock.

Mother is going to write to you, but if this letter reaches you before her's I should act before then, by either coming up as she is asking you or telling her to leave before it is too late. As you see mother is not willing to leave, and as she thinks show the white feather.

Why I am writing to you at all, is because just a little while ago we heard two bombs or a dump or something blow up in the distance and mother called for me and said we would leave, but in about a quarter of an hour she wasn't sure.

I made up my mind before this happened that I would write to you as there are too many distractions for me to work steadily, but now I see how mother is, I am not going to leave her till I hear from you. I send heaps of love.

Your loving son,
JESSE

[*From Jessie to Henry*]

WEDNESDAY
May 29 1918

MY DEAR HENRY,

Your telegram came Monday and we took it, Jesse and I, that you were coming up here to see for yourself how things were.

I went to Marché and got fish and meat and Jesse went to the station and waited until 7:30 for the Paris train which after all would not arrive until 9:33. We waited dinner for you until 11, as I had made a nice fish dinner for you. Then your letter from Paris of Monday came and then we saw what your telegram meant, that you were leaving Vosges again, as I did not know you were in Paris until I got your telegram. So we had a mix-up and a disappointment. Well, it will be for another time. I hope soon. We are OK after our big shakeup. You have no doubt received both mine and Jesse's letters add. to Neufchateau.

If you left Paris yesterday you missed a big raid. I see by the "Telegram"—I hope you got out of it OK. Poor Daddy, he is now in town! Poor old man. How I wish he was home in N.Y. with Elna—it was very unfortunate he returned when he did after we sent him home and a war on over here—but really, I cannot worry about him. We have enough hell here. I am so glad you are out of Paris as much as you are. The moon is now on the wane thank goodness, and we will have a wee respite and get some sleep.

Night before last we slept over at Mme. Charmiers, she has a good cellar and further away from bridge than we are. I hope before next moon we will have a good dug-out on one of our dunes.

As the Germans moved closer to Paris, Atherton and Ingeborg Curtis thought it best to go further south, but they were anxious not to lose touch with Henry and Jessie.

[From Atherton to Henry]

MONTIGNY-SUR-LOING
SEINE-ET-MARNE
Sunday June 2, 1918

DEAR HENRY,

Here we are at last at Montigny. We came out on the afternoon train on Friday. No trouble and no difficulty. No crowds at the station. Fewer people, in fact, than in ordinary times. We sent you Jessie's letter as soon as it came and asked Gillespie to telegraph you. Hope you got both all right. I fear that they are having rather a bad time of it up there from what Jessie writes. I wish that they would get out; but Jessie will know how to take care of herself and she does not lose her head. I am sorry for you having to worry about them so far away and news so slow in coming through. What terrible times we are passing through! Who would have thought that after four years it would all begin over again in the same way! It would be perfect calm down here if it were not for the uncertainty of the future. If we have to leave we will go to M. Georges Thirion, 59 quai Ulysse Besnard, Blois, Loir-et-Cher; and if we could not stay there for any reason, I would let my cousin Louis C. Taylor know of my change of address. His address is "Tastet Baita," Saint-Jean-de-Luz, Basses Pyrénées. I think that I gave you these addresses but there is no harm in repeating them. With these two you can always get in communication with us.

Love from us both,
ATHERTON CURTIS

Within a matter of days Jessie decided, or Henry decided for her, that the time had come to leave Trépied, and she joined her husband at Vittel.

[*From Atherton to Henry*]

CHEZ M. GEORGES THIRION
59 QUAI ULYSSE-BESNARD
BLOIS, LOIR-ET-CHER
June 13, 1918

DEAR HENRY,

We were very glad to get your letter and have some news in detail of Jessie and Jesse. What an awful time they must have had and how glad I am that they are in safety and that you are all together once more. I hope that they will soon recover from the shock. It must have been a terrible strain on their nerves. These are bad times but I hope that the tide will turn before too long. It does seem as if we must have reached the final grand uproar of the war. I cannot see how things can go on at this rate much longer without the collapse of one side or the other or both.

We are here staying in the Thirion's house and have a wing to ourselves so that we can keep house on our own account. They have a beautiful garden and a lovely wood. One feels much farther away from the war than at Montigny and we should be very quiet and comfortable if it were not for the tormenting events that leave peace of mind nowhere to anyone.

We should like to have news of you all once in a while. It is best for you to write direct to us here and not to Paris. I don't know whether I gave you the address of my cousin

Louis C. Taylor
Tastet Baita
Saint-Jean-de-Luz
Basses-Pyrénées

It is well for you to have it as I keep informed of my change of address and through him my friends could always get into communication with me if we were obliged to leave here, which I hope will not happen.

We both send you all much love and sympathy in your troubles.

Affectionately,
ATHERTON CURTIS

The Tanner's reunion was of short duration, for after Jessie's arrival at Vittel Henry was sent almost immediately to another depot.

[*From Jessie to Henry*]

HOTEL DE FRANCE
VITTEL — *June 18, 1918*

MY DEAR HENRY,

Your short note at hand. I hope you have received mine I wrote you a few days after you left.

I had a bad cold again after you left but am OK now. I am getting on nicely and feel quite like my old self again.

Mme. Bertrand is here which makes it very nice for me.

The 4 July is going to be a great day here. I hope you will try and be back here.

Lots of rain today. It will do a lot of good.

I weighed the other day, 60 kilos 800—just under 61 kilos. I think I am getting a little *fatter.*

I trust you are keeping well—Papa wrote you a letter which I have opened. He hopes to get that room at 70 bis about now as the man has come up. He seems very pleased about it.

All for now. No news as yet from Trépied which I am anxiously awaiting.

*Went to a real American dance Sat. night and had a fine time. Everything done AI—you bet—*real American.

Love from both,
Yours,
Jessie

Hotel de France — Vittel, *June 20, 1918*

My dear Henry,

Just a line to say I got your letter of Sunday last from Chaumont. I am all O.K. now and Jesse is doing very well indeed at R.C. . . .

When do you think you will be here again?

An English officer was in to lunch today with a French interpreter and they both told me of another terrible air raid at E. 850 people and soldiers killed and the hospitals terribly bombed. 8 nurses and 11 officers killed—is it not terrible? I hear the H's are all now evacuated from there. How strange it must be not to have any nurses around—poor E is being hit more ways than one.

Had a letter from Mr. Nelson—He said the torpedo did not do any damage to the garden. The garden is being worked and put in AI shape. Our house is not rented yet.

The ex. Force Canteen is after it but found the rent rather stiff. I think I will let it go for 375 frcs, not a sou less. Mme. Marsch's is now free so I had better hurry up—I would like them to sign for at least 6 months at that rent. I shall write Mr. N today to that effect. Had a lovely long letter from Mme. M they are at Carbourg (?) Calvados for the summer. If we find a good school for Jesse she will try to send Jacques too as she wants to send him now to a boarding school. Letter from Papa. He is O.K. One from Denny in answer to mine. I asked for Jesse's bread and sugar card and he sent them and he felt greatly relieved we had left and were safe as he knew all about what we had all passed through up there. The Geo. Magazine also came as usual was very fine.

With love from us both for you,
Yours,
JESSIE

In August Henry was stationed at Neufchâteau, and Jessie was given permission to visit him there. The following month he applied to the Red Cross for permission to sketch scenes in the war zone, and in October he left the Farm Bureau to be attached as an artist to the Bureau of Publicity. The day of the armistice, November 11, he was sent his *carte d'identité*—W.P. 646—by the headquarters of the American Expeditionary Force, and an authorization to go, by railway and auto, to Chaumont (Hts. Marne), Neufchâteau (Vosges), and Toul (M. et M.) to make sketches, subject to the usual censorship.

Three pictures that Tanner painted from sketches made at Toul and Neufchâteau were sent to the American Red Cross Headquarters in Washington, D. C., in October, 1919, and are now there in the War Museum. They are interior and exterior scenes of Red Cross canteens. As a record of the realities of war these pictures leave much to be desired. Brutality and suffering were subjects alien to Tanner's comprehension as an artist. The figures of the soldiers are stiff and flat and seem to have little relationship to their setting. Nevertheless, in the cool blue-green tonality of the night scenes and the blurred outlines of the forms, Tanner conveys something of the poetic feeling that gives character to his Biblical paintings.

Tanner also made some "unofficial" sketches during his travels. One of these so impressed Capt. Carter Harrison of the A.R.C. that he wrote Tanner about it on March 22:

> I hope to see you in Paris and to be allowed the privilege of looking over your work. And, by the way, if you feel like disposing of the little sketch of Jeanne d'Arc's home at a figure I feel I can afford to pay, please bring it to Paris with you.

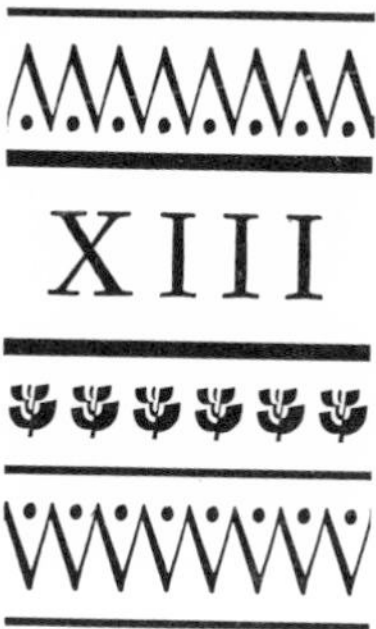

Aftermath of the War

Henry Tanner's wartime experiences, though harrowing at times and unproductive of memorable paintings, were nevertheless valuable to him. His work with the soldiers helped him to overcome the feeling of futility that had plagued him so miserably during the first years of the war, and his association with members of the Red Cross and the convalescent soldiers gave him a broader and, perhaps, sharper view of Americans.

But the benefits were not all one-sided. There is evidence that Tanner came to mean a great deal to the men with whom he served, both in his farm work and later, as an "official" artist. This is deserving of special note since as a Negro, as Tanner was counted, he occupied an unusual position in the American forces. American Negroes in World War I were segregated by regiments, and it was rarely that a Negro officer, even in the Red Cross, worked exclusively with white men on an equal footing. But Tanner, though older than most of his associates, was not only accepted, but extremely popular. One of his fellow artists, W. J. Aylward, put into writing the opinion of his colleagues when he wrote Tanner:

> I wonder if you know what a warm place you have made for yourself in the affections of the official artists? We often speak of you those of us who are left, for we are only four now and it is the concensus of opinion among us that we not only respect you as an artist but love you as a friend.

Mr. Aylward was so drawn to the life that Tanner described at Trépied that he wrote of his intention to "run down to Etaples and look over the studio situation" before leaving for home. It was his desire to bring his wife and child from America the following spring and become a permanent member of the art colony to which Tanner belonged. He did indeed return and settled for a time at Les Sables, but postwar France was very different from the France Tanner had described before the war.

It is possible that some of the men with whom Tanner worked did not know of his Negro blood. He was no darker than many Latins, and as a cultivated gentleman he was at ease in any situation; he had none of the qualities stereotyped in the minds of many Americans as "Negro." But he made no effort to disguise his race. It would be interesting to know whether "Capt R——" in the following "jotting," which refers to an incident that happened at Neufchateau in 1918, knew of Tanner's racial background.

> It had been a rather gay dinner when Capt R——continuing his accounts of a trip to the front which had fired us all said "but we will have to kill several of those niggers down home before we will be able to get them back in their place." Now I had not known that the —— Regiment which they had been talking about was a N—— regiment.
>
> Capt R—— and I had seen I to I on many subjects and had become quite friends which surprised me—as I knew the

first time I met him that he was from the South. He came from Miss—— and like a good many people from the South he talked a great deal on religion. After the remark called forth by I have forgotten what he continued quite a tirade against the Negro. There was little said for or against his leading remark, as nearly all forgot to apply any of Christ's Spirit upon a subject in which their own prejudices and weaknesses were concerned. I do not think I took any part in the further discussion of religion that evening but nevertheless it continued hot and heavy until a sudden look at his watch made Capt R—— hurry away. The alleyway between the tables was small and to let him out we all leaned forward over the table to give room. He passed two or three putting his hand upon their shoulders. When he arrived at me he put his big hand upon my head in the position of a blessing—somehow I felt I had God's blessing as far as mortal erring man could give it. He was I know as blind as when Isaac blessed Esau. It would seem that men have to give God Bless signs when they should prefer not to—but as in Biblical times a blessing once given could not be easily changed.

Tanner's description of this incident is written with understanding and pity—and even a touch of humor—and is a testament to the objectivity that he had achieved toward his fellow man.

Tanner's work with the Red Cross ended during the summer of 1919. On his Foreign Service certificate, signed by Woodrow Wilson, the severance date is given as June, 1919, although a permit exists that shows he was sent on a special mission by the Red Cross to Boulogne in July of that year.

Once out of the service Tanner did not immediately resume his own work. He felt that he needed a rest from the pressures put upon him by his war work, and he wished to tie together some of the loose ends that had been left by the war. At Trépied the house needed repairs, and he had to consider the possibility of selling or renting "Les Charmes" and building a new home on some land, half dune, half pine, that he bought in 1912. Then there were professional as well as personal matters to attend to, particularly in regard to the sale of his paintings in America.

Although art, except that of propaganda, had come to a virtual standstill in France during the war years, in the United States it had remained a going affair, and Tanner's paintings had continued to attract attention. In 1915 at the Panama-Pacific Exposition a large proportion of the honors had gone to American artists in Paris. Frederick Frieseke was awarded the only grand prize, but medals of honor were awarded Richard Miller, Walter Griffin, and Lawton Parker, and gold medals went to H. O. Tanner, Elizabeth Nourse, Myron Barlow, and Max Bohm.

In February, 1918, Tanner had received a letter from E. W. Ericson, director of the Artists' Guild in Chicago, telling him that he had sold one of his pictures, *The Shepherd*, to Dr. I. M. Cline of New Orleans for $600.

> We promised Dr. Cline to write to you and ask you to address a letter to him direct, telling where the picture was painted and anything that you can that would be of particular interest to you and your work. It will be a good "shouter" if you can give him something to shout about.

But just then Tanner was engaged at the convalescent hospital at Vittel and had no time to think of his own work, even to give an art connoisseur "something to shout about."

During his preoccupation with war work, some valuable paintings that he had placed in storage with the Art Packing Company in New York at the beginning of the war were nearly lost. The warehouse owner had died in 1917 and unknown to Tanner the pictures were put up at auction and sold. In February, 1919, a friend of Tanner's, J. S. Carpenter, the president of the Des Moines Association of Fine Arts, who had purchased his *Christ Learning to Read* a few years before, saw one of the pictures, a *Holy Family*, on sale at a dealer's in Chicago. Learning that the owner had bought it at auction and wished to remain unknown, Carpenter suspected something irregular and wrote Tanner about it. Through Carpenter's friendly assistance the pictures were ultimately redeemed and two of them purchased by Mr. Carpenter, but the negotiations took many months and were a source of worry and expense to Henry Tanner. It was J. S. Carpenter whose enthusiasm for Tanner's art aroused the interest of Robert C. Vose, of the Vose Galleries in Boston.

Mr. Vose wrote Tanner on September 22, 1919, proposing that he exhibit with them. At this time some Tanners were already being shown in the United States, part of an exhibition by a "Group of American Artists" held at Knoedler's Gallery in New York. Following its close on the 29th of March this exhibition went on circuit to several cities in the Midwest and East, ending at Portland, Maine. It was a great success from the point of view of attendance and press coverage, but sales were few, for people in America were not yet spending money in the lavish manner that was to become characteristic of the twenties.

During the summer of 1920 a Tanner was also shown at The Museum of History, Science and Art in Los Angeles. In the same show were paintings by Gari Melchers, Robert Henri, Childe Hassam, E. W. Redfield, and William M. Chase, but the honors went to H. O. Tanner for his *Daniel in the Lions' Den,* his Salon success of 1896. The painting had just been purchased by Mr. and Mrs. William Preston Harrison and was temporarily on loan to the museum, although it was to become part of the Harrison Collection of Contemporary American Art.

> As soon as the proposed addition to the Museum is made and a permanent and fitting gallery to house the collection is ready, this painting, together with several others, among them the E. W. Redfield now being shown in the present exhibition and the lovely bronze "Bacchante" by Frederick

MacMonnies, also recently purchased and loaned for the present, will be formally presented to the people of Los Angeles.[1]

In January, 1921, the exhibition at the Vose Galleries became a reality, and ten pictures by Tanner were shown in Boston. Most were prewar pictures, but among them was one done by Tanner during the war that was unrelated to military activities, a small picture entitled *Home of Jeanne d'Arc*, possibly the one that Lieutenant Harrison had hoped to buy.

In August and September Tanner was represented by his *Christ Washing the Disciples' Feet* in an unusual art exhibition in New York City. This exhibition, held in the public rooms of the 135th Street branch of the New York Public Library, had been arranged by a group of prominent Negro citizens. It consisted of 198 works of art by Negro artists. It was not the first art exhibition by Negroes in New York. In 1912 there had been one by the "colored students of greater New York" and in 1915 one by "colored folk," sponsored by the Phi Beta Sigma fraternity. But the 1921 exhibit was larger and more comprehensive than the two earlier ones and marked a milestone in the American Negro's bid for cultural equality.

Tanner's contribution to this exhibition is evidence of his continuing interest in promoting Negro achievements in America. His interest was not limited to art; he had been for a number of years a loyal member of the National Association for the Advancement of Colored People. He and W. E. Burghardt DuBois were friends and had discussed, both in New York and Paris, the problems of the Negro in America. DuBois had the greatest admiration for Tanner. In his *Gift of the Black Folk* he called him "one of the leading painters of the world," as well as the "dean" of the group of young Negro artists then rising in the United States—a group that included Edwin Harleston, Richard Brown, and Laura Wheeler.[2]

1. *Bulletin of the Museum of History, Science and Art*, 1, 4 (July, 1920, p. 25.

2. *The Gift of Black Folk* (Boston: The Stratford Co., 1924), p. 313.

All Negroes who knew of Tanner felt a pride in his success, but artists were his most ardent admirers. In 1922 a group of Negro artists and art teachers in Washington, D. C., honored him by organizing a Tanner Art League, which sponsored an extensive Negro art exhibition, including paintings by Tanner himself, in the studios of Dunbar High School. The Tanner Art League was merely one expression of the emerging solidarity of Negro thought in the twenties, a solidarity to which Henry Tanner had unconsciously contributed. To Bishop Tanner, who years before had worried about Henry's selection of art as a career, this was a matter of heartfelt satisfaction. In 1922 he was eighty-seven years old and within a year of his death; he had not seen Henry since before the war.

Bishop Tanner died in January, 1923, the last of Henry's and Jessie's parents to pass away. John Olssen, after spending the war years in relative safety in Paris, went to visit Elna in 1921 and died while with her in New York. His body was cremated and, at his own direction, the ashes brought back to France and buried in the cemetery at Sceaux next to the remains of his wife. His death cast a shadow over the Tanner household.

Jessie herself was not in very good health. Though her spirits were still full of the old gaiety, she found that since the war her strength was greatly depleted. Yet the summer of 1921 was a happy one. She and Henry had sold "Les Charmes" the year before to Mrs. Urzalz, of Darien, Connecticut, and were in the new home they had built which they called "Edgewood." Like "Les Charmes" it was beautifully situated amid tall pines and had a lovely garden.

Few of the old artist crowd had come back to Trépied after the war, but the Tanners had their usual round of summer visitors. Among them was the daughter of Wesley Clifford, Henry Tanner's old colleague at Clark University in Atlanta. Margaret Clifford was in France with a group of French teachers at the invitation of the French government to see the destruction of war and to encourage American contributions toward restoration work. She spent a week with the Tanners, and a letter from her mother to Jessie expresses some of the pleasure that Margaret felt at their hospitality.

> Already she has written most delightful things about you all. What elixir do you use for she says you look no older than when you were here? She also said she felt as though she had known you all her life which shows that a real spirit of friendship prevailed. She has the greatest admiration for Mr. Tanner, of course, and Jesse very brilliant and full of promise. We were so pleased to think he was to come to Columbia, and yet your new plan is better, for Columbia is a big place and really more of a graduate school so that a youngster (begging Jesse's pardon) is lost for a while. And the Atlantic is horribly broad when one wants to get home in a hurry.

The "new plan" mentioned by Mrs. Clifford was Jesse's decision to attend Cambridge University in England, a decision made possible by Atherton Curtis, who took the financial responsibility for Jesse's education. It was Jesse's intention to become a mining engineer.

It may have been a desire to be home for Jesse's first Christmas vacation from Cambridge that made his mother decide not to accompany her husband on his next trip to America, a trip necessitated by an exhibition he was to have at the Grand Central Art Galleries in New York. But before he left they received some wonderful news. Jessie heard it first, for Henry was not at home the afternoon some of their French acquaintances dropped by to say they had seen a notice in the *Journal Officiel* that "Ah O Tannaire" had been made a chevalier of the Legion of Honor for his work as an artist. "We thought it must be your husband," they said. A belated letter in the post office at Etaples confirmed the news. This citation by the French government was considered by Tanner to be the greatest honor of his career.

Henry sailed for the United States toward the end of December, and while on shipboard he wrote a long letter to his two "Jessies."

Sunday—I started this letter on a little piece of paper and will now continue it on S.S. paper—when I commenced it was not yet out—but it seemed better or safest to use all the time that I felt like writing in writing.

Sunday aft.——

The weather keeps not bad, if anything a little better than this morning. You know after all—the company did very well by us. We left the G. St. Lazare at 3.45, seats reserved. In each reserved seat was a buffet box lunch—very, very nice, wine and water, beef, ham, cheese and a sweet. We arrived at Cherbourg near 11 o'clock, an omnibus took us and our small baggage to Hotel, awakened at 5½ and coffee and rolls and butter. All this gratis. We only paid R.R. fare from Paris to Cherbourg (2nd Class 52 frcs.) So while they charge you enough initially—they are not all the time adding to it with little pin pricks of charges.

Monday—

It quieted down a little yesterday aft. and I took advantage of it to have a good dinner, roast duck, celery, etc., ice cream. This morning it is however a little rougher, but by quite a little management I am still all O.K. Sunday morning when we got on the boat I saw a big commotion on the dock and went to see what was up. I found them distributing letters and telegrams and unexpectedly received one too, from my dear Jessies (can't guess how it ought to be written). It is quite mild today. I hope you both are keeping warm. If we had anthracite I would feel more sure.

Xmas day

The weather still keeps good, and I am therefore all right. My room has again been changed and I am now in a room with one other man (whom I have not seen so far) instead of with 3 others—It was too crowded. It is now 2.30 by Trépied time and I see you—I hope—having a good time—I hope you are comfortable. Such quantities of food and good food, and such terrible waste—How I would enjoy having you both with me—I am sure you would do justice to a good table—In the dining room is a Christmas tree with electric lights and glistening silver tinsel—pretty but not much like on shore, after all. We have dinner tonight. We make about 330 to 350 miles a day—They could make easily more and get in Jan 1st but as Customs are closed, it would do no good. So we expect to get in Wednesday Jan 2nd.

Wednesday

As you will see by enclosed menu, I had a very good dinner, put on my dress suit, because I am sure my Jessies would have wanted it, went to dance at 9 o'clock and stayed till midnight. The weather had gotten a little heavy and since 3 a.m. we have been pitching a little, but she does not roll at all. Had my breakfast all right though dining-room a little thin.

Thursday and Friday

Yesterday (that was Thursday) weather got suddenly rather rough and with a little respite has continued today with such rough weather—I have never before been on my feet. I went out on deck a little while and the great waves were terrifying and now while I am writing it is rough. So far I have not lost a meal, though I eat carefully. Day after Xmas I ate a big piece of Xmas cake and it nearly laid me up for repairs.

Saturday

It is now 5 minutes after 8 p.m. Trépied time or 5.30 on shipboard. We have had all kinds of weather in the last 24 hours. I mean bad weather and even a little sunlight—but it has grown much colder nearing the Banks—I am growing used to it and it is rough. I am not unhappy (until I have some more paper, aurevoir)

Sunday

We are one week aboard today. We only made 262 miles yesterday—headwinds and high seas, and it is now blowing "great guns" off Newfoundland—if it keeps on we will hardly arrive Wednesday as we have expected. Had church service this morning and I went. I have met a lady who seems to know my work. It snowed this morning and is getting cold. I shall write a little more when it is quieter. (D.V.)

Monday New Years Eve

At last the bad weather seems gone and are bowling along hoping to get to N. Y. Wednesday aft. So far I have been to the table to every meal.

Tuesday Jan. 1st 1924

This is to hope you have a pleasant though quiet New Year. I have kept Trépied time so that I knew when your New Year came in. On shipboard it was the Captains dinner, afterwards a dance and a very ladened "buffet"—Sorry you two were not here—The cold in my head which I had at Trépied is gone. Have met some people who knew my work.—I hope to mail this tomorrow afternoon to you to Trépied in New York—and I should think if there is a fast steamer leaving Thursday or Saturday you should get it before leaving T.

I hope Geology and Crystology have gone to your satisfaction. It seems a long while since I saw you, and should pictures go well you can be assured it will not be long before I wend my way homeward. About 40 or 45 passengers—17 different nationalities so the Captain said last night. Among them 2 young men Italian and Swiss engineers but mechanical and civil engineers.—There seem to be plenty of engineers but few "mining"—and I now know why,—I shall very likely only add a word or so upon my arrival (D.V.) in NY tomorrow.

Since writing the above have received a Radio from Elna: "Happy New Year Will meet you Elna Charles"

Jan. 2nd

We are now nearing New York and this may be sealed up and sent off without further ado.

With my love to you two and hoping you all are O.K. Cold

HENRY

At the end of his letter he added a note in pencil:

> *Elna and Charles met me at dock and took me home in a big Cadillac. I am staying at Hotel Lafayette. Charles and Elna had engaged a room for me—Saw Barrie and go again today.*
>
> *Love*
> HENRY

"Barrie" was Mr. Erwin S. Barrie, director of the Grand Central Art Galleries. Tanner's relationship to this organization was relatively new and was considered by the galleries to be a feather in their cap, for, as Walter Ufer, the painter, remarked to Mr. Barrie at the time of Tanner's acceptance of membership, "Tanner is an international ace."[3]

His exhibition at the Grand Central Art Galleries in February, 1924, did nothing to contradict this judgment. Because of it, as well as his election to the Legion of Honor, a few of Tanner's artist-friends were inspired to write letters to Robert W. DeForest, president of the Metropolitan Museum of Art, urging him to consider acquiring a Tanner for the Metropolitan. As Harrison Morris put it:

> France has just given her testimony with the Legion of Honor, and has two of Tanner's earlier pictures in the Luxembourg.
>
> Ought we over here in his home to be less sensible to his merit?

The following year Atherton Curtis gave a *Sodom and Gomorrah* by Henry Tanner to the Metropolitan Museum.[4]

Henry Tanner remained in New York until late March, living most of the time in Brooklyn, where he rented a studio.

3. Related to me by Mr. Barrie, director of the Grand Central Art Galleries, New York.

4. *Metropolitan Museum Bulletin*, 20, no. 11 (November, 1925): 275. The picture was subsequently disposed of by the Metropolitan Museum, but no record exists as to its present whereabouts.

He also visited members of his family in Philadelphia and, while there, went down to Swarthmore to give Margaret Clifford Bryant a little picture of *Etaples* as a wedding present.

During his stay in New York he was interviewed by Jessie Fauset, who wrote an article about him for the *Crisis*, the magazine of the NAACP. She described him at that time as a tall, slender man with grizzled hair and a "chuckling" sense of humor who was fond of wearing gray.

> Henry Ossawa Tanner is of all the great men who have achieved, undoubtedly the least affected and the least conscious of personal glory.[5]

Two important commissions were given Tanner during his stay in the United States. One was from Bethel Church in Philadelphia for a bronze tablet, and a small replica of it, commemorating Richard Allen, founder of the African Methodist Church. The other was a painting, *Nicodemus Coming to Christ*, to hang in the Cheyney Training School for Teachers at Cheyney, Pennsylvania. Both were to be major works of art and, accordingly, to pay very well. But both were doomed to cause Henry Tanner great unhappiness: the first because Bethel Church retracted on its commitments, after Tanner had fulfilled his; the last because of personal tragedy, which made painting for a time difficult, if not impossible.

Henry returned to France by late spring and was delighted to be reunited with his family. Summer was always the most beautiful season of the year at Trépied, and the summer of 1924 was especially lovely. An old artist-friend of Tanner's, Charles H. Pepper, and his wife, from Concord, Massachusetts, visited the Tanners in June and in Pepper's letter of thanks wrote of "those pleasant days and the talks and rides and friends" that gave them so much pleasure.

In August Jessie went on a little trip to England with Elna and Charles. While on their travels "Aunt Elna" wrote Jesse

5. "Henry Ossawa Tanner," *Crisis*, 27 (April, 1924): 255, 256.

a card from Cambridge, where the three of them were having luncheon, and commented, "Your mother returns to France tonight."

Jessie found that she tired easily, but thought it due to extended war-weariness. Neither she nor Henry dreamed there was anything seriously wrong. They had always had so much happiness and so much luck, that it seemed impossible anything could darken the bright years they believed still lay ahead of them.

Time of Change

Life at Trépied was never to be what it had been before the war. An artists' colony still existed, and Henry and Jessie, in their lovely new home, enjoyed their many friends in and around Etaples. But something was missing. Many of the old crowd did not return, and those who did were less in step with the times. The war had left in its wake a cynicism that was unknown in the old days.

The change was not regional. All of France was affected. The war had been a traumatic experience, and old values were upset. In Paris, in the Latin Quarter, it was difficult on the surface to see what made the difference. Foreigners had returned in greater numbers than ever, and writers, artists, and the usual hangers-on of art overflowed the academies and were as conspicuous as formerly at the Rotonde and the Coupole. The physical appearance of the city—the gay boulevards, the flower-bordered parks, the sidewalk cafés—was the same, but there was a new pretentiousness, a multiplication of barrooms, a noisiness, a so-called "Americanization" that grated on the sensibilities of the old timers who had known prewar Paris. Sisley Huddleston reflected on the old atmosphere in his book, *Bohemian Literary and Social Life in Paris.*

> Montparnasse was, not many years ago, a quiet suburb, in which the artists lived almost a village life. When I first knew the Rotonde, for example, it was a tiny, low-ceilinged room in which poor folk gathered to while away the hours. There was hardly space for two score of us. We played chess, we smoked, we sketched, we talked. We were ambitious and confident in our future, but in the meantime our pockets were empty, and we would linger over our little horseshoe-shaped rolls and our black coffee, and speak comfortingly to each other out of the thick clouds of tobacco.[1]

Ambroise Vollard, the picture dealer, wrote feelingly of the changed atmosphere:

> The new Montparnasse was a Babel, where the painters for the most part talked in dollars, piastres, pesetas, kroner, pounds sterling. What a contrast with their elders, who painted simply for the joy of painting. Not only the snobs and profiteers had "gone in for painting," the more enlightened collectors were no less ardent in their pursuit of the artists.[2]

Art as well as the tempo of life was changed. The former rebels—Picasso, Dufy, Chagall, Matisse, Braque, and all the prewar "*nouveaux*"—were becoming the leaders in the art world of Paris. World War I did not create a new set of art values, but it did lay to rest those of the academicians. In 1924 Leo Stein wrote:

1. Sisley Huddleston, *Bohemian Literary and Social Life in Paris* (London: George C. Harrap and Co., 1928), pp. 149–50.
2. *Recollections of a Picture Dealer* (Boston: Little Brown and Co., 1936), p. 310.

> The change in balance between the Academy and the insurgents is so remarkable that whereas twenty years ago everyone knew the names of the great "official" painters, men like Jean-Paul Laurens, Bonnat, Carolus-Duran, Benjamin-Constant and Roll, today no one knew [*sic*] whether there are such, and when I asked a number of painters the other day to name some, no one could give me any other name than Besnard.[3]

The older painters were not happy with the transformation. Gilbert White, who had lived in Paris in the old days, expressed the bitterness that many of them felt:

> When I was a student in Paris, we lived in the Latin Quarter and never crossed the river. In those days it took two hours to reach the Etoile, and we had too much work to spend so much time on travelling. But then our ideas were entirely different. We considered an exhibition was the crowning effort of a man's work, the result of years of study and labor. Now, young painters begin by gathering up a sufficient number of indifferent canvases, to give an exhibition. The basic training is lacking. Besides, everybody is analysing, with the result that painters are self-conscious. What they produce is affected, and honestly done work is rare. Few modern painters measure up to the despised artists of the Eighteenth Century. They knew anatomy, they understood how to work, even if they did choose banal subjects, whereas the artists of today have neither the inspiration or the technique.[4]

The atmosphere of postwar Paris was not one to inspire religious art. New religious symbols, sadly needed in a world lately emerged from a holocaust, were notable for their absence. In 1920 at the Salon of the Société Nationale a section was given over to *tableaux de piété*, but the pictures for the most part were puerile efforts to inject a contemporary spirit into old forms. Artists resorted to such devices as angels with tri-

3. "A New Salon in Paris," *New Republic*, July 30, 1924, p. 271.
4. Huddleston, *Bohemian Life in Paris*, p. 161.

color wings supporting the dead from the Battle of the Marne and offering them to God. Or Christ carrying his cross on top of the trenches, showing heroes how to die. Supernatural visions were no longer needed, presumably because they were no longer believed in.

Henry Tanner shunned these false heroics as well as the new styles of art that blossomed in the uninhibited atmosphere of postwar Paris and continued to paint the traditional themes that had borne him successfully to his peak of popularity. In his sixties he was not apt to follow a new path. Yet his art was not static. He made no innovations but carried to further development trends begun before the war. His forms became more ghostlike, his colors more suggestive of the mysticism that, to him, was the essence of life. He painted slowly and laboriously, which he believed was the practice of most good artists.

> As to the making of a picture after it has been conceived, it seems to me that they all go through nearly the same stages. A "brilliant idea," a great rush, great excitement, great pleasure in work. Then one by one the great hopes you have had vanish, the various qualities you knew you were going to get fail to materialize, the lights go out—what misery—then it is that determination to succeed has to be evoked, work is a "drudge"—but again light begins to appear and with it a picture, sometimes quite a little different in details from your original idea, but one on which work is a pleasure.

In the United States during these postwar years, Tanner's stock was very high. Money was plentiful, pictures were in demand, and "modern art," that had been introduced to Americans at the Armory Show in 1913, had not yet seized the public's imagination and submerged in its popularity the more traditional forms of art.

Tanner's affiliations with the Grand Central Art Galleries

and with dealers throughout the Midwest gave his pictures a good market. Yet he was not a rich man, and it may have been to save money, since he had agreed to go to Chicago later in the year in connection with a new exhibition, that he did not accompany his wife on her trip to New York in January, 1925. A friend, probably Atherton Curtis, wishing to spare Jessie as much red tape as possible, obtained a letter from the consul general in Paris to the inspector of customs in New York introducing her as the wife of Henry Tanner, "a very prominent American artist."

> Mrs. Tanner has not visited the United States in the past fourteen years and assures me that she does not maintain any residence in the United States and is only taking with her personal effects, wearing apparel, etc., which are absolutely necessary and appropriate for her use during her sojourn of three months in America, after which she will return to her home in Paris.

Jessie's illness turned out to be more serious than anyone had anticipated. She suffered from what was diagnosed as acute pleurisy and seemed unable to gather the necessary strength to combat her ailment. She underwent treatment in New York, and a telegram sent from Elna to Henry on March 11 was heartening: "Progressing wonderfully." Ten days later he received another: "Responded beautifully latest treatment expect leaving hospital ten days."

This was wonderful news to Henry, who believed the worst was over. On April 2, probably the day she left the hospital, he cabled: "Jessie God Bless You."

Jessie received other messages, rejoicing at her successful recovery. One friend wrote:

> Your lucky star has been with you, Jessie dear! . . . Yes, I should think you would long for your nearest and dearest, for the beauty of your own little place, with its simplicity, sweet perfumes and quiet.

Chapter Fourteen

Jessie did long to get home. She had told the Cliffords, who had gone to New York to see her at Elna's, that she would pay them a visit before returning to Trépied, but she decided to forego this and get home as quickly as possible. She sailed for Boulogne from New York on the *Rotterdam* on May 2.

For a brief time she was better, but on June 9 Atherton Curtis wrote to Henry:

> Your letter has come and I don't need to tell you how dreadfully sorry we both are and Miss Oliver too to hear that Jessie is having more trouble. We do most sincerely hope that she will show improvement in a few days and not have to undergo another operation. . . .
>
> We don't know how much Jessie's sister may be helping you out in money matters so we do not know just what to say or do ourselves. We are afraid that you may be finding yourself in some difficulties as regards money if Mrs. Tough is not helping you out. We supposed that she paid the expenses of Jessie's illness when she was in New York though you did not say so. At all events, whether she did or did not, it may be that she is not helping now since she supposes Jessie is all right. Now, Henry, you must tell us frankly if you need help and we will do what we can. You know that we should not want to see you in money difficulties and especially at such a time as this.

Jessie's condition continued to grow worse, and Henry took her to the hospital at Berck-Plage, where she could get better care than at Trépied. He remained constantly at her side. Jesse too was with his mother, but in early September he made a brief trip to Bourron to see the Curtises at their summer home near Fontainebleau. While he was there he received a telegram from his father telling him to come back at once. The following day, September 8, Jessie Tanner died. Her son remembers that a few hours before she passed away she turned to her husband and said, "Henry, I have never regretted one moment of our marriage."[5] Jessie was buried beside her mother and father in the cemetery at Sceaux.

Letters of condolence poured in from all sides to Henry and Jesse, from French and English and American friends at Boulogne and Etaples and Paris and London and from friends and relatives across the sea, including the Cliffords and Henry's old friend and benefactor, Bishop Hartzell, now retired and living near his son in Ohio. But perhaps no letter came that was written with greater feeling than the one from Atherton Curtis.

DEAR HENRY AND JESSE,

There are times in life when sorrows so great come that one does not know what to say to those who are suffering. I feel that such a time has come to you now and I am so overwhelmed by the thought of what you are both going through that I do not know what to say. . . .

Atherton and Ingeborg both wanted Henry and Jesse to come to them at Bourron, though Atherton said he would not press the point, for Henry might not wish to come just then, "but you know that you will be welcome if you want to come."

There is no question that Jessie Tanner—sweet, outgoing, and affectionate—endeared herself to everyone who knew her. But her most outstanding trait, to those who knew her best, was her devotion to her husband. As Elizabeth Clifford wrote to Henry, referring to her last brief visit with Jessie:

> Her face lighted up as she talked with me in New York of "Henry and Jesse" and it was easy to see that she lived for you and loved you both with a love rare among women.

Jessie's death left a vacuum in Henry Tanner's life that was

5. Jesse O. Tanner to me, May 6, 1966, Archives of American Art, Detroit.

never to be filled. Although he did his best to work, for months he found himself incapable of it. In May he had received a letter from Leslie Pinckney Hill, the principal of the Cheyney Training School of Teaching, asking about the commission, *Nicodemus Coming to Christ.* "We have been hoping that you might be able to let us have this painting towards the end of the present year." But Henry could not work. His son Jesse was his only consolation, but Jesse, who had completed his work at Cambridge University, was now finishing his education at the London School of Mines.

Tanner's unhappiness was increased the September of Jessie's death by the loss of two old friends, the artists Henry Boddington and Paul Bartlett. Henry Boddington, especially, had been very close to him and Jessie. With his death, at seventy-six, was gone one of the strongest links with the past.

In October Henry received a letter from Ellen Cohn, an artist he had known many years, suggesting he join a party going to Spain. "It would be delightful if you could come and I fancy it would help you through a gloomy winter." But Tanner felt no inclination to go. And he took little interest in the exhibition held in October and November at the Gallerie Charpentier of the work of twelve "American Artists in France," including Frederick Frieseke, Walter Gay, Alexander Harrison, and H. O. Tanner. His faith and the devoted affection of Atherton and Ingeborg Curtis were the source of what little strength he had, but it was little indeed. The trip he planned to Chicago was never made.

Yet Tanner was not completely unaware of other needs besides his own. On December 31, 1925, James Weldon Johnson, secretary of the National Association for the Advancement of Colored People, wrote him from New York:

MY DEAR MR. TANNER,

It was especially gratifying to us to receive your contribution of twenty-five dollars to the Legal Defense Fund which we are establishing. I think that the published report of your contribution stimulated others to give.

I know you will be gratified to learn that we have reached the $50,000 goal; in fact, we have passed it. It is probable that the Fund will reach $60,000 before the contributions cease.

I hope that you are quite well and that it will not be long before you will visit the United States again.

With best wishes, I am
Yours sincerely,
JAMES WELDON JOHNSON,
SECRETARY

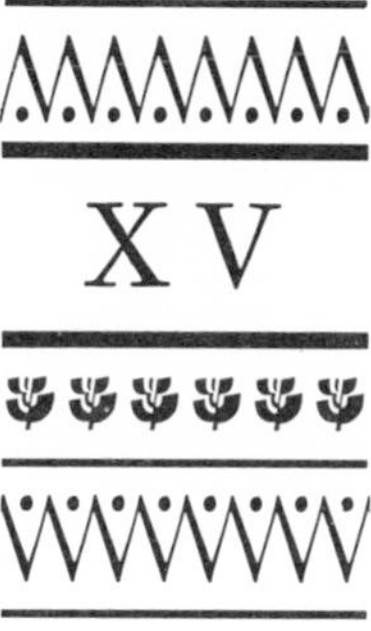

XV

Years of Stress

THE THREE THINGS THAT FOR SO MANY YEARS GAVE MEANING to Henry Tanner's life—his wife, his art, and his son—were, with Jessie's death, reduced to two. His art, however, had always been a heavy drain on his emotions, and after Jessie died the physical strength from which it drew was greatly diminished. He found that he could work only a few hours at a time without suffering complete exhaustion, and there were times when he could not work at all.

When Jesse left for England in the fall of 1925, following his mother's death, Henry returned to his studio on the Boulevard St. Jacques, unwell in body and spirit. At Christmastime Jesse went with him to the Riviera, where it was hoped the warmth and sunshine would restore his general well-being. The change of climate seemed to help him, and when Jesse's vacation ended, Henry stayed on. He had rather thought he might go to the United States in the spring, but as the months passed he felt unable to make the trip. A letter to the Cliffords in January reflects his feelings of this period:

NICE, ALPES MARITIMES
Jan'y 24, 1926

MY DEAR CLIFFORD, MRS. CLIFFORD AND MARGARET,

I should have answered your kind letter a long while ago—but I have written to no one not even my sister Mary.

There is little to be said. I have been far from well myself and came here with Jesse a few days after Xmas—he has now returned to the university—he has 5 months more and I shall be very glad. I shall not come over as soon as I expected, this depending somewhat on my ability to work.

We have beautiful sunlight here and I am better. I may stay a few weeks longer or I may return to Paris soon. I do not know.

Hope you all keep well, especially that grandson.

Believe me, as ever,
HENRY TANNER[1]

In June, 1926, Tanner was again at Trépied with Jesse, whose work at the London School of Mines was now completed and who had accepted a position in London with the geophyscial department of the Anglo-Persian Oil Company. Henry did not look forward to the separation from his son, but he could have borne the idea more cheerfully had he not been concerned about Jesse's health. Jesse had always been a fine athlete, but his father noted that he was unnaturally tired a great deal of the time. There was no indication of organic trouble, however, and after a summer at Trépied he seemed better. Tanner too was almost his old self. He was painting with greater regularity and was interested in some

1. Tanner to Clifford, January 24, 1926, Atlanta University, Atlanta, Ga.

exhibitions that were to be held in New York. Atherton referred optimistically to Henry's health in October:

> We are glad to know that you are really better and that your tension has become normal. There isn't any "nearly normal," as you say in your letter, because I am told that tension varies a little in different people. I am sorry that Jesse is not well but I suppose it is only natural that after working so hard for five years in England he should be tired. I hope that he will soon be all right again.

Although Tanner had his personal worries professionally he had every reason to be pleased. In January, 1927, for the first time since the war his pictures were on display in New York City, and while the response was not as enthusiastic as it had been in years past, the reviews were laudatory.

> One of the rooms at the Grand Central Art Galleries is occupied by a group of pictures by H. O. Tanner. Mr. Tanner rarely exhibits in America. He has lived for many years in France, and the last exhibition of his pictures held in New York was at Knoedler's something like ten years ago. Mr. Tanner still cultivates the field of religious subjects which have always been his specialty, a specialty in which in these days he finds little competition.
>
> The artist's work seems to have changed hardly at all since his last appearance here. He still sticks to the cool color arrangements, in which blue predominates, and within its limited range plays slight variations in closely related tone and color.
>
> In the Oriental scenes and the heavily swathed figures, bathed in an unearthly light, he expresses the mood of brooding mysticism that has always been the keynote of his work.[2]

In February Tanner was represented at another New York exhibition, this one at the National Arts Club Galleries in Gramercy Park. His painting, *At the Gates*, was singled out

2. *New York World*, January 27, 1927.

for the National Arts Club bronze medal and a prize of $250, honors that no doubt contributed to his election in the spring of 1927 to full academician in the National Academy of Design.

Tanner also resumed work in March on the commission he had undertaken of *Nicodemus Coming to Christ.* The principal of the Cheyney Training School, on being informed of this, was deeply gratified.

> It is a very great joy to all of us to know that you are again at work and that we may be looking forward to the completion of our picture within a few months. I am immediately notifying the Richard Humphreys Foundation at Philadelphia through the President of our Board of Trustees, Mr. James G. Biddle, and I am certain that they will join us in the pleasant emotions stirred up by this expectation in which you are encouraging us.

James Biddle expressed regret that Tanner felt he would be unable to come to the United States for the presentation of the picture.

> Perhaps, however, when the time comes, you will feel differently about it—and I want you to appreciate how much it would mean to all of us to be introduced to the picture by the master who painted it.

But Tanner did not feel up to the trip, and the picture was delivered in May from New York by the Grand Central Art Galleries. In return he received a bank draft for $3,000.

Times were good in America in the twenties and apparently getting better all the time. Charles Tough assessed the situation for Henry shortly before the "crash" in the following words:

> The whole city and in fact the whole country is like a baccarat room at Le Touquet. Everyone from boot blacks up is taking a hand at gambling. I shudder to think what would happen if a big and sudden break were to come.

But few people expected a break, and art works found a ready market. Tanner made arrangements with Carson, Pirie, Scott in 1927 to display his pictures at their large Chicago department store, an outlet that seemed to offer promising sales. And in 1928 J. S. Carpenter, in Des Moines, wrote cheerfully of sales in the Midwest.

Because of "good times" Tanner was urged by his friends in America to come to the United States. Carpenter believed the trip would encourage him to work at a faster pace.

> You have a great place in the art world, and I feel that from now on you will do your greatest work, and I hope you will feel that you owe to the world as many of your pictures as you possibly can paint.

His brother-in-law, Charles Tough, thought a trip to the United States would bring Tanner's name before the public and thereby increase his sales. He and Elna visited Henry at Trépied during the summer of 1928, and the following was written on his return:

> I do want to tell you once more how much enjoyment I got from my stay with you. It is no exaggeration to say that it has been the most enjoyable summer trip I have ever made. Being in your home and genial presence was a constant enjoyment. . . .
>
> I am sure you are on the track to turn out pictures regularly as you used to and I am also sure you will find a good market for them in your prosperous native land. We will benefit incidentally by seeing you more often in New York. As I have said to you before, there is nothing like having the author or maker on the spot to sell the product. I am sure when you get over this Fall you will sell the few you have completed and then you can come over every Fall or at least every second and you can be putting money in the bank instead of steadily drawing it out.

There was one person, however, who did not think of Tanner's visit to the United States in terms of money or professional advancement. This was his sister Mary. Although she and her older brother had seen relatively little of each other during their lives, there was an intuitive bond between them that endured through their long years of separation. She understood better than anyone that Henry did not wish to leave France, and she did not urge him to do so.

> I never, however, forget you and while I am sure you feel more like over there is home than you do here, I cannot keep the wish out of mind that you could be home here. But this is not the way of the world. It would be a strange world if families stayed huddled together.

His sister's letters did not refer to the changes that were taking place in America in regard to the Negro. But changes were taking place, albeit slowly. Tanner's friend, John Nail, wrote him from New York:

> Negro artists are getting considerable recognition. A man named Motley from Chicago has just had a one-man show at the New Gallery, and received very favorable newspaper criticism.
>
> O. Richard Reid specializes in portraits. He has painted a portrait of John Barrymore in the character of Hamlet for the United Artists Association and also Mr. George Arliss is sitting for a portrait in the character of Shylock.
>
> In fact, in all the arts, the Negro is forging ahead.

Nevertheless, Tanner knew that gifted Negroes who could afford it still preferred the freer atmosphere of Europe. Among those who had found a haven in Paris was the poet, Countee Cullen. He and his wife visited Tanner at Trépied during the late summer of 1928.

> 4 rue du Parc de Montsouris
> Paris, France
> *Sept. 23, 1928*
>
> My dear Mr. Tanner,
>
> *I have been waiting before dropping you a note of thanks for your kindness to us, until I should have received proofs*

to send you of the pictures taken at your place. Both my wife and I are extremely indebted to you for the hospitality of a most enjoyable weekend.

We know you will be busy on your return to Paris, but we hope you will allow us to see a little of you off and on during the winter. We want very much to have you visit our little apartment, and hope it will be soon after you return to Paris.

Very sincerely yours,
COUNTEE CULLEN

While older expatriates like Henry Tanner and Atherton Curtis felt themselves less at home in Paris than in the old days, there was still much to enjoy. Atherton found his print collecting as absorbing as ever and, with the monetary exchange in his favor, wrote Henry in high spirits about his acquisitions.

BOURRON, S. ET M.
June 29, 1928

DEAR HENRY,

. . . *We got the things that I wanted most at the Deltiel sale and had to pay something in the way of prices too. The chief things that I wanted I divided by giving orders to the two dealers and as I did not bid myself, people did not know what I wanted. I bid myself on one Corot and lost it. Le Garrec, the expert of the sale, said he already had a bid on it and preferred to have me do my own bidding. I suspected that it might be for M. Thomas, one of the big collectors, and watched his face during the bidding. I could see from his expression that he was the man who was against me and so dropped it at 6000 fr. for bidding against him is uphill work. I told him afterwards that he got a beautiful impression and that I could see from his face that Le Garrec was bidding for him. Do you remember that last winter I just missed getting a Zorn nude which a small dealer had for sale at 3000 fr.? I saw it in his catalogue and telephoned at once but another collector had got in ahead of me. Well, one was sold in the Deltiel sale for 65000 fr. which makes over 77000 fr. with the 19½% tax added. The dealer who sold his for 3000 fr. must feel sick and the collector must be chuckling. I may add that I didn't buy the one in the Deltiel sale.*

We are having lovely weather and I hope that you are having as good. If you are, I should think you might leave off your sweater. The thermometer is 28 in the shade outside our window at this moment. . . .

I hope that news from Jesse continues good. This weather ought to keep him warm, if nothing else. I should think it might be 60 or more down his way.

I enclose a cheque for 3500 fr. plus Jeannette's studio rent and money for the concierge. . . .

Much love from us both and our love to Jesse when you write,

Atherton

Because of pressure from his friends in America, each fall Henry Tanner planned a trip to America, and each spring, to their great disappointment, he postponed it to some future date. His excuse was invariably his health. While it is true that his health was not good, there was a more important reason for not making the trip, a reason that only Atherton and Ingeborg Curtis fully appreciated. This was Jesse. Henry's fears in regard to his son's health had been substantiated. In October, 1926, Jesse was forced to give up his work with the Anglo-Persian Oil Company and return home because of nervous exhaustion. There was nothing wrong with him that time and care could not remedy, but in the meantime he needed quiet and rest. For the next few years Tanner's own health problems were compounded by concern over his son's health.

Tanner had to spare himself all unnecessary fatigue in order to work as efficiently as possible to help Jesse over this crisis in his young life. In March, 1928, much to his sorrow, he was unable to participate in the memorial service in Paris given for his early benefactor, Rodman Wannamaker, who died on March 9 at the age of sixty-five. But Tanner did not forget his old friends, as may be seen in a letter from the man most responsible for his residence in France—Bishop Hartzell, now eighty-six years old.

> Thank you very much for saying that you will make a "small sized portrait of Mrs. Hartzell." I should like to have it as a memento from you. Both of us, as you know, were greatly interested and rejoiced in your remarkable success and if living, you would have her sincere sympathies in all your trials. Take very good care of yourself my dear friend and go slow until you build up physically.

It was his generosity of spirit that endeared Henry to his friends. When Ingeborg was ill during the summer of 1928, Henry, putting aside his own problems and worries, invited her and Atherton to come to Trépied for a visit, thinking she would benefit from the sea air. They could not come but were nonetheless appreciative of his kindness. Ingeborg wrote Henry in September while he was visiting Jesse in a nursing home at Saujon, in central France.

RUE PASTERU, SEPT. 30, 1928
Bourron, S. et M.

DEAR HENRY,

I wish to add to Atherton's my thanks for the invitation to visit you at Trépied. I know that it would mean to you a lot of extra trouble to house and feed us, and it was indeed very kind of you to be willing to disarrange your quiet daily life for us. I am sure the sea air and the lovely pine woods would have done me a lot of good, but as Atherton has already written you, this year it was not possible for us to come.

Yesterday we received your letter written the 17. I am

glad you have gone down to Jesse, it will do him good to see you. . . . It is awfully hard on you both that this illness lasts so long and it must take no end of patience and courage on Jesse's part to spend month after month in inaction when there is so much he would like to do. Fortunately, he inherits from his mother and you a wonderful vitality and an inherent love of life, and that will help him more than anything. . . .

We are all well. I have improved a great deal these last months. . . .

Atherton will write soon. We hope to hear from you and Jesse soon and to have good news.

Love from us both to you two.
Affectionately,
Ingeborg

Henry and his son spent many months at Saujon and in southern France during the winter of 1928–29, and Ingeborg and Atherton showed great concern and affection for them in their letters.

Paris, Jan. 22, 1929

Dear Henry,

We were very glad to get your letter yesterday, we had begun to worry a bit about you both because we heard nothing from you and we had decided to telephone to Saujon after supper last night but at noon we received your letter. . . .

I don't wonder that Jesse feels he has had hard luck lately. There is no denying that he has, but that certainly does not prove that he always will have bad luck, and from all that you say (as for instance that J. bicycled 11 kilometers the other day) it is very evident to me that he is ever so much better and that he is decidedly on the good road towards recovery.

I am sending this to Nice and I hope you will be there soon and that the weather will be everything that it ought to be . . .

Lucy[3] *is well as are the rest of us. Life hums along in its usual way with little ups and downs, on the whole perhaps more ups than downs.*

We both send you both our love, and we wish you good health, and good weather and a very pleasant time in everyway. I hope you will enjoy your painting, Henry. . . .

As ever affectionately,
INGEBORG

Paris, Feb, 3, 1929

DEAR HENRY,

I hope you have found a satisfactory place to stay in and that you are both getting better and having some good weather. After two mild days the thermometer has gone down to three below this morning. . . . Ingeborg is still in bed but very much better with temperature now 36.6 to 37. She still has a trained nurse because a nurse knows better than I what to do for her and how to do it. . . . However, things are getting better now and I hope that Ingeborg will be all right in a few days. She joins me in much love to you both.

Good luck to both of you.

Affectionately,
ATHERTON

Possibly because of Ingeborg's illness little Lucy Curtis, Atherton's niece, was sent with her Nannie to the south of France, and in March, 1929, Henry Tanner made a trip to Juan-les-Pins to see her. In regard to the visit Ingeborg wrote:

We heard from Juan-les-Pins of your nice visit to Lucy. Miss Clausen told me about it at her return and Nannie also wrote about it. It was so nice of you to go over. Nannie and Lucy are planning to send you an invitation to come again

3. Lucy Curtis was the Curtis's niece, the daughter of Atherton Curtis's older brother.

> for a longer call that they have some plans for making happy and festive, but when it will be I don't know, for last night, I am sorry to say, I had a letter from Nannie in which she told us that Lucy has the grippe, she has a sore throat and back of the nose. They seem to have a good doctor, he was not alarmed about Lucy, but I confess that my heart went in my boots when I read that letter. . . .

In her letter Ingeborg referred to Henry's mention of Elna's plan to buy a "place in the south"—presumably, Florida. "I suppose you both feel tempted to buy a little piece of land yourselves in that sunny country," she wrote. But Ingeborg did not seem to take the matter of Henry's leaving France very seriously. It is doubtful whether he did himself.

The summer of 1929 he and Jesse were back at Trépied, enjoying the beauty and quiet of their own home. Ingeborg wrote in July:

> I was glad to hear that you are painting and that Jesse seems better. The times of "going ahead as if he were perfectly well" will surely increase in number as time goes by and finally he will feel altogether his old self.

Art sales in America continued to be good, and what hints of business decline there were, were not taken seriously. J. S. Carpenter wrote Tanner in February, 1929, about his picture *The Three Wise Men:*

> I sold this more than a year and a half ago, and only today have I been able to collect for it. The man I sold it to got caught in the decline of real estate, and I guess was not very flush for the time being, and while I could have had the picture back any time, I felt eventually I would get the money, and it has so turned out. The picture you priced me at $1200.00 and I made this man a discount of twenty-five percent, or a price of $900.
>
> I have the two pictures which you sent me from New York, and I am very happy to have them, and hope to be able to place them for you. Your work is much admired

here, and these two pictures are especially admired. You wanted my opinion on the large one. I think it is a beautiful canvas, and a beautiful feeling in it, and there are some things about it I admire more perhaps, than some of your others. But still I cannot conscientiously cast any reflections on your other pictures. However, I enjoy them all, and this is a very beautiful canvas.

In June he sent Tanner a draft for $897 for the larger picture of the two and in July one for $300 for the other. The last was sold to a Mr. Huttenlocker, who wrote Carpenter: "Two years ago I had no idea I could sit before a picture an entire evening and enjoy it as I have this one."

In July the Grand Central Art Galleries sold two of Tanner's smaller paintings to a businessman in Atlanta, Georgia—J. J. Haverty, vice-president of the Atlanta Art Association. Mr. Haverty was pleased with his purchases and wrote Tanner the following letter:

SIR:

I have recently acquired two paintings of yours, both from the Grand Central Art Galleries of New York,—one entitled "The Road to Emmaus," and the other "At the Gates," which received the National Arts Club prize at a recent exhibition.

Will you please interpret the story of these paintings for me? The one, "At the Gates" is interesting, and I would like to have your idea of it. "On the Road to Emmaus" is an interesting painting, and I am greatly pleased with it. A note or line from you concerning the story of the subjects will be interesting I am sure.

I gave a letter a few days ago to a friend of mine who is going to Paris, an artist from one of the Atlanta newspapers, the Atlanta Constitution, to study art for a year. I called his attention to your paintings, showing him the two pictures to which I refer above. The letter I gave him was to my friend, Mr. Fredrick Frieseke, and in this letter I suggested that Mr. Frieseke invite the bearer, Mr. Lewis C. Gregg, to visit your studio.

I hope you will find time to give this gentleman some of your views upon coloring, in which he is particularly interested, and in which you are particularly distinguished.

Very truly,
J. J. HAVERTY

Public recognition in Atlanta, where he had once lived for two years as an unknown, undoubtedly brought back memories long dormant in Henry Tanner. But he did not refer to them in his correspondence with Mr. Haverty who, at that time, knew nothing of Tanner's early years, possibly not even the fact that he was a Negro.

Before answering Mr. Haverty's request for an interpretation, Tanner had to ascertain just which paintings he had purchased, for the titles of his pictures, even in exhibits, were sometimes changed without his knowledge. He was especially dubious about *At the Gates* and asked to have a photograph of it sent to him. Mr. Haverty sent the photograph along with the following comment:

> I wish you would give me an option to purchase the new painting on the 33 verse of Chapter XXIV of St. Luke, referred to in your letter. I would like to have this painting in my collection with the other two which I now have. I have long wanted a picture on this subject by a good master, and it will please me very much if we can come together on this painting.

Henry Tanner did not realize when he wrote Mr. Haverty, giving him the option, that it would take him several years to finish the painting and that in that time a great financial blight would have settled over the United States. Never a fast worker, the inevitable "slowing down" brought on by age and ill-health, as well as his continued determination to never consider a picture finished until it met his own high standard, made his output very meagre.

It was doubtless for this reason that he did not respond to

a request by Mr. Erwin S. Barrie for a contribution to the Members Prize Exhibition at the Grand Central Art Galleries in October, 1930. Nevertheless, a Tanner—*Etaples Fisher Folk*—was awarded the Walter L. Clark prize of $500, the highest honor in the exhibition given a figure painting. His friend, Mr. Barrie, manager of the galleries, wrote him in explanation:

November 7, 1930

DEAR MR. TANNER,

I was certainly very pleased that the Jury awarded you the Walter L. Clark Prize at our annual show. As a matter of fact I went in the stock room and picked this painting out and entered it in the show so that you would be represented. We will mail you a check in the very near future.

Can't you send us four or five paintings as we are doing our best to represent you here in this country?

With kindest regard I am,
Very sincerely yours,
EDWIN S. BARRIE
MANAGER

The notice of Tanner's prize in the New York newspapers was read with pleasure by his old friends in New York. Among them was his first studio companion in Paris during his "Julien" days, Hermon MacNeil:

December 9, 1930

MY DEAR TANNER,

Just a little reminder that we are occasionally thinking of you, particularly now that the holiday season is on and also that last evening at the Arts Club Round-table dinner I was sitting beside Roy Brown chatting about your own good self. The surprise both he and I had when we both ran across Bontwood up there in your metropolis.

I had hoped things might work out that Mrs. MacNeil and I might come over there and do some work again with the inspiration of your and my other friends' surroundings but fate seems against it for the moment as I am loaded up this winter anyway with several "major jobs" and some minor ones. The things pile in and as long as we are living, I suppose we have to work, provided there is work. In fact the hard times over here although it seems to curtail picture buying, yet the monumental things are so often in preparation with committees for years and culminate most any old time.

I want particularly to congratulate you on your Grand Central Gallery prize which I see by the papers was awarded to you. Also hope this finds not only you but your big boy in good health. . . .

Various of your friends here often speak of you in a most choice way. I will not stop to make you blush at this time. I am simply sending you the most pleasant greetings that I am able to wish for a pleasant holiday in which Mrs. MacNeil very cordially joins.

Ever yours,
H. A. MacNeil

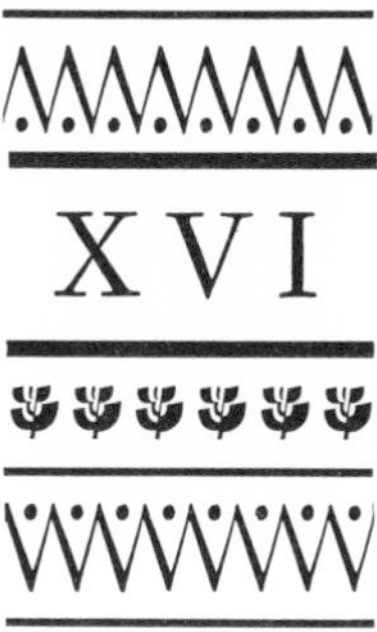

XVI

The Depression

BY 1930 THE AMERICAN COLONY IN PARIS, OF WHICH TANNER had been a part, was a thing of the past. Homer St. Gaudens, in his book *The American Artist and His Times,* referred to the dwindling group. He commented that Frederick Frieseke, one of Tanner's contemporaries who outlived him by only two years, was "the last of that Paris colony that I recall as a boy, the only man to bridge the gap from the early 1900's and the 1920's when I returned to France again."[1]

That St. Gaudens remembered Frieseke as "the only man to bridge the gap" indicates an unconscious overlooking of Tanner as part of the mainstream of American art, for he knew Tanner and mentioned him in his book in connection with the eighteenth-century Negro painter, Joshua Johnston. But there were others he also overlooked, among them Walter

1. *The American Artist and His Times* (New York: Dodd, Mead and Co., 1941), p. 217.

Gay. In 1935 Gay was old, confined to a wheel chair, and living in his magnificent "little Versailles" not far from Fontainebleau. One afternoon in August he and his wife drove over to Bourron to see the Curtises, and Atherton wrote Henry about their visit.

> Mr. and Mrs. Walter Gay came over for tea with us Thursday. They have a place between Barbizon and Melun about 25 kilometers from here. They both admired your paintings greatly and Gay remarked. "Tanner is a great painter." He was much impressed by the landscape "Abraham's Oak" and by the big picture in the little Salon with Christ by the wall of a house. He said of both, "Very beautiful. Beautiful color." He had no reason for saying so much if he had not wanted to. He made no remark at all about Ulmann's picture and I don't wonder particularly at that. Well, at any rate, he was enthusiastic about your work, and he knows something about painting himself; knows how to paint and how to select great things. Of course, I knew that about you already but it was pleasing to see him so enthusiastic.

The following month Ingeborg and Atherton returned the visit.

> I told Gay that I wrote you what he said of your picture and that you answered that you would rather have his good opinion than that of any other painter. He was so moved at this that he almost cried—that is to say tears came to his eyes. Well, the fact is you are both of you great painters.

As their circle grew closer it was a pleasure to hear occasionally from an old friend who had long been out of sight.

October 22, 1930

MY DEAR OLD FRIEND TANNER,

It was bully to get another view of your familiar "hand" a month or so ago and to know that, like myself, you are still alive and kicking. I constantly see your works in the Grand Central Art Gallery, with no falling off in their inspiration and familiar color. This keeps me in your touch, but the letter is a good deal better for the offices of friendship.

How good it is to find you having the same views of what is alleged to be modern art, as I have. I made an address in Newport at the Art Association in the summer, of which I have only a limited report, that I am going to enclose. If there are any traces left from this schism, they will not justify it; any more than the outbreaks into bad taste in the history of English literature have left any justifiable improvement in that great stream.

I wonder if you are ever going to come back and see us? The old fellows are so far apart, and there are so many gone forever—as Alexander Harrison just now—that I think we ought to foregather. There will always be, as you know, an open door in our new house, where I hope you and your wife would repeat the dinner we once had in the old house long ago. It is just around the corner.

It is a poor mildewed period in American painting, without new inspiration except in a very few oncoming painters and what is left of the old men of genius.

I hope you have seen my book, "Confessions in Art," as I have set down there what I am sure would please you.

With my warmest regards to your wife and a whole lot more to yourself, I am

Yours truly,
HARRISON MORRIS

Tanner did not share Morris's pessimistic view of "the poor mildewed period in American painting." While there was much in contemporary painting he did not like or understand he tried to keep an open mind toward the work of younger men, and he had little sympathy for the attitude of his old friend, Walter Griffin. When Tanner wrote Griffin about joining the European chapter of the American Artists' Professional League, Griffin replied:

The tempting offer of membership in your new venture with subscription of the Art Digest for three dollars per year

> I regret to say does not appeal to me for the reason that I have subscribed to that interesting paper for years past but have finally concluded that for reasons personal to me that I can become a past number subscriber. *All* this! My dear Tanner may give you the impression that I am not actively interested in the art interests of today—but to confess the truth as far as I know it—I'm getting damn tired of conditions and the present-day tendencies. I am always pleased and charmed when I read or hear your name spoken of as an "artist of our epoch."

The American colony had grown smaller ever since the 1914 war, but the final blow was the depression, which cut nearly in half the value of the dollar. Only the wealthy, like Walter Gay and Atherton Curtis, could stay in France and hope to maintain anything like the old amenities. Artists were particularly hard hit. The Art Club, for lack of support, had to close its doors, leaving the few remaining members no place to meet or discuss their mutual interests. By 1930, when Charles Tough wrote Tanner to congratulate him on winning the Clark prize, the depression was in full swing.

> In this country we used to regard $500 as almost small change. Now we look upon it as a fortune. It will no doubt come in very handy to you and it is mighty fine to feel that they think you still do good work. It at least ought to make a better market for that particular picture and as soon as people begin to feel that the country is not going to the dogs they will think of buying more of your pictures.

Sales were so far down that Carson, Pirie, Scott priced a large picture that Tanner had on display with them at $450, so far below the $1500 he usually received for this size painting that when he heard about it he had it shipped to J. S. Carpenter in Des Moines. In spite of hard times Carpenter thought that he might place it.

> We have a man in Des Moines who is very anxious to buy one of your pictures. He already owns a small one, and he has expressed a desire to own a larger one.

But in the spring of 1930 even the depression could not dampen Tanner's spirits. He was feeling more cheerful than he had for years, for Jesse was much improved and was back with him at Trépied. In May Henry wrote Carpenter optimistically about his work:

> I have 5 or 6 pictures under way—all unfinished—but I hope soon to remedy this state of affairs. I have not changed my principal at this date—unless I believe in a canvas I do not send it out—However, things are beginning to change and I have two which I hope to finish within the month.... I have been working upon a tempera mixture for the last 5 or 6 years and have finally a wonderful binder. I am now using it exclusively and I am sure you will find no loss of quality in my painting.

Tanner felt so encouraged about his ability to paint again that he wrote Atherton saying he thought it would not be necessary to send him any more money. But Atherton felt otherwise. He knew that money was scarce and that Jesse's health was still precarious. Money was seldom mentioned in Atherton's letters to Henry, but Ingeborg wrote:

> Your letter, Henry, has just come and Atherton wishes me to say to you that he thinks—and so do I—that it is better to continue the 3500 fcs. for the present. Later on we can discuss the matter again.

Early in the summer of 1930 Ingeborg and Atherton visited Henry and Jesse at Trépied. It was the first time they had seen "Edgewood" and both were delighted with it; Atherton wrote enthusiastically:

> I think it is one of the loveliest houses I have ever seen, a really beautiful house. It seems to me perfect. I don't see what could be done to improve it. You were both of you very good to us and gave yourself much more trouble than you needed to, to make us comfortable. We could not have been uncomfortable in such a house as yours if we had tried.
>
> When we got back I told Lucy we had been to see her

friend Mr. Tanner and she said, "I like my friend Mr. Tanner."

P.S. Here is something else of Lucy's. She pointed to your picture of "Abraham's Oak" and said "Thats by Mr. Tanner. You and I know its blue but other people think its green. Even Mr. Tanner hisself thinks its green." Which is one on you.

In July Tanner gave his annual tea for his friends at Trépied, an event that was usually exhausting to him. But this year he was less tired than usual. He remained at Trépied until October, getting back to Paris about the same time as Ingeborg and Atherton from Bourron.

Henry's cheerful frame of mind was not to last. Jesse's improvement was temporary, and he had to return to Saujon. In America, to cloud the picture still more, the financial situation was growing worse. In September, 1931, Carpenter wrote Tanner:

> The times in this country are very strenuous.... In fact, we are in the worst depression this country has known for many years, and it has almost reached the stage of a panic....
>
> Our Art Association has suspended activities for the year. That is, we are not going to ask our members for any membership dues, and will simply fill our gallery with a loan collection of pictures, and let it hang through the year.

Nevertheless, there were a few bright spots. Carpenter wrote that he was hopeful of selling his picture, *Etaples Fisher Folk*, which had been sent him by the Grand Central Art Galleries:

> A Mrs. Don McGregor was interested in it and there are a number of other people somewhat interested in the painting, but up to the present time I have refused to make them a price.... I do not agree with you that the picture turned down in Des Moines means no one would be interested in it. Our people buy their pictures pretty much on their own judgment and the picture collectors know a good Tanner when they see it, and I consider it a very fine one.

About the same time, Jessie Bateman, Jessie's cousin from San Francisco, wrote from New York that she and Elna had been to the Grand Central Art Galleries to see his prize painting. She wished she could afford to buy it, but since this was not possible she would be pleased and happy to buy the *Fisherman with the Lantern* that she had seen in Tanner's studio the previous summer. Would he please send it to her?

And, Mr. G. T. Nelson, of the Grand Central Art Galleries, reported "There was a party in our Gallery recently interested in securing one of your paintings of a religious subject."

But these bright spots did not compensate for Jesse's setback or for the bad news that his sister Mary wrote him from America. His brother Carlie was seriously ill, and she herself was not at all well. In her letter she added:

> I wish I could think you were going to come to America again. I however realize you have been away so long there would be little to draw you here—But how I would love to see you and talk with you.

Any hope that Tanner may have had of returning to the United States was now gone. It seemed to him that his strength grew less each year. And what Mary said was true—there was little to draw him any more. It saddened him, however, to think of his favorite sister growing old and dying without him seeing her again.

Atherton perceived the depth of Henry's sadness and when he was away from him wrote letters designed to bring a smile to his lips. In the following, written in May, 1932, he enclosed a photograph of a vase, modelled in the form of a grotesque human head, that had been dug up at Jericho.

Paris, May 27, 1932

DEAR HENRY,

You said you had never heard of Jericho in the Bible but only of Gericault the painter. Well here is a picture of him.

Hope you are getting on all right. We are freezing here—even Ingeborg. This morning we decided to start the furnace going again but the sun came out for a few minutes after lunch and we changed our minds—which was a mistake for now we are freezing again. Ingeborg is shut up in her salon with a fire going and door closed. She even puts a light shawl on top of her blanket at night. Well the world is in a pretty mix-up anyway and I suppose it really doesn't much matter whether we are a little too cold or not. There is one consolation. It is a darn sight colder out in Neptune. It must be really cussedly cold out there so far away from the sun.

Yesterday morning we did three exhibitions. First we went to see the Retrospective show at the Salon—Jerome, Cabanel, Bouguereau, Laurens, Puvis de Chavannes, Fantin-Latour, Ziem, Manet, Renoir, Dagnan-Bouveret, etc. Well, we came to the conclusion that they are not any of them any worse than present day painters and that no matter what time or what school or what group one considers they don't any of them know how to paint anyway. I don't see any choice between Bouguereau, Manet, Renoir, Cabanel or Matisse. Each paints in a different way from the other, that is all, and each one is just as bad as the other. Then after walking our feet off going through the Artistes-Décorateurs where we saw awful furniture, awful objets d'arts, awful interiors, we went to the Doré show. Doré as a painter could hold his own with Bouguereau, Manet, Matisse or any of them for badness. O là, là! What painting the world has had inflicted on it and all painting that it admired while it was going. Isn't it lucky that fashions change? Suppose the world had to go on for ever admiring all the things it had once admired! Think of it!

Hope the news from Jesse continues to be good. Much love from us both,

Atherton

Some weeks later he commented:

Of course, I can't judge as to whether you have become a Harrison this summer, not having seen your work. Besides, as I can't see paintings well anyway, my opinion couldn't be much good. But there is this to be said of you. You are much younger than Harrison; in fact, quite young compared to old fellows like me even.

For youth or age are not counted by years as Shakespeare would have said if I hadn't got in ahead of him. At all events, it is encouraging to see Jesse more optimistic about himself and I hope they will soon let him go from Saujon and get back to you.

In the spring of 1933 Henry had further trouble. One dark night he was out walking in Paris and fell into a hole in the sidewalk. He was badly shaken up, and Ingeborg and Atherton took him immediately to Bourron, then had him moved to the American Hospital at Neuilly. While he was there Ingeborg sent the following "pneumatic":

DEAR HENRY,

We feel very badly because we have not been able to get out to see you for so many days. The chief reason is that Dhos has had a bad cold. Today he is better and by tomorrow he will be so well, I hope, that we can get out to see you. You may wonder why we don't take a taxi. As a matter of fact we have been using taxis for two or three days, but I won't let Atherton out alone in one because I am afraid he might get dizzy, and then be badly off with a strange chauffeur, and he won't let me go alone in one—Well, Heaven knows why! . . . Atherton telephoned out last evening to ask at the Hospital how you were, and the report was, of course, very satisfactory. Nevertheless a telephone conversation always leaves a great deal to be desired, and one never has a chance to ask much, so of course, we are coming out as soon as we can come and get you and bring you back here. Netta's room will be ready for you, and we will make you as comfortable as we can, and not freeze you as we did the Sunday morning after the fall. And you can take the lift both to your room and to the top floor, so you will not have to walk much if you are stiff. Netta has a room downstairs—her father's room

—and she will use that if she comes in. So you see we can be very comfortable.

As soon as he was able to leave the hospital Tanner went to Bourron for a rest, but he was back in Paris by June 18 and able to walk, though slowly, to his studio.

Jesse was again making progress. By summer he was better than he had been for several years, indeed so much better that he was hoping to find a business that his limited strength would permit him to operate. With this in mind, as well as for financial reasons, Tanner decided that the time had come to dispose of "Edgewood." Summer seemed the best time of the year to sell, though Atherton was not optimistic about a sale. "Things seem to be picking up just a little, which may help, though I can't say that the improvement such as it is, goes with any lightening rapidity either in Europe or in America." Atherton was also sympathetic with Jesse's problems in locating a business to buy.

> I can understand the difficulty for Jesse to find anything worth while for sale just now. If I had a good business that was paying me a profit, I certainly would not sell now when placing the proceeds in anything safe would be extremely difficult. . . . And naturally Jesse does not want to buy a poor business that is not paying. . . .

In July Henry received an urgent plea from J. E. Spingarn, president of the National Association for the Advancement of Colored People, for a contribution. For years Tanner had been a contributing member, and it was no doubt with a heavy heart that he sent the following letter, knowing that the need for money in America was dire.

Dear Mr. S——

It seemed to me that your personal appeal on behalf of the N.A.A.C.P. should have from me a reply. I am sorry that this year I shall be absolutely unable to make a contribution for its most excellent work. I am completely in sympathy and feel its vital importance, but this year my affairs are such that I cannot send my usual subscription.

Believe me,

———

During June and July Tanner exhibited three of his paintings—*The Governor's Palace, Tangiers, Moonlight* and *The Good Shepherd*—with the American Artists' Professional League at the Simonson Galleries in Paris. These were old pictures, but they were praised above the work of the younger artists, above that of John Allen Wyeth, Aston Knight, and Janet Scudder.

The winter of 1933 Tanner spent mostly in Paris. He moved into a small apartment at 43 Rue de Fleurus, near Atherton and Ingeborg Curtis. He was not at all strong. In January he received a letter from an artist-friend in America, James R. Hopkins, who was now teaching art at Ohio State University and who wrote to say that under a grant from the federal government several artists had been put to work in Columbus on various projects for the beautification of public buildings. One of the public schools which figured in the project had requested a portrait of Henry Tanner. They needed a photograph to work from, and Hopkins asked Tanner to send him one as soon as possible. But Henry was too tired to look for a picture of himself, and it was April before he answered Hopkins's letter.

April 14, 1934

DEAR HOPKINS,

Your letter of Jan. 15th received a long time ago. It was not answered because I had no photos here in Paris and have been expecting to go up to Etaples, where are all my effects, such as photos, etc. Then I had a bad cold which confined me to the house, besides I have few photos except small snapshots from which a painting would be very difficult to make. My young friend has very likely grown weary of waiting, and done something nearer at hand.

An art school—twenty-three on the staff—some school—

Nearly all the people you and I knew over here have gone home and most of them who remain wish they were in the U. S. Since our $ has lost 40% of its value it has indeed been difficult. We over here heard that our govt. was giving $2 million to needy but otherwise that was all.

You indeed were wise to accept a teaching job, and I do not doubt you get a real kick and pleasure out of it and give value received in return. Besides, it makes a very nice surrounding to live in and each month comes pay envelope with living assured. And not like some of us, struggling to make a picture, and struggling to sell it or orders ahead, when picture is completed by blood and tears, our patron has lost his money, and is too poor to pay for it.

The American Club after W—— death had no money and was disbanded. So that one now has no place of meeting. Greatly missed *indeed.*

Tanner's comment about "struggling to make a picture, and then struggling to sell it" was a direct reference to a situation that was very much on his mind. The painting that Mr. Haverty, of Atlanta, had ordered some years before Tanner had, by dint of the hardest work, finally finished in February. But when he wrote Mr. Haverty that it was completed he received the following answer:

Dear Sir,

Your letter of February 11th was received a few days ago in my absence from the city.

I do not feel at this time that I should buy a picture from you. It is now three years since this picture was ordered. At that time I was flush with money. At this time I am in the gutter in money matters. The depression has made us all poor in the country, and I do not feel that I should take upon myself the investment of another picture, although I know that this picture was ordered from you, but so long a time has elapsed that if it please you, I would prefer not to have it sent to me.

The following month, in March, Tanner got word that his favorite sister Mary had died. His brother Carlie had died three months before.

During the spring and winter of 1934 Jesse spent some time with his father in Paris, but he was investigating the export business and looking for a suitable headquarters in central France. He wanted a house that he and his father might also use as a home. During these months Tanner spent a good deal of time with Atherton and Ingeborg, and in return for their hospitality he gave them a new little painting. In June Ingeborg wrote him:

Thank you a thousand times for the painting, it was awfully nice and thoughtful of you to send it over before we left. I took it right along, and am enjoying it every day. It is not up on the wall yet, but I think I have found a place for it and in the meantime I have put it in a place where I see it several times a day. I am very, very glad to have it, and I thank you ever so much.

The Curtises urged Tanner to stay with them at Bourron that summer, but Henry was reluctant to impose on them for so long. Ingeborg made an arrangement, however, that won his consent. Tanner wrote Jesse about it from Bourron in July:

I began to hunt up a place and Uncle A—— and Aunt I—— have offered me in the little cottage across the road a room with a little kitchen for three weeks or a month until I am ready to go South to you. I shall be most comfortable and I shall not be, I am sure, in their way either. You know Miss Oliver has one end of the house. It is one house but two separate little houses with nice little garden. I have accepted it and shall be able to paint some too. I shall come back to

Paris Wednesday or Thursday. What day are you coming through Paris? I should prefer to come up and see you the day you are going through. I hope you took the woman's address so that I can find her in Fall or sooner.

I hope you are feeling better.

If you should be coming to Paris before Wed or Thurs send me a telegram please.

Jesse found a château at Belvès, in the Dordogne, that he thought would suit his purposes, but it needed repairs. These turned out to be more costly than he had anticipated. From Bourron, where he was still staying, a letter from Henry in September indicates his concern for Jesse and his anxiety to help him. He wrote that he would send him "the whole 1500 frcs. received from Uncle A—— *this month*."

I am not strong as I should like. I do not feel badly, but have no strength to paint or to do much work around as I am in the habit of doing. I was thinking of staying here, where my expenses are small till about Sept 15th then go to Paris to about the 20th and see the Batemans for a day or two and see if there is a chance to sell them a small picture (if I can get some small picture done) for about $100 or $150—but I do not feel there is much chance this year. Each time before I have sold them something but it does not look hopeful to me this year—but as it did not look like I could be of any use to you now I thought I would try and see. If it was costing me money here I would certainly come and save it.

What will it cost to do the repairs you will be forced to do in Oct. so as to pass the winter—or have you any other plans? Have you seen Monsieur et Madame de Bonfils? Since you left has only been about 10 days but it seems like a month to me. I sent off 2 letters to you this morning. The Dr. has given me some mixture for my nerves, it seems to be slowing up my strength too and I do not feel so strong as usual. I think I shall take a half dose for a while....

Tanner went to Paris, as he suggested, and had a pleasant

visit with the Batemans. In November, after reaching San Francisco, Jessie Bateman wrote Henry that "we often speak of our visits to the Coupole and smile when my thoughts go to the evening of the struggle we had to get our favorite table in the corner." She wrote that, after living with the *Fisherman at Etaples* for two years, she wished to buy it and would also like to own the *Disciples at Emmaus* but could only afford to pay $500 and so felt it was beyond her reach. The *Disciples at Emmaus* was the painting that Mr. Haverty had turned down, and Tanner wrote he would be glad to sell it at this price.

Henry was now seventy-five years old and growing quite frail. In the *New York Herald* of April 15, 1934, a full-page spread was given to photographs of "Americans in Retrospect"—those who had lived in Paris for many years—and among the faces of James Hazen Hyde and Morton Fullerton and other prominent Americans was that of Henry O. Tanner. He was sitting with a group of young art students in the garden of the old Art Club. The picture was taken in 1895 and was the only one Tanner could find when asked for a photograph of himself to include among the celebrities.

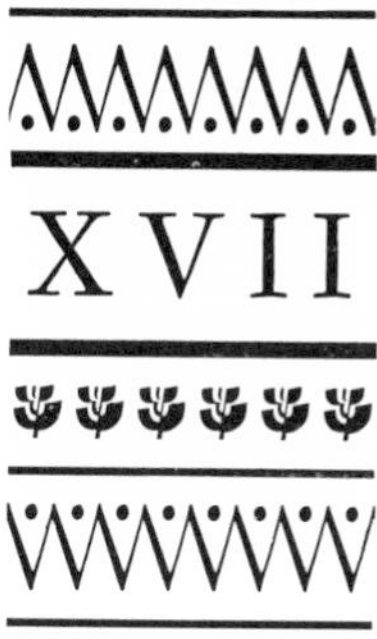

XVII

Last Years

TANNER REMAINED IN PARIS IN HIS APARTMENT ON THE Rue de Fleurus through the winter and early spring of 1934–35 waiting for the repairs to be made on the house at Belvès. He painted a little and sold a few small canvases. One of these was to a cousin he had never met, Maudelle Bousfield, principal of the Stephen A. Douglas School in Chicago and the daughter of Menie Tanner Brown, Tanner's first cousin. The sale was an unexpected boon. Tanner wrote Mrs. Bousfield in January:

> I do not think I ever met your mother. I have been in France so many years except for short visits to the U. S. which are all the time becoming farther apart so that I have lost many of my old friends.
>
> To buy a picture you come in a very good time. I have two small pictures, a "Hiding of Moses" and "The Flight into Egypt," size about 24 x 28 inches, for which in ordinary

> times I would receive from \$350 to \$400 and which I believe are very good examples of my work. I would take two hundred. Being an American artist there is no duty on the picture. The Consular certificate and packing as well as small duty on frame will be at my expense. I am making it especially easy not only on account of the times but because I should like some of my family to have some of my work.
>
> On account of the hard times all over the world even some of the most successful artists have temporarily reduced their prices. This is my case.
>
> If you should prefer a larger picture I have one not yet quite finished. I hope—D.V.—to have it finished in about two months.
>
> I can especially recommend the "Flight into Egypt". . . .

Mrs. Bousfield bought the *Flight into Egypt* and was very pleased with her purchase. She wrote that she hoped to be able to buy a companion piece later on, but because of the depression her hope was not realized. She wrote in 1936, "the truth is I just cannot afford it."

In January, 1935, Tanner also received an inquiry from Miss Josephine Sharkey, who wrote him on behalf of Bennett College, a Negro college in North Carolina that wished to purchase a *Good Shepherd* from him.

> As you know we are very hard up these days and the Negro colleges do not come in for any large amounts but they would like more than anything to have a picture by one of their own people in the new building. Please write me by return sending me a photograph of the painting and the dimensions. Does a painting of that sort come through free of duty?

Tanner assumed from her letter that Bennett College wanted the picture as a gift, and in view of his incapacity to work he did not feel in a position to give away any of the pictures he had on hand. He delayed answering the letter, not knowing what to say, but Miss Sharkey was not to be put off. On March 28 Charles Tough wrote Henry:

The reason for my answering your letter so promptly now is that I just received a letter from Miss Josephine Sharkey on a business matter in which she mentions negotiating for the purchase of one of your pictures by a school in her neighborhood. She says the school was interested but before buying it wanted to know the dimensions of it and see a small photograph of it. She says that she has had no reply from you on this subject and wonders if you are "so rich you do not care."

Tanner was hurt by Miss Sharkey's attitude and wrote Charles:

No, I am "not so rich" I do not care, but I judged from her letter that while it might interest them they had no money and besides I thought by what right do I ask Miss Sharkey to trouble herself on such a thankless job. True she did ask for a photo and the dimensions of the canvas—a kind letter, but it seemed to me at the time she was trying to let me down easily and while I wanted to sell I felt it was asking too much, and so dropped it. I should have thanked her for her kindness and told her to not have too much trouble about it. You know my pictures do not yield very good photos and I have had little success with photos of them.

It is doubtful whether Atherton Curtis fully appreciated the extent of Tanner's straitened circumstances at this time, for Tanner did not complain. That he was hard pressed for money may be seen from a letter he wrote to his nephew Ben Johnson about the sale of some property they had both inherited from Bishop Tanner.

I hope you will conclude to sign the deed for the sale of the Washington property. I hear your reason is that you consider the price too small. I have had to lately sell some pictures for ½ of what they were ordered for and certainly 30% less than they had cost in good $'s, without counting my labor for everything.

Times are very hard over here and the exchange value of the $ having dropped 40% has so decreased my income that if you could sign and let it get through quickly it would be a personal favor to me. I believe that every one of the heirs have signed except you and your brother. The sum could not be so large that you would personally gain by any ordinary increase in sale price.

But Ben Johnson did not sign, and the money, so badly needed, was not added to Tanner's account.

On Christmas Eve Tanner received a letter from Mrs. Bryant, the little Margaret Clifford he had first known at Highlands, North Carolina, when he was a young man with his future still ahead of him. He answered it that night.

Paris, Dec 24th, 1935

Dear Mrs. Bryant,

Your very kind letter received this morning and you will know how glad I was to receive it, that I am answering the Xmas eve.

I so often thought of you and your mother and wondered how time was using you. Jesse is not home this Xmas—I think for the first time and it hardly feels like Xmas. We often see your photo—on the beach at Paris-Plage and wonder how are you and yours. I am beginning to feel my age, but I do not complain. Times have been very bad here and our money going off the gold standard has quite upset our calculations—the 40% decrease in the value of the $ is felt very severely by Americans who are left here. We are glad to hear that times are improving in U. S., may the good work keep up. It is still not a time when pictures are being sold.

I am sure if Jesse were here he would with me wish you and yours a merry Xmas and a Happy New Year.

Believe me
as ever

H. O. Tanner

43 rue de Fleurus
Paris

We have rented our Trépied house and Jesse is in the centre of France, but unmarried.

Please excuse this short note.

In early May Tanner finally made the journey south to Jesse's "Château de Lascaminade" at Belvès. Atherton wrote on May 13:

> Glad you got down there O.K. and found the place not too bad. It is a great thing not to find it damp. I am glad that there is one view from the Château that you like. Long views over great stretches of country can be very grand. They can also be very paintable. But they are not intimate and are not to me pleasant to live with.

But Atherton was lonesome for Henry. He too was growing old and was not very well. Because of bad health he and Ingeborg had to remain later than usual in Paris that spring. He wrote Henry "You seem dreadfully far away, down there in the Dordogne." And, a few days later:

> Every night when I go to bed I look at your window to see if the light is burning and you are home. It's a habit and I can't get used to not seeing a light.

Henry was happy to be with Jesse, and Jesse was glad for his company, for there was a close relationship between father and son, but there is no doubt that in the Dordogne Tanner missed the familiar sights and sounds of Paris. Nor did his health improve as rapidly as he would have liked. Atherton wrote him in July:

> I am glad you are getting better but sorry that you do not pick up faster. I am sorry you are not in Bourron where you picked up so quickly last year. If you find that you are not getting on as fast as you think you ought the cottage at Bourron is still there and we can offer you the sitting-room and bedroom you had last year.

Ingeborg also urged him to consider coming back to Bourron. But Tanner was reluctant to leave Jesse. By August he was painting again, though his paints were in short supply. Apropos of this difficulty Atherton wrote him in a mischievous vein:

> Too bad about those paints. I hope there was some blue or green among those you had unpacked. It would be a pity if you had to substitute red for blue and paint sunsets or things on fire instead of moonlight. But if there is no blue in the lot there may be some green, which would do just as well for you though others who saw your picture might be a little surprised.

Atherton wrote more seriously about another aspect of his art:

> By the way, when did you begin your new methods of painting by mixing oil and egg colours—or rather by using the two on the same canvas? It seems it was the Van Eycks' methods and "Beaux Arts" says that it was lost until discovered again by a chemist in 1931. My impression is you discovered it before that and used it. If I am right I will write to "Beaux Arts" and tell them so.

Tanner's answer is lost, but it is apparent that his method was not that of the Van Eycks. To recapture that medieval technique would have been beyond the grasp of any twentieth-century artist. On November 8, 1935, he wrote down on a slip of paper the process he was then using[1] and made no

1. Among Tanner's personal letters is a formula for his paint that is dated 1935. It is as follows:

> 150 gr. of the water or syrup from ¼ lb. of best linseed, soaked for 24 hrs., slightly cooked or raw.
>
> 300 gr. of newly made glue from parchment (sheep skin) soaked 24 hrs., heated slightly 2 or 3 hrs., simmered for ½ hr. but not boiled hard.
>
> 200 grs. of mastic varnish into which shall be added 25% of linseed oil of best quality or 10% poppy oil. The last is added to slow up boiling. This 200 grs. is to be 75% of mastic varnish and 25% of oil as directed.
>
> 15 grs. lanoline dissolved in essence mineral.
>
> Add to above mixture 15 or 20 grs. of alcohol 90% This is added to make a better emulsion, too much will injure the glue but it also adds to the keeping quality of the mixture as will a little essence mineral.
>
> Mix in the above order or glue can be added if the mixture in cooking is not like soft butter. Mixture to be used warm equal parts of color.

mention of egg as a binder. Nevertheless, in the care with which he prepared his painting medium he was close in spirit to the Van Eycks.

Tanner never acquired Jesse's love for central France, and as the days became shorter again he decided to return to Paris for the winter months. He had not benefited as much as he had hoped from the country air. He would miss his son, as he always did when the two were apart, but Jesse was in good health now and had his business to preoccupy him.

On September 19 Ingeborg wrote Henry from Bourron:

> This is just a line to say that we are delighted to know that you are back in Paris and once more in your small apartment. It has not the spendours of Lascaminade, but it is a cozy house-like corner, easier to manage and to live in in autumn and winter weather. Your letter to Atherton came just now. I thank you for it and Atherton will do so later, I know.

By the end of the month Atherton and Ingeborg were also back in Paris. Henry Tanner, at seventy-six, was old for a man who had never been in robust health. He did not suffer any pain, but he felt debilitated and tired much of the time. The walk to and from his studio on the Boulevard Saint-Jacques he found a great strain, and in November he rented it to Jean Hélion, an artist. He no longer needed the space of a large studio, for his paintings were small enough to be done in his apartment, and he did not wish the responsibility of two establishments. He still had "Edgewood" on his hands and this was a minor worry. During the summer of 1935 heavy rains had damaged the house so badly that it had needed a new roof. Tenants, he knew, did not care for a place as well as its owner.

Despite his decrease in strength he kept up his affiliation with the American Artists' Professional League, and in December he exhibited with them for the last time. Leslie Cauldwell, the secretary of the league, was pleased to have some Tanners in the show.

We were so glad that you decided to expose with us and as usual your pictures have been very much admired. I am told that there are a few visitors who have asked about prices of some of the pictures, promising to come back and decide.

The matter of racial prejudice in America, that had impelled Tanner originally to make France his home, had long since faded into the background of his life. But once in a great while it was brought into new focus. In September, 1935, he received a letter from a clergyman in America asking permission to use his painting, the *Two Disciples at the Tomb*, in a religious service that was to be held for the improvement of racial relations. Tanner was progressively slower in answering his correspondence, but in December he finally wrote the clergyman.

Paris, Dec, 1935

DEAR REVEREND THOMAS II,

Yours under date Sept 25th to hand. I am very sorry to have been so long in answering. I can assure you however it was due to no lack of interest.

That at first your letter and programme caused me surprise I cannot deny, even though it was agreable, it was a surprise. I knew there were some people in the U. S. who were trying to make race relations more Christian but that special *services were held was unknown to me. As I think it over it does not surprise me. We are supposed to be a very practical people, and if race prejudice and race hate are vices why not treat them as we would other evils that are more generally recognized as needing the grace of God to cure. That you will finally win the day, there will be little doubt. For you cannot have a Christian religion without it winning the day. The Pilgrims once thought they could drive out the "Quakers" and be only more devout Christians. How few still have such erroneous thoughts. The problem is a different one, but perhaps harder for man in his own strength. But who dares limit the power of the grace of God to his erring children?*

I personally see no reason why you should not use the picture in any flight of imagination that might add power to the subject in hand. I only think myself fortunate if the picture will in a however small degree bring the thoughts and actions of my fellow man closer to the teachings of our Lord and Master.

Of course occasionally one is hunting for some color scheme and chooses the subject he does because he finds the chance he is looking for.

Thanking you for your kind letter
Believe me
Very sincerely,
H. O. TANNER

43 RUE DE FLEURUS
PARIS, 6

In 1935 Tanner also received a visit from James A. Porter, a Negro artist from Howard University whom Tanner knew from two previous visits. He came to discuss the possibility of obtaining one of Tanner's pictures for his school. As a token of their friendship Henry Tanner gave Porter a treasured possession that his father had given him, a small pastel of Richard Allen, the first American to fight actively for civil rights and the founder of the church to which his father had devoted his life. On the back of the picture Bishop Tanner had written the following words:

Richard Allen at 25. Founder of the Bethel Church, Sixth St. Erected in 1793. Elected Bishop of the African Methodist Episcopal Church A.D. 1816. The above picture executed in 1785 consequently 89 years old, and is the only picture of Mr. Allen painted during his early manhood.
Given by Bishop B. Tanner, 1874

James Porter knew it was Tanner's hope that this unique gift would be placed where many Negroes could see it, and he presented it to the Moorland Room, Founders Library, at Howard University. Walter G. Daniel, the university librarian, acknowledged the receipt of the picture on January 29. The day before, Dorothy Porter, the wife of James Porter and a librarian at Howard University, wrote him the following note:

DEAR MR. TANNER,

I want to thank you for your gift to our special collection on the Negro. The picture of Richard Allen will certainly be one of our proud rarities. It has already been placed on our wall. In another two years we expect to have a new library. It is our aim to obtain everything concerning the Negro.

I was very much disappointed that I did not meet you this summer while I was in Paris. My husband has told me so much about you. He enjoyed every minute he spent with you. You will always be the greatest Negro artist.

Yours very truly,
DOROTHY PORTER

Being the "greatest Negro artist" did not insure Henry Tanner against professional involvements that caused him great pain at a time of life when he wanted, above all, to enjoy peace and quiet. One of the pictures that Mr. Haverty, of Atlanta, had purchased from Tanner, *The Road to Emmaus* had flaked rather badly, and he wished it replaced with another. Tanner's letter to Mr. Barrie, who was handling the negotiations, expressed the artist's anguish over the transaction:

Paris, March 22, 1936

DEAR MR. BARRIE,

My health is quite a little better so that nearly every day I work on small pictures *and with some success but I am not able as yet to commence new pictures of any importance, and do not see myself doing so this summer, but if Mr.*

Haverty would send me the picture I am fairly sure I should be able to put it in condition this summer.

As to the matter of transportation I should hope Mr. Haverty would be willing to pay it—besides this there is duty demanded by the French on returned pictures, and if Mr. Haverty would give a small value, *less than he paid for it as it is damaged, I will try to pay duty.*

I have given up my studio in Paris, which I have had for 30 years and it is only in the summer I could work on a picture like Mr. Haverty's. I am then in the country and have more room. This does not mean that the quality of the work has lost but that I am not so energetic and can do less—and also that I have financial worries along with it. The exchange value of the $ being only 60 cents has very much upset me financially. The money I had been able to save I had put into property and now my property is mostly rented to work people who cannot find work and those houses which formerly made a good income now bring only enough to pay taxes and not always enough.

All this has nothing to do with Mr. Haverty though I still think he treated me rather badly about the order he gave me. On one other order the man died and generally I have had a rather worrying time for the last couple of years.

But my small pictures I am sure have not gone off—only for the moment I am not strong enough to worry with large ones. I was just on the point of writing you if I might send you 3 or 4 small pictures priced from $200 to $300 and see whether you could help me out. No sales over here. *We have just maybe escaped a new war with Germany.*

Could you tell me what Mr. Haverty paid me for that picture, please. It is quite worrying as I believe it is the only time I have had trouble with a purchaser of paintings.

Please excuse this wandering letter, What I mean to say is that though I am better than last summer I still have to avoid any strain that would overdo myself and that though Mr. Haverty does not like to send it over I still believe it would be best. I would like to know what Mr. Haverty gave for picture. I believe it was quite a reduced price—but that has nothing to do with making it good.

Thanking you for your kindness.

Believe me,
H. O. TANNER

Mr. Haverty was not satisfied with Tanner's offer to repair the painting, and, in some desperation, Tanner cabled Mr. Barrie to give him one of his large paintings in the Grand Central Art Galleries, either the prize-winning *Etaples Fisher Folk* which Mr. Carpenter had been unable to sell in Des Moines, or *The Destruction of Sodom and Gomorrah.*

If my life were to hang upon it I could not make a large picture as you suggest. I have not the strength to do it and certainly I never could have done it in the time you suggested. . . .

It seems a rather hard bargain that I should give the "Etaples Fisherfolk" for a picture that I only originally offered for one thousand, but I have to have a rather quiet life to do my work at all so that what I consider exhorbitant demands, as I do Mr. Haverty's, so upset me for quite long periods I have concluded to make the sacrifice so as to have peace of mind.

Mr. Barrie wrote in September that Mr. Haverty was "perfectly satisfied" with Tanner's offer and that he considered the deal closed. Nevertheless, Tanner was troubled by the affair, the more so as times seemed to be getting worse in France and the future looked dim. In June a meeting of the American Artists' Professional League was called off by Gilbert White, the president, because of the political situation. He was afraid the restaurant where they usually met would be closed because of street disorders.

It seemed terrible to Tanner that after all of the suffering endured during the First World War Europe should again be on the threshold of war. He was not alone in this thinking. Ingeborg wrote him in late June:

> I am glad you are painting. I am sure it is very necessary that some people at the present time should believe in beauty and try to create some. Atherton reads stacks of newspapers, but in between he works with his prints, and he and the world are better for it.

During the early summer of 1936 Tanner was again with Jesse at his château, but he returned to Bourron in July. He seemed to be marking time, waiting for some unkonwn culmination of events that would set at rest forever the disturbances that were troubling the peace and security of the world.

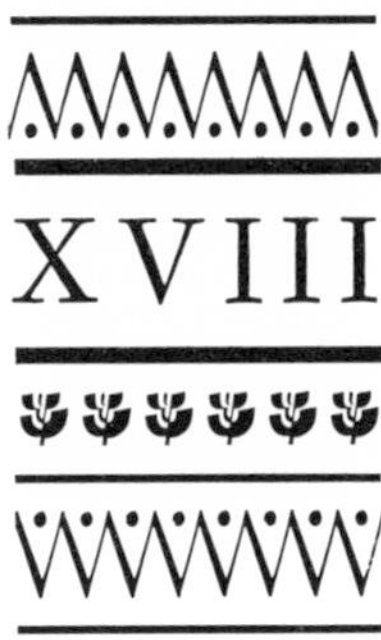

The End

Henry Tanner had been singularly lucky all of his life, and his luck did not forsake him at the end. It is true that he had financial worries, but money had never been the alpha and omega of life to him. He was still able to paint a little each day, to enjoy the beauties of nature, to visit with his close friends, and to look forward to a happy married life for Jesse, now in good health and doing well. On April 8, 1937, Jesse was married at Belvès to Colette Chaperon, the daughter of Emile Alphonse Chaperon, Officier d'Académie.

Jesse wanted his father to make his home with them, but for the time being Tanner remained in Paris. He was not ill, but felt quite weak at times. Sometimes this forced him to forego gatherings he would have liked to attend. One of these was a dinner given by the American Artists' Professional League in honor of their secretary, Leslie Cauldwell, an old friend. Mr. Cauldwell wrote him on April 28:

My dear Tanner,

I have been promising myself to go over and see you, to thank you personally for your very charming little note I received on the evening of the dinner the members of the American Artists' Professional League gave me.

To tell you the truth I was more touched by your few words than the very festive and much appreciated honor of the dinner. Those few words warmed my heart and I will never forget them.

Thank you sincerely,
Leslie Cauldwell

Tanner's capacity for making and holding friends was, next to his art, his greatest talent. One of the last letters that he ever wrote was to Margaret Clifford Bryant. He had received a Christmas letter from her which he misplaced. He found it several months later and answered it on May 3, 1937.

My dear Mrs. Bryant
of other days
Dear Margaret—

It is only the other day that I found your kind letter of Xmas time. You know I put it away so carefully that for a long while I could not find it—You know I have the way sometimes of putting things away and forget where I have put them—So that it was only a very short while—unless I wanted to confess to the truth—I was going to send you this announcement and that made me write on its back my little message.

You know I am getting to be quite an old man and cannot hop about so lively. I still work each day—but not so many hours as formerly—but I am happy to say that I have a good many friends who think my work has not dropped off. It is only within the last year that we sold the place at Trépied.

I am very glad your mother is still enjoying life and I

imagine that Swarthmore is a very lovely place for her. Please remember me to her. I am very glad you can give such a good report of your children. It is a pleasure to see them opening out with good minds and health. Do bring the children over in a few years—it will mean much to them and will be a great education to them. Bring your husband along at the same time, it will be a great pleasure to him, and especially he will enjoy the children—So many American women leave their husbands at home. It will add much to your own enjoyment. I know with me I have more pleasure in seeing beautiful things when I can see them with congenial spirits—but of course it is sometimes due to expenses are nearly doubled, but not quite—

Jesse is as you possibly know a graduate of Cambridge and London University School of Mines—He had a lovely position in the Anglo-American Oil Company—where he was in the Geophysical Dept and as he had specialized in petroleum in the University—where I believe he was the 1st American to get a prize given by a London Petroleum Society—in the University—but over work in University and with Co. so soon after a very stiff course, with Athletics thrown in, as he won the Cambridge colors—he thus lost some years and had to leave the Co. and is only coming to life again, I am happy to say. You will excuse this scribble but you may be able to find out what I am trying to say. I shall however send it off and hope I may see you when you come over with the children, if you don't put it off too long.

With tender remembrances
as ever
H. O. Tanner[1]

43 rue de Fleurus
Paris 6e

About two weeks after writing this letter Tanner visited Atherton and Ingeborg Curtis and, in the course of a conver-

1. Tanner to Bryant, May 3, 1937, Atlanta University, Atlanta, Ga.

sation with them, said, "How beautiful spring-time is in Paris! The earth is awakening once more." If he had been able to select the place where he should die he undoubtedly would have chosen Paris. There he had found all of the things that meant most to him—his wife, his success as an artist, and, above all, the freedom he had yearned for as a youth.

Henry Tanner died in his sleep on May 25 in his apartment on the Rue de Fleurus. No death could have been more peaceful or less free of suffering. When his friends read in the newspapers that he was gone they were shocked by the suddenness of it. They knew Tanner was old and not very strong, but death had seemed far away. Yet they knew it was the way he would have wanted to go, with the paint still fresh on his last canvas.

Of his friends none felt the loss as severely as did Atherton Curtis. He had been closer to him than anyone except his son. The following letter, written to Atherton and Ingeborg by a mutual friend the day of Tanner's death, expresses the sympathy that was felt for these devoted friends.

PARIS LE 25 MAI 1937

MES CHERS AMIS,

Mourir pendant qu'on dort est une trop belle mort pour qu'on puisse être triste du départ de celui qui s'en va. Il faudrait que nous puissions tous avoir la même fin sans souffrance. Aussi, je ne veux pas pleurer sur M. Tanner; je suis d'ailleurs sûre que vous qui l'avez beaucoup aimé, malgré tout le regret que vous pouvez avoir, vous êtes contents pour lui.

Que va t'on faire? Y a-t-il un service religieux? J'irai bien volontiers l'accompagner s'il n'y a pas trop a marcher.

Et, en attendant, vous savez que je suis avec vous *dans le vrai sens du mot, et de tout coeur.*

Votre,
L. DÉSORMONTS

Tanner was buried on May 27 in the cemetery at Sceaux, next to his beloved Jessie and just a stone's throw from the resting place of the famous Marie Curie.

To his son Jesse went letters from many old friends to whom the name Tanner represented the best of an era. Leslie Cauldwell wrote to Jesse on behalf of his father's professional colleagues:

MY DEAR MR. TANNER,

In the name of the American Artists' Professional League and in my own name, I wish to express to you the very real sorrow the death of your remarkable father causes us.

Apart from his great talent as an artist, which is universally admitted, was his beautiful Faith, a Faith that shone through all his pictures and in every little act, so that a hand shake seemed like a benediction and made one feel the better for it.

His serenity was something to be envied by us all, in our hurry and struggle to achieve some little success.

It was a privilege to have known, to have some association with such a rare character as his was; no, is, *for our memories of Henry O. Tanner will live with us until our own time comes to answer the last call.*

With our deep regrets, yours sincerely,
LESLIE GIFFIN CAULDWELL, *Secy.*

Mr. Cauldwell expressed a sentiment felt not only by the American Artist's Professional League and himself, but by all of Tanner's artist friends and those who knew him best. In their estimation he was a man of magnetic and endearing personality, as well as an artist of rare talent.

The *New York Herald Tribune* ran a long obituary of Tanner. The headlines were:

HENRY TANNER, 77, DIES IN PARIS
WAS AMERICAN NEGRO PAINTER

The term "Negro painter" was a tribute to his race. Yet it is also suggestive of the separateness that Tanner deplored and that had nothing to do with his art.

But Tanner cannot be held within the framework of race. If he is little known today it is because his art, like that of other artists of his period—J. Alden Weir, Frederick Frieseke, Childe Hassam, to name but a few—has suffered from the almost extravagant wave of popularity of postimpressionist and abstract art that all but submerged every other style of painting during the decades following his death.

Today the tide is turning, and a broader view of art is asserting itself. Once time is allowed its judgment there can be little doubt that Henry Ossawa Tanner will have a lasting place in American art, not only for his early studies of Negro life but for his landscapes and, more especially, his biblical paintings on which his reputation was won.

Nevertheless, Tanner will always have a special place in the minds and hearts of American Negroes, for he was the first among them who with single-minded intensity pursued a path of excellence and rose superior to most of his white contemporaries in the highly competitive field of art. It is true that his success came first in Europe and that he lived abroad most of his life, but in spite of success and exile he never lost his feeling of Americanism or his sense of identity with the Negro race.

James A. Porter writes that

> Four generations were required to produce the first genius among Negro artists. But the interval prepared the way for Henry O. Tanner. His predecessors, white and black, had shown the possibilities of realistic and impressionistic landscape, of portraiture, history painting and genre, according to the fluctuating canon of taste in the Nineteenth Century. Now it was for Tanner to find an original field and explore new paths of feeling. He was well prepared for his mission and his success greatly affected other Negro artists.[2]

2. Modern Negro Art (New York: Dryden Press, 1943), p. 64.

Romare Bearden, another well-known Negro artist, whose sensitive abstract pictures are very different from the romantic-realist paintings of Henry Tanner, gives a personal as well as universal appreciation of his art.

When I was a small boy attending Public School 5 in Harlem, each year my class would make its hegira to the Metropolitan Museum of Art. I was always more impressed by the marbelized grandeur of the great museum than by the art works, but on one visit a teacher stopped the class in front of a painting and said, "Now you colored boys in the class should know that this painting was done by a Negro artist, Henry O. Tanner."

The painting was "Sodom and Gomorrah" and I would look for it on each trip, until, finally, Tanner, along with Gérôme, Meissonier, and other masters of the 19th century Salons, was sent to his artistic graveyard within the museum basement. By the time of the socially conscious mid-30's, as a young artist, I was disenchanted with Tanner. I felt that he had divorced himself from the task of developing a statement which reflected the crucial social problems of his time. I understand now that Tanner was marked forever by his early religious experience. I understand, also, that external responsibilities were not so compelling as was Tanner's exploration of his self, and of his relating religion to art. In his religious painting, especially the last works, Tanner tells us much of what he thinks about the world and of man's place in it. This kind of self-exploration when integrated by a personality of real proportion can be both vital and transcendent.

Booker T. Washington, who admired Tanner's "Banjo Lesson," felt that at last Negroes had a painter who could depict their lives in a human and dignified way. However, when Washington visited Tanner in Paris, he found Tanner adamant to all entreaties that he return to America, or that he return to painting Negro subjects. It is to Mr. Washington's credit that he finally understood the nature of Tanner's personal vision and that Tanner's religious painting was not necessarily the artist's refuge from the burdens of the world, or his responsibilities as a Negro artist.

Chapter Eighteen

It is time now, in Tanner's case, to sound the trumpet call of artistic resurrection. Some of Tanner's late works evolve such beauty in the integration of method and subject matter that when more of them are assembled the art world will rediscover one of the great, but neglected, American painters.

INDEX

Index